The Limits of Trade Union Militancy

THE LIMITS OF TRADE UNION MILITANCY

The Lancashire Textile Workers, 1910-1914

JOSEPH L. WHITE

Contributions in Labor History, Number 5

G P *GREENWOOD PRESS*

WESTPORT, CONNECTICUT ● LONDON, ENGLAND

Library of Congress Cataloging in Publication Data

White, Joseph L.
    The limits of trade union militancy.

    (Contributions in labor history; no. 5)
    Includes index.
    1. Strikes and lockouts--Textile industry--
England--Lancashire--History. I. Title.
II. Series.
HD5366.T4W47 331.89'287'700942769 77-87965
ISBN: 0-313-20029-7

Library of Congress Catalog Card Number: 77-87965
ISBN: 0-313-20029-7
ISSN: 0146-3608

First published in 1978

Greenwood Press, Inc.
51 Riverside Avenue, Westport, Connecticut 06880

Printed in the United States of America

10 9 8 7 6 5 4 3 2 1

To Delsa

Contents

Abbreviations

AWA	Amalgamated Weavers Association
BPP	British Parliamentary Papers
BSP	British Socialist Party
CFT	*Cotton Factory Times*
CWA	Cardroom Workers Amalgamation
ILP	Independent Labour Party
SDF	Social Democratic Federation
UTFWA	United Textile Factory Workers Association

Tables

Preface

Many people helped me write this book.

In Lancashire, Fred Hague, Harry Kershaw, and the late Lewis Wright of the Weavers Amalgamation, Joseph King of the Cardroom Workers, James Milhench of the Oldham Weavers, Albert Shaw of the Burnley and Nelson Weavers, Stanley Iveson, and Mavis Williams shared with me documents in their possession and their wide and deep knowledge of the Lancashire trade union and Socialist movement.

Staff workers at the British Museum, Public Record Office, L.S.E. Library, Manchester Central Reference Library, University of Manchester Library, Burnley Public Library, Blackburn Public Library, and the Lancashire Record Office provided that amalgam of friendliness of professional expertise that transforms research from a burden to a joy.

David Montgomery, Eric Hobsbawm, and Edward Thompson read drafts of the manuscript and offered invaluable comments and criticisms, as did Perry Curtis, who stands as at least one counterexample to the generalization that professors give their students nothing but headaches.

Financial support for research was provided by a Ford Foundation Western European Fellowship. Gerry Katz typed the manuscript with style, flair, and unswerving good humor.

For moral and intellectual support I am indebted to my students at Pitt, Bernie Yadoff, and Delsa, Eugene and Robin White.

Despite all this help, weaknesses remain, and I take full responsibility for them.

A mule spinner at work. The spinner is piecing up a broken end.
(*Photo by Joseph L. White*)

Wilton Mill, near Bury, scene of the 1911 ring spinners' strike.

(Photo by Joseph L. White)

Loading raw cotton into the Coldhurst Mill, near Oldham.
(Photo by Joseph L. White)

The Limits of Trade Union Militancy

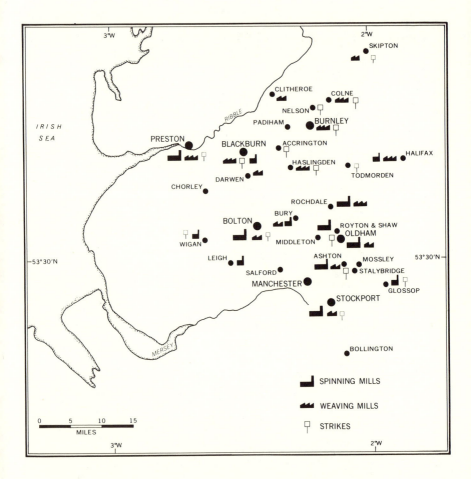

Map The Cotton Region, 1910-14. *(Map by Howard Ziegler)*

Introduction _____ 1

For historians of British working people, the early twentieth century has constituted a "natural laboratory" of impressive proportions. However measured and evaluated, the period was one of unprecedented growth, militancy, and the spread of new ideas and perspectives within the labor movement—not only in Britain, but for workers throughout the industrialized world as well.

The classic interpretation is that the workers had risen in syndicalist revolt, and that revolution or Armageddon were only a matter of time. Claud Cockburn exaggerates only slightly when he writes in his autobiography that contemporaries, including his immediate family, thought the revolution was already under way. They were quite wrong of course as far as Britain was concerned, but the debate over the causes and meaning of the labor unrest have continued right down to the present. Elie Halévy and George Dangerfield, writing in the late 1920s and mid-1930s, retrospectively developed in full the classic thesis of a massive workers' revolt against the capitalist state and industrial structure;[1] and in so arguing they remained very close to the contemporary assessment. Not until the 1950s and 1960s did a new generation of labor historians attempt to ask new questions and employ new methods—influenced as they undoubtedly were by their perceptions of a working class for whom full employment, the welfare state, and levels of overt industrial conflict far below the early years of the century were the norm. Dismissing such vague formulations as "labor unrest" and "workers' revolt," these scholars have looked for short- and medium-term factors to explain the timing, scope, and intensity of the upsurge. In his splendid *Growth of Industrial Relations*,[2] E. H. Phelps Brown advanced the thesis that the industrial conflict of 1906-14 was the outgrowth of a unique conjunction of economic, demographic, and institutional factors. Oppressive poverty for unskilled workers, inflationary pressures on pay packets, and a system of industrial relations that was not very responsive to shop floor and plant grievances were for him the main causes of the unrest. Following along in the attempt to be more specific and cut events down to size, Henry Pelling has argued in a spirited polemic that the industrial struggles of the workers in the years just before World War I were rigorously isolated from other agitations of the period—notably the "Tory Revolt" in Parliament, the Irish question, and the women's suffrage movement.[3] The failure of the insurgents to link up casts into grave doubt the possibility that British society was undergoing a general crisis. Recently, Standish Meacham has speculated that the turmoil of the prewar years expressed the forebodings of a working class already in historical decline.[4] There was a strange death all right, but the corpse was not quite the same one Dangerfield had in mind.

We may speak then of a revisionist reply to the classic thesis. However, it would be inaccurate to say that the revisionists have imposed a new orthodoxy upon the evidence of the period. In an interesting monograph Peter Stearns has argued that, compared with the situation in France between 1900 and 1914, the industrial struggles waged by British workers were indeed massive and influenced or thought to be influenced by syndicalist ideas and élan, though Stearns goes on to suggest that throughout western Europe workers were becoming more moderate and what he calls progressive in their demands upon economy and society.[5] We shall be dealing with Stearns's notions of what constitutes moderate behavior and demands by workers in several different contexts along the way in this book. In essential agreement with Stearns, Robert Holton[6] has shown that for the early twentieth century, he who says syndicalism also says Britain, for in terms of organization, numbers, and influence workers in no other country—not even France—were seen as constituting the international center of syndicalist theory and practice. Finally, James Hinton has added an incalcuably important new dimension to the debate by showing how engineering shop stewards during World War I picked up where the prewar movement left off, and through their struggles and experiences forged a revolutionary vanguard and the active nucleus of the British Communist Party.[7] The notion of a neoorthodox interpretation is not altogether misplaced.

At this point one is tempted to say, "Well, the historians don't agree and that's all there is to it." Such pessimism is misguided. What all three interpretations—classic, revisionist, and neoclassical—have failed to come to grips with is explicitness and accuracy in defining the representative components of the prewar labor unrest as well as a remarkably uneven treatment of the question of how industrial conflict is best analyzed. What questions need to be asked? Which quantitative measurements are the most relevant and enlightening? How is workers' consciousness to be gauged? This book, by focusing on the Lancashire cotton workers, seeks to shed new light both on the period just preceding World War I and on the nature of industrial conflict in a mature capitalist or industrial society.

The first reason that the cotton workers have been selected is that they shed a decisive light on the question of how widespread was the prewar labor unrest. Every historian takes as his starting point the fact that in Britain the number of strikes, striking workers, and "days lost" reached an (up to that time) all-time high, peaking in 1911-13. But to say this does not settle the question of the relative propensity of specific kinds of workers to strike. During the very same period millions of workers engaged in no strike action whatever and possibly had no great desire to join in the unrest. The vagueness of previous attempts by historians to pin down the extent of the unrest can be seen in their treatment of the cotton workers' participation. The only mention Halévy made of the cotton workers was that the spinning lockout of 1910 and the weaving lockout of 1911-12 were "important."[8] They certainly were that, as will be shown, but the lone adjective is not very helpful. Dangerfield, basing his account wholly upon secondary sources, singled out for more detailed narrative treatment the same two disputes as major instances of the irrationality that institutions, classes, and sexes were exhibiting in the management of their affairs.[9] Phelps Brown, on the other hand, minimized the significance of disruptions in the cotton textile industry as part of his larger project of reducing the insurgency to more modest proportions.[10] H. A. Turner, looking for features in the historical development of the cotton unions in order to shed light on the growth and structure of the entire British trade union movement, also noted the two industry-wide lockouts, "many minor disputes," and "general unrest" in the weaving districts of northeast Lancashire, but found the period before the war significant for other reasons and did not attempt to explain the unrest.[11] G. D. H. Cole and Raymond Postgate's only reference to the cotton workers in *The British Common People* was the mildly ironical comment that the spinners' unions' withdrawal from a collective agreement with the employers, "which would once have astonished the industrial world," was thoroughly eclipsed by more militant developments elsewhere in the labor movement.[12] The most reliable quantitative guide continues to be Knowles's reminder that, after coal miners, textile workers were the most strike-prone sections of the British work force for the period 1911-47, with most of the strike action taking place before 1932,[13] At the first level, then, when we speak of the extent and limits of trade union militancy, we mean that the prewar unrest extended at least as far as the cotton workers.

Set in proper theoretical perspective, this last point has several important implications. For much of their history the cotton workers were anything but representative and typical. In the first half of the nineteenth century they often stood apart from the rest of the working class. First, in no other industry had the factory system made such deep inroads. Second, the cotton workers were unambiguously among the leaders of the working classes with respect to both industrial militancy and political assertiveness and sophistication, as seen by their massive political campaign for protective legislation and a shorter workday. For different reasons they were exceptional for much of the twentieth century as well, due mainly to the decline and radical restructuring of the industry—including the move away from cotton as a raw material. But in the early twentieth century the cotton workers and the industry were a remarkably representative cross section of the British working class and as fine a candidate for an extended case study as the student is likely to find. They came as close as they ever would come to sharing many (though as we shall see not all) the features common to other sections of organized labor at that time: urbanization, employment in medium-sized firms with an export orientation, and a history of trade unionism.

Better yet for analytical purposes, typicality does not imply monolithic homogeneity. However the cotton region might appear to the urban historian or economic geographer, the labor historian is struck by the diversity within the region, industry, and work force itself. Depending on which group of cotton workers one is talking about, they ranked among the best paid (e.g., male mule spinners) or the worst paid (e.g., female ring spinners) in the entire pre-1914 British economy. If the yarn-spinning side of the industry was marked by many sharp occupational demarcations wherein no more than 36 workers in a mill employing 200 might be engaged on the same job at the same rate of pay, cloth manufacturing firms had as high as 75 percent of the operatives engaged in the common task of power loom weaving.[14] The parliamentary constituency of Preston ranked among the most reliable of urban and predominantly working-class Conservative seats with the exception of Merseyside during the period 1886-1918. The constituency of Clitheroe, barely twenty miles away, was just as consistently Liberal, and after 1903, Labour.[15] Skilled tradesmen, semiskilled operatives, unskilled laborers, women and children—the cotton region, like the policeman in Andy Capp's neighborhood, "got 'em all." Seldom has one industry provided such a broad range of workers and experiences.

We shall be considering the cotton workers mainly while on the job and, specifically, their responses to life on the job. Since a frequent response of theirs was to go on strike, the analysis of strike dynamics will constitute the bulk of this book. In part the choice of strikes is dictated by the type of evidence the workers themselves generated: That is, had their activities taken different forms, or had they engaged in few or no public protest activities, other matters would have been awarded precedence. Accordingly, it is necessary to look closely at the assumptions, concepts and methods that historians and social scientists have used to explain strikes past and present.

Two points may be made at the outset. First, all serious students are agreed that strikes are both amazingly complex and deeply rooted phenomena in the life of industrial capitalism. The notion of strikes as aberrant instances of "social pathology," whose overt manifestations can be eliminated by the judicious use of carrot or stick, is no longer regarded as a serious interpretive option. (Indeed, the unheralded assumption that workers who engage in industrial conflict should be assumed unless proved otherwise to display just as much substantive rationality as their opponents may well be the single most important reason for the post-World War II advance in labor studies.) Second, the thesis that strikes are a direct and an unmediated response to movements in real wages is also trading at a heavy discount—again for the best of reasons. Historians no longer need to be convinced of the very wide range of issues, motivations, and broad economic contexts in which strikes have actually been fought.

If one had to summarize the post-World War II trend in explaining strikes, one could accurately say that vulgar economic determinism has given way to a *sociological* interpretation. The pioneering study was un-questionably Alvin W. Gouldner's *Wildcat Strike* (1954), which dealt with a two-week wildcat strike by gypsum mine and factory workers in the Middle West.[16] Although Gouldner fully acknowledged that the postwar boom had come to an end (the wildcat occurred in 1950) and that man-agement's top priority was to increase labor productivity, nevertheless he strove mightily to show that the strike could best be explained in terms of expectations, authority, and legitimacy. Of particular interest to Gould-ner was the way in which structural, ideological, and power constraints inhibited the workers from articulating formally to management what was "really" upsetting them. Thus a duality between manifest and latent dis-contents was built into the situation itself; and equipped with the right analytical tools, the researcher could uncover what the wildcat strike "really" was about—in this case the violation by management of an "in-dulgency pattern" that the workers had come to expect as a matter of decency and fair play.

A similar quest for underlying sociological factors also informs the hypothesis of the "isolated mass" advanced by Clark Kerr and Abram Siegel in their article, "The Inter-Industry Propensity to Strike" (1954).[17] Despite obvious differences in scope—Gouldner studies one strike at one workplace, whereas Kerr and Siegel cast a wide net across time and space—both studies are agreed that at bottom sociological determinants were paramount in explaining industrial conflict. Kerr and Siegel argued that where historically large-scale modern industry developed in isolation from the rest of civil society, workers are much more likely to display a chip on their collective shoulder and develop a tenacious solidarity against out-siders, in whose ranks management is often included, and to hold these outsiders responsible for their discontents and keenly felt sense of exploi-tation. Kerr and Siegel have received considerable criticism, not all of which is in our opinion fully justified. But the immediate point is that for Kerr and Siegel political economy has decisively given way to sociol-ogy. We shall return to this point presently.

Despite their being severe critics of Kerr and Siegel, Charles Tilly and Edward Shorter in *Strikes in France, 1830-1968*,[18] also belong unmis-takably in the sociological camp. One cannot be sure whether this book was intended as a contribution to labor history or an extended set of working papers undertaken in order to place strikes empirically, and to a lesser extent, theoretically, within the framework of modernization theory. However this may be, Tilly and Shorter argue vigorously that in

France strikes are best understood as essentially consisting of political demonstrations. To be sure, wage and wage-related demands were overwhelmingly the most frequent manifest issue over which French workers struck. But by constructing three ideal types of French workers—artisans, semiskilled factory proletarians, and modern science sector workers—they show to their satisfaction that all three groups went on strike in the pursuit of "power," both at the shop level and the state level. This is their answer to the big question that every student of strikes must ultimately address himself to: Why do workers strike? In response to a second and related big question—Why do some groups of workers strike more frequently than others?—Tilly and Shorter conclude that organization and urbanization are the main determinants. The better able to organize workers are, the greater the degree of urbanization, the more frequent in number and size strikes will be. In this way they are able to attack the claim that strikes are caused by absolute deprivation and ignore altogether the hypothesis that *relative* deprivation experienced by the working classes vis-à-vis the propertied classes in industrial capitalist society is of any theoretical importance in understanding why workers strike. Although they recognize that the occupational history of many industries and groups of workers has not yet been written, they are nevertheless confident that strikes in France can be adequately explained without recourse to concrete factors such as short-term technological and organizational change, changes in working conditions, changes in consciousness within and among groups of workers, and methods and styles of industrial relations. To cite just one example, students of strikes know that many short strikes, and especially wildcats, are fought over "perishable disputes." That is, unless workers take immediate action, say, over the preemptory firing of a fellow worker, the possibility of redressing their grievance will be irrevocably lost. Since Tilly and Shorter make no mention at all of perishable disputes (perhaps because they are too mundane and low level to make an impact within the capacious categories of modernization theory), the reader is left wondering how, if at all, French workers dealt with such grievances.

Fortunately, the economic and sociological approaches to strikes can be combined. Michelle Perrot has done this brilliantly in *Les Ouvriers en Grève, 1871-1890,* arguing that strikes are both means of expression and calculated efforts to change economic relationships. The language, manifestations, and gestures of strikes can thus be analyzed for the rich insights they provide into the consciousness of class, whereas the timing, scale of organization, and formal demands of strikes reveal the ways in which workers have learned to battle effectively for their own interests within the framework provided by industrial capitalism. Perrot's approach clearly rejects any efforts to reduce strikes to a single cause. Moreover, she devotes special attention to textile workers, since "France on strike was above all the France of textiles, its capital Roubaix, its leading actors the weavers, who alone monopolized 23 per cent of the conflicts."[19]

British workers on strike should be approached in the same spirit. Curiously, they have been until recently rather neglected by specialists— possibly owing to the Webbs' singular reluctance to count, measure, or significantly comment on strikes aside from assuring their readers that strikes and lockouts are a glaring example of capitalist waste and inef- iciency and of unquestioned detriment to the community. What follows is a clarification of our assumptions and methods.

In the first place, strikes must be placed in the context of political economy. By this we mean much more than merely sketching in an eco- nomic "background"—as Gouldner does and as Tilly and Shorter do in such broad strokes as to turn the exercise into a caricature. Rather, we insist that work, authority, power, money, and class must be seen as form- ing an interrelated whole and that one abstracts out "factors" only with great caution and for limited and specified purposes. Self-evident though it may appear, the class component of striking is frequently ignored in the attempts to analyze strikes and even to define them, as can be seen in the frequent failure to observe that workers are literally the only group in industrial society that in fact goes on strike. Other groups strike only metaphorically—most notably students, whose strikes by our definition are really demonstrations, much like Tilly and Shorter's strikes. Infre- quently, there can be strikes in which withdrawal of labor is not the pri- mary activity, for example, rent strikes, though here too working people appear to account for a large majority of all known rent strikers.

Secondly—and most importantly—strikes are profoundly Janus-faced activities. On one face, they are without doubt a violation of the domi- nant value system in any society, capitalist or socialist, where production is held to be the primary goal of social life. This formulation applies with equal theoretical force irrespective of the legal status of strikes and strikers, and irrespective of the bitterness or equability with which they are fought. This is why only social revolutionaries declare strikes to be a positive good thing in general and also why the oldest interpretation of the prewar labor unrest—namely, that it was also a workers' *revolt*—is not to be totally dis- missed.

But if all strikes interrupt "business as usual," it is equally important to observe that the vast majority of strikes that workers have fought since the Industrial Revolution, and all of the strikes of the cotton workers that we shall examine, have a side to them that can with full justice be called limited or reformist. That is, strikes and their spokespersons make demands upon an economic and a political system that, with very few exceptions, are believed to be realistic in the here and now. Granted, a certain degree of flexibility is called for. It may well be the case that learning which demands to make realistically and who to make those demands upon is part of the "maturing" process that labor movements undergo, and may possibly be what Stearns had in mind in arguing that between 1890 and 1914 strikes by western European workers became more "moderate," though his generalization is not particularly helpful in understanding the cotton workers' participation in the labor unrest. This idea of the inherent reformism in strikes by workers in mature industrial capitalism is another implication of the limits of trade union militancy.

The here-and-now concreteness of strikes and the demands of strikers suggest a third major point about strike analysis, namely that strikes provide what is perhaps the most accurate data the historian can marshal by which to probe the norms and expectations of workers acting within their social role as workers. Strikes fought from a position of hopeless weakness are a partial exception, but even they show where workers have defined the "last ditch." Despite the clear importance of the distinction between latent and manifest issues, the important fact remains, which Gouldner underemphasized, that very few totally inexplicable strikes have ever been recorded. Accordingly, the historian can gauge the moods, opinions, and attitudes of workers who actually down tools and walk out, with far more accuracy than can be done in the case of nonstriking workers. This is not to suggest that other types of data and behavior cannot be analyzed to good purpose—for instance, inquiries, demographic movements, voting behavior, participation in politics (including demonstrations and other agitations), data on absenteeism, turnover rates, and industrial sabotage. The point is, rather that when it comes to pinpointing exactly what workers will and will not tolerate, and what they expect and hope to achieve in the present or immediate future, the light that strike data shed appears to be in a class by itself.

What then were the causes and initial conditions that led to the unrest of the prewar cotton workers? Cotton workers differed markedly by district and occupation with respect to the propensity to strike and the goals for which they struck. But within the diversity common elements can be identified. To state our thesis briefly, the period from 1910 to 1914 presented the workers with a unique set of grievances and opportunities to remedy them. On the one hand, workers struck against the hardness of their work and against their lack of control over the factors determining whether work would be manageable or difficult. And indeed the evidence suggests that, rather than being merely a subjectively perceived phenomenon, the work that many operatives had to perform had become measurably harder over time. On the other hand, they were able to strike with a high degree of frequency and success because the period 1910-14 witnessed the greatest production and employment boom in the entire history of the Lancashire cotton industry, a boom during which post-World War II levels of employment were reached. The result was a workers' offensive that aimed not only at mitigating long-standing grievances but that pressed for new rights as well—a militancy owing little to syndicalism or revolutionary Marxism. Although political and ideological influences were far from absent, the unrest was in the last analysis industrial and economic in its origins and scope. The outbreak of World War I brought the unrest to an abrupt end; and just as the cotton industry lost its prewar prominence in the economy, so also did the cotton workers never regain their aggressiveness of 1910-14. An offensive outlook gave way to the defensive and conservative outlook of workers in a declining industry.

However, before the strikes of the cotton workers can be analyzed, they must be placed, as we have said, in the context of political economy. In Chapters 2 and 3, work intensity, wages, and the internal stratification of the workers are looked at. Chapter 4 brings quantitative methods to bear upon the questions of workers' shareholding and upward mobility into management. Chapter 5 deals with the cotton union leadership's response to economic fluctuations and their impact upon industrial relations, and as such is the part of the book furthest removed from workers in the factories. Chapters 6, 7, and 8 analyze the strikes that broke out from January 1910 to the outbreak of World War I. Chapter 9 deals with politics, first in the traditional sense of voting behavior and party allegiance, and, secondly, in showing the ways in which workers' politics were a response to union policies and Industrial problems. Finally, Chapter 10 presents our findings and conclusions.

The Cotton Workers in the Early Twentieth Century: An Economic and Social Profile

2

WORK

The basis of our wealth, intelligence and culture is broadening; the pauper cotton "hand" of the thirties and forties is rapidly becoming the respectable middle class citizen of today, whose intellectual and moral elevation are the greatest safeguards against anarchism, outrage and violence. The patience and fortitude, the orderliness of the cotton operatives and coal miners under the recent [1892] lockouts were the admiration of the civilized world and deservedly enlisted the sympathy of their fellowmen. A complete change has come over public opinion and the press; the despised Trade Unionist of 40 years ago is a recognized power in the State today. "The Organizations of Labor in England," says Professor Schulze Gaevernitz, "have become veritable peace societies," and indeed the number of labor struggles has steadily diminished in the last 50 years. The strongest adherents of the "supply and demand" doctrine will no longer maintain that Trade Unions are injurious to the prosperity of trade. It is entirely owing to organization that Labor has been able to sell its only commodity in so good a market and has secured the high remuneration it enjoys today. The wisdom and moderation shown so far by Trade Unionists encourage the hope that they will not push their demands beyond reason and the best interests of the country. They fully recognize the importance of our foreign trade and are not likely to injure their own condition by driving it into the hands of our competitors.

The remuneration of capital is yearly diminishing. The prosperity, health, happiness and comfort of our workers, however, are constantly increasing, and we can but wish them "God speed" in their course . . . .

. . . By shortened hours and high wages we have previously outdistanced all competition, and shorter hours will again increase the energy, the vitality, the productiveness of our workers on which depends the victory in the industrial struggle.[1]

Taken as a whole, the cotton industry was expanding during the period 1896-1914. In terms of productive capacity there were 42.7 million spinning spindles in 1896 compared with 59.3 million in 1914; and the number of power looms had also increased from 638, 469 in 1896 to 805, 452 in 1914.[2] Statistics for the consumption of raw cotton show a similar upward trend: 1,637 million pounds in 1895 compared with 2,178 million pounds in 1913.[3] Expressed in terms of average decennial movements, the figures indicate a 29.0 percent increase in spindles for 1906-14 over the decade 1896-1905, a 15.0 percent increase in looms for the same period, 17.0 percent for cotton consumption, and 18.8 percent for cloth exports, whether measured in linear yards or pounds. Sharpening the focus by one more setting, one notes further that the rate of growth of industrial production for the United Kingdom as a whole was 18.0 percent for the decade 1905-1914 compared with 1895-1904.[4] Cotton then was unambiguously holding its own in the growth league tables,[5] and as such constitutes a case in point of the propensity of the British economy in the late nineteenth and early twentieth centuries to develop along already well-worn lines.

The absolute number of workers in the industry was also increasing (see Table 1). More surprising than the tendency of cotton workers to fall as a proportion of the population between 1881 and 1901 is the modest reversal of the trend between 1901 and 1911. Here again the statistics available to the cotton workers themselves gave them no reason to fear that the trade was in danger of decline or collapse, and in fact there is no evidence that workers or trade union leaders seriously entertained any such notions.

Table 1

Number of Cotton Workers per Million of
Population Aged Ten and Older

	1880	1891	1901	1911
Men	51,762	49,001	40,561	41,718
Women	61,300	57,542	50,284	50,065
Men and women	56,699	53,440	45,625	46,067

Source: British Parliamentary Papers, 1913, vol. 78, "Census of England and
Wales," Cd. 7018, p. 557.

However, it is not our intention in this chapter to write either a comprehensive or a potted economic history of the industry, David Landes's
call for the former notwithstanding.[6] Rather, the goals are the more limited and specific ones of asking what sort of living, in a broad sense, the
trade provided for its employees. How many workers received how much
in wages? How hard did they have to work for what they got? Did cotton
workers cooperate with, or compete against, one another? What opportunities for social mobility existed? It might be thought that once the facts
of the industry's growth have been established, the question answers itself
in the affirmative in the forms of high wages, more comfortable working
conditions, fringe benefits, job advancement, and the like. But is this what
happened? Or, to revert to the opening quote, did Frederick Mertten's
predictions and analyses hold up the subsequent generation of cotton
workers?

In "The British Gas Workers," E. J. Hobsbawm constructed a model
that enabled him to relate the gas industry's output and productivity to
wages in such a way as to measure changes in work intensity. Hobsbawm
was able to show that in a context of (1) expanding production that, however, saw (2) no major changes in technique or works organization and
in which (3) wage *rates* remained unchanged, the result was an increase
in productivity far in excess of increases in earnings. Moreover, the increased productivity must have meant that gas workers simply had to
work harder—both bodily and psychologically—in order to get the job
done. Table 2 brings this out clearly. The point was to explain the "explosion" of 1889, in which the gas workers struck for a reduction of the
workday from twelve hours to eight, and it is easy to see that the model's
simplicity and powers of explanation stem from the number of variables

Table 2

Work Intensity in the British Gas
Industry, 1874-88

Year	Coal Carbonized	Gas Produced	Wages
1874	100	100	100
1888	176	187	148

Source: E. J. Hobsbawm, *Laboring Men,* New York: 1964, p. 163.

that could be held constant, not the least of which being that the end
product is uniform manufactured gas, irrespective of when and where it
was produced.

Table 3 is an attempt to adapt Hobsbawm's work intensity model to
the two main branches of the cotton trade. Unfortunately, the accuracy
of the statistics leaves much to be desired. In the first place the sources
for all of the statistics for 1829-93 and for the production figures for 1912
were not indicated by the authorities citing them, and accordingly there
is no direct way to double-check them. In the second place the results of
the one test that is possible to make easily do not inspire confidence. As
is pointed out in note 5 of this chapter, raw cotton was processed into
yarn throughout the whole period in such a way that the ratio between
the weight of cotton consumed and the weight of yarn spun should come
out as a constant—more specifically, one should theoretically expect the
ratio to be a number slightly above 1.0. But the results of this test, given
in Table 4, fluctuate entirely too much for comfort, particularly for the
year 1907, which is all the more disturbing because the 1907 figures are
from the Census of Production. In the third place, it has been necessary
to use the 1911 census for the number of workers in 1912, and there is
no telling how many persons replied to the enumerator that they were
cotton operatives when they were not actually employed at the time or
later on, or vice versa for that matter. A final drawback inherent in the
data is that, unlike manufactured gas, it is not correct automatically to
assume that in terms of time and effort inputs, one sort of yarn or cloth
is equal to any or all others. Luckily, however, one can reckon productivity
in terms of value produced as well as amount, and this offers a partially
effective means of making allowance for changes in end products.

Imperfections in the data in Table 3 do not mean that they are altogether worthless, if only on the grounds that they contain no prima facie

Table 3 Work Intensity in the Spinning and Weaving Industries, 1829-1912

Spinning

Year	Spindles	Workers	Workers/ 1,000 Spindles	Wages/ Week	Production/ Year (Pounds)	Pounds Produced/ Worker	Value
1829/31	10,000,000	140,000	14.0	126d.	216,500,000	1,546	n.a.
1844/46	19,500,000	190,000	9.74	132d.	523,300,000	2,754	n.a.
1859/61	30,400,000	248,000	8.16	150d.	910,000,000	3,671	n.a.
1880/82	42,000,000	240,000	5.71	204d.	1,324,900,000	5,520	n.a.
1891/93	45,270,000	220,000	4.86	234d.	1,465,600,000	6,662	£291.19
1907	52,585,362	237,890	4.52	n.a.	1,519,842,000	6,389	£332.26
1912	58,140,220	225,664	3.88	236d.	1,983,000,000	8,787	£608.69

Weaving

Year	Looms	Workers	Workers/ 1,000 Looms	Wages/ Week	Production/ Year (Pounds)	Pounds Produced/ Worker	Value
1859/61	400,000	203,000	507.5	142d.	650,870,000	3,206.0	n.a.
1880/82	550,000	246,000	447.3	180d.	993,540,000	4,039.0	n.a.
1891/93	660,000	310,000	469.7	198d.	1,321,000,000	3,972.0	£222.25
1907	725,221	334,040	460.6	n.a.	1,265,733,211	3,789.2	£236.62
1912	758,712	379,513	500.2	233.2d.	1,467,800,000	3,867.6	£280.76

Note: n.a. = not available.
Sources: Merttens, op. cit., p. 134, for the years 1829-93; for 1907, BPP, *Census of Production of 1907*, p. 22; for 1912, R. Robson, *The Cotton Industry in Britain* (London, 1957), pp. 332, 343.

Table 4

Ratio of Raw Cotton to Yarn Produced

Year	Cotton Consumed (Million Pounds) (1)	Yarn Produced (Million Pounds) (2)	Ratio (1) ÷ (2)
1829-31	243.3	216.5	1.1238
1844-46	588.3	523.3	1.1242
1859-61	1,022.7	910.0	1.1238
1880-82	1,416.3	1,324.9	1.0690
1891-93	1,549.3	1,465.6	1.0572
1907	1,985.0	1,519.8	1.2977
1912	2,142.0	1,983.0 °	1.0822

Source: Same as Table 3.

implausibilities. Looking first at spinning, one notes that the "scissors movement" of a decreasing number of workers per machine and an increasing number of pounds of yarn produced per worker, which continued unbroken for the entire nineteenth century, is checked by 1907, but thereafter increases to an all-time Lancashire record of 8,787 pounds per worker in 1912. The long-term increase is attributable to four main considerations: (1) larger mules, many of which were installed during the mill building boom of 1905-07;[7] (2) faster running speeds;[8] (3) a slow but steady increase in the number of ring-spinning spindles; and (4) a reduction in the number of ten- to thirteen-year-old half-timers.[9] The assertion that other factors must have been negligible is warranted by the facts that the period 1891-1914 saw no other changes in technology except as noted, or in works organization or job demarcation. Although one is free to argue that an improved psychological and physiological state of the work force also helped to send productivity upward, it is difficult to see what kind of research design would shed a decisive light, save in the vaguest of senses that healthier, better-educated, and more "affluent" workers should be expected to produce more. As for the slight decrease in productivity per spinning worker recorded between 1891-93 and 1907, there is no satisfactory explanation if one assumes that the mix of end products remained constant throughout the period. It is significant to note in this connection that value produced per worker does register a gain between 1890-94 and 1907, which could easily have resulted from a shift in production away from coarser yarns toward finer yarns.[10]

In weaving, the first point to notice is that, unlike spinning, the number of workers per machine steadily increases from 1881-83 to 1912, particularly in the years after 1907. In the absence of major changes in technology, it is not clear why this should have happened. It may have been the case that an increasing number of adult operative weavers were adopting the practice of employing a juvenile tenter—*mutatis mutandis* the equivalent of a piecer of mule spinning. Unfortunately, the census does not subdivide workers engaged in weaving processes, so that an explanation can only be advanced in the spirit of an unproved hypothesis. In any event, the impact upon the amount of cloth produced per worker was such that the figures for 1912, while showing a slight increase over 1907, do not get back to the high-water mark of 1880-82. On the other hand, the value produced per worker shows the same upward movement as for spinning, though not as great. Even when the lack of technological innovation is taken into consideration, the sluggishness displayed by the productivity figures is surprising, given the expansion of the trade. Equally surprising is that employers did little or nothing to improve matters, particularly with regard to their practice of not always giving weavers a full complement of looms to tend. Unlike during the interwar years, when industrial conflict in cloth manufacturing turned on the unions' resistance to employers' attempts to rationalize the trade by increasing the number of looms a weaver had to watch, a major bone of contention before the war was the employers' practice of leaving the warps out of anywhere from one to three of the weaver's usual four looms. This alternative to organized short-time working was particularly annoying to weavers, because in addition to loss of earnings it also meant that workers had to hang around the mill for the whole day, whereas if short time was imposed, the workers reaped the benefits of a half-holiday. Indeed, strikes broke out over employers' making weavers "play for warps," but statistically speaking the strikes appear not to have had a deterrent effect.[11] A final point on productivity that relates both to spinning and cloth manufacturing is that sharp fluctuations in the trade cycle must have kept productivity lower than would have been the case had it been possible to maintain steadier employment, so that the short-term analysis provided here may well contain a bias toward understating the effects of the boom years 1905-07 and 1911-13 as a key reason for such gains in productivity as were recorded.

Do the facts of sharply higher output per head for spinning workers and the slight rise after 1907 for weaving workers necessarily mean that their work was becoming physically more arduous? In theory this need not always be the case. New and improved technology, better plant layout, and higher-quality raw materials can often result in both high productivity and less burdensome working conditions. However, in the cotton industry between 1910 and 1914 we find no marked tendencies in these directions. The machines in newly opened mills were indeed fresh from the textile machinery works, but in ease of operation represented no recorded improvement over older models. Nor was management in these years disposed toward innovation and experimentation in plant layout and other nontechnological aspects of works organization. As for the quality of raw materials, there are strong reasons for supposing an actual deterioration; and, as is shown later, complaints over the quality of material constituted the single largest cause of strikes among mule spinners and power loom weavers. Accordingly, the evidence points to the conclusions that spinning workers definitely and weaving workers possibly found themselves working harder year by year.

Did the wages paid to the workers rise in direct proportion to the increased work effort and output per head? For spinning, the answer is that they did not. Indeed, spinning wages for the depressed year of 1910 averaged 25.8d. per worker per week *below* the figure for 1891-93 calculated by Merttens, and even the prewar peak of 244.9d. in August 1913 does not amount to labor and management "splitting the difference that arose from increased productivity. Weaving money wages, on the other hand, rose steadily to a peak of 250.4d. in January 1913, which means not only that weavers' wages caught up with and overtook those of the spinners, but also that wage increases outstripped the rise in productivity per worker by a handsome margin. The figures seem to show that weavers were in fact being paid for their added exertion.

The figures suggest that wage increases do not always buy off workers' discontent. But there is an added complexity. On the first payday of July 1912 a 5 percent addition to the piecework lists took effect in firms that recognized the union.[12] Employment was brisk and rising. Other things being equal, one should expect at least the full 5 percent increase to turn up in the statistics of money earnings. But as Table 5 shows, this did not

Table 5

Earnings of Spinners and Weavers,
1912-13

Month	Spinners				
	1912		1913		
	Earnings	Change from June 1912 (%)	Earnings	Change from June 1912 (%)	
January	237.7d.		240.3d.	+0.2	
February	210.6d.		239.6d.	0.0	
March	238.6d.		235.3d.	−1.8	
April	235.1d.		241.2d.	+0.6	
May	242.2d.		244.3d.	+1.9	
June	239.7d.		230.1d.	−4.0	
July	238.8d.	−0.4	240.4d.	+0.3	
August	237.3d.	−1.0	244.9d.	+2.2	
September	236.2d.	−1.5	243.6d.	+1.6	
October	238.6d.	−0.5	241.6d.	+0.8	
November	236.3d.	−1.4	244.0d.	+1.8	
December	240.3d.	+0.2	242.4d.	+1.1	

Month	Weavers				
January	237.7d.		250.4d.	+4.9	
February	170.3d.		239.9d.	+0.1	
March	228.3d.		238.7d.	0.0	
April	231.8d.		241.2d.	+1.1	
May	236.3d.		245.3d.	+2.8	
June	238.6d.		235.9d.	−1.1	
July	235.8d.	−1.2	244.4d.	+2.4	
August	241.7d.	+1.3	248.4d.	+4.1	
September	242.0d.	+1.4	239.9d.	+0.1	
October	247.2d.	+3.6	242.6d.	+1.7	
November	245.1d.	+2.7	237.6d.	−0.4	
December	243.2d.	+1.9	233.4d.	−2.2	

Source: Board of Trade *Labour Gazette,* January 1912-December 1913.

happen. Taking the *Labour Gazette* figure for June 1912 as the base, representing the wage level for the highest-paid month before the increase went into effect, one notes that in no subsequent month did weavers realize the full 5 percent, although for one month, December 1912, they almost did. The explanatory task is to locate the thing that was not equal. It is submitted that the source of this downward pressure on earnings was the brittleness of yarn with which the weavers were supplied to weave into cloth, an argument that draws its reinforcement from the strikes of 1912 and 1913 over the issue of bad spinning. If anything, a purely statistical approach must have the effect of understating the discomfort and annoyance workers felt as the result of breakages stemming from bad yarn; for as the union spokesmen frequently put it, the ideal remedy was not cash compensation, however generous, to restore earnings to a putative norm, which was the way bad weaving and spinning disputes were actually resolved, but rather attention to quality control to avoid bad materials in the first place. If our argument is correct, compensation paid out (which as additions to wages would be included in the *Labour Gazette* statistics) did not in the aggregate even fully restore earnings, much less compensate for the added effort.[13]

If, on the one hand, work in cotton mills was not becoming any easier, on the other hand, employment opportunities were certainly plentiful. As Table 6 shows, in every month but one from January 1911 to September 1913 the industry employed more workers than in the same month of the preceding year. It is significant that upward of 90 percent of the strikes that took place between January 1910 and the outbreak of World War I were clustered within this period of rising employment. In no sense was high employment (which by 1912-13 was as clear an instance of full employment as the pre-1914 economy ever attained) a cause of strikes: Workers simply do not walk out solely because jobs are available. Instead the high employment level represented an initial condition that enabled —but did not cause—workers to strike over a wide range of issues.

The evidence presented so far indicates that deteriorating working conditions occurring in the context of full employment caused the strikes of 1911-14, but that technological change was not an important factor. There is another hypothesis that must be considered, that of falling real wages as one cause of the unrest. J. H. Porter has presented evidence that real wages for the Oldham spinners (which he implicitly assumes to be representative for the entire spinning trade) fell markedly between 1908 and

Table 6

Monthly Increase or Decrease in Employment,
January 1911–December 1914,
Compared with Previous Year (Percentages)

	1911	1912	1913	1914
January	1.4	1.4	0.8	−0.4
February	3.2	1.0	1.5	−0.8
March	3.9	1.0	1.0	−1.0
April	4.1	−0.8	2.4	−1.2
May	3.2	1.0	2.4	−1.2
June	2.1	1.7	0.5	−0.9
July	3.5	1.6	0.3	−1.1
August	5.2	2.0	0.4	−1.4
September	4.8	2.0	0.3	−42.1
October	6.6	1.2	−0.3	−23.8
November	3.2	1.1	−0.2	−18.3
December	1.7	1.2	−0.4	−12.1

Source: Board of Trade *Labour Gazette,* January 1911-December 1914.

1913. His figures are reproduced in Table 7. However, rates can be deceptive. If earnings are used, as has been done in Table 8, a very different picture emerges. We see instead that as the trade cycle turned upward at the end of 1910, money earnings actually kept up with the cost of living until the beginning of 1914 and indeed in 1913 slightly outran the moderate inflation of the last prewar years.[14] Accordingly, falling real wages cannot be considered as a cause of the cotton workers' industrial unrest.

All things considered, our adaptation of Hobsbawm's work intensity model reveals an inventory of factors that appears to be as volatile as those affecting the gas industry in the late 1880s. However, this conclusion cannot be the resting place for the analysis; on the contrary, it is precisely here that the real problems of interpretation begin. The point is that in gas the explosion actually happened in one sharp blast, whereas in cotton the record to be explained is a much more discontinuous series of small and medium-sized explosions, unevenly distributed with respect to time, district, social, and occupational structure. Having established the existence of economic pressures felt by all or most cotton workers, one must now look for differences that made for the wide range of re-

Table 7

Real Wages in Coarse Spinning, 1908-13 (1880 = 100)

	Oldham Spinning List	Cost of Living	Real-Wage Rates
1908	129	89	145
1909	129	89	139
1910	124	92	135
1911	124	92	135
1912	124	96	129
1913	124	98	127

Source: J. H. Porter, "Industrial Peace in the Cotton Trade," *Yorkshire Bulletin of Economic and Social Research,* May 1967, p. 60.

Table 8

Earnings of Lancashire and Cheshire Cotton Operatives
and the Cost of Living

Year	Money Wages	Index No.	United Kingdom Cost of Living (1900 = 100)
1900	221.0d.	100.0	100.0
1906	237.0d.	107.2	—
1910	211.75d.	95.8	105.7
1911	232.72d.	105.3	105.9
1912	238.43d.	107.9	109.8
1913	244.61d.	110.7	109.8
Jan.-July 1914	239.32d.	108.3	—
Jan.-Dec. 1914	224.46d.	101.6	111.5

Sources: Column 1, G. H. Wood, *History of Wages in the Cotton Trade,* London, 1910 (for 1900); BPP, 1909, Cd. 4545, p. xxviii (for 1906); *Labour Gazette,* January 1910-December 1914 (for 1910-14). Column 3, computed from figures in Column 2. Column 4, S. Pollard, "Real Earnings in Sheffield, 1851-1914," *Yorkshire Bulletin of Economic and Social Research,* May 1957, p. 57.

sponses to the problems inherent in being a cotton worker in the early twentieth century. If it is true that the Lancashire cotton workers were the world's first factory proletariat, it is also true that sectional differences among the cotton workers showed a remarkable depth and tenacity. The measurement and analysis of this diversity form the remainder of the chapter.

WAGES

British and foreign observers alike thought that Lancashire cotton towns in the 1890s and early twentieth century were prosperous places.[15] This was not a wholly tendentious conclusion, drawn as it was from several different "stacks" of evidence. First and most impressive was the wage level of operative mule spinners, which compared favorably with that of the most skilled trades in the economy. For example, in the fine-spinning center of Bolton full-time wages for mule spinners averaged 45s. 9d. in September 1906 and 32s. 0d. for all adult men cotton workers; for the same period pig iron workers and shipbuilding workers averaged 33s. 4d. and 30s. 7d. respectively.[16] Indeed, viewed in terms of the world cotton industry, Lancashire was unique in having the vast majority of its mules staffed by men, irrespective of the size of their pay packets.[17] Second, it was unequivocally true that female power loom weavers were the highest paid women manual workers in the entire country. In Burnley and surrounding districts of northeast Lancashire their wages averaged 24s. 11d.; and for the entire United Kingdom cotton industry, 20s. 7d. By contrast, women workers in metalworking, engineering, and shipbuilding received on the average 12s. 8d.[18] Third, there was a fairly widespread impression that pooled family earnings could make possible incomes of £5 a week and up, thus enabling luxuries such as pianos and holidays at Blackpool.[19] A fourth consideration is that pauperism rates in the cotton towns were consistently below the national average for England and Wales: Oldham's 17.1 per 1,000 population and Blackburn's 16.8 compared favorably indeed with the national average of 21.0 per 1,000 recorded for January 1, 1911.[20]

Although not totally wrong, the conventional assessment as surveyed previously suffers from major defects, regarding both its accuracy in depicting historical reality and its usefulness to the labor historian. As a starting point, it should be noted that that if the wages of all cotton workers—men, women, and children—are taken together, the average wage comes to 19s. 11d. As Table 9 shows, the most that can be said for cotton is that it was the highest-paying textile trade and, with the exception of boots and shoes, workers in the rest of the factory sector of the British economy simply were paid higher wages. Yet one must be careful not to overemphasize the gap separating cotton from the "honorable" trades, since the gap separating cotton from the rest of textiles was just as wide and, moreover, showed signs of growing even larger. Except for the still miserably paying jute trade, even after taking into

Table 9

Average Full-Time Weekly Wages in Selected Industries

	Textiles		
	1886	1906	Change (%)
Cotton	15s. 8d.	19s. 11d.	+27
Woollen and worsted	14s. 4d.	16s. 2d.	+13
Linen	10s. 1d.	12s. 3d.	+21
Jute	10s. 6d.	14s. 4d.	+37
Silk	12s. 8d.	14s. 2d.	+12
Hoisery	17s. 0d.	15s. 11d.	−6

	Other Industries, 1906
Ready-made boots and shoes	19s. 5d.
Building and woodworking	26s. 7d.
Public utilities	
Gas supply	31s. 7d.
Electricity supply	29s. 6d.
Water supply	28s. 3d.
Tramway and bus workers	29s. 3d.
Adult male agricultural workers,	
England only, 1907	18s. 4d.
Pig iron	33s. 4d.
Iron and steel	36s. 0d.
Engineering and boilermaking	25s. 11d.
Steam railways, 1907	
Adults	26s. 8d.
Lads and boys	11s. 11d.
Paper and printing trades	20s. 0d.
Pottery, brick, glass, and chemicals	23s. 6d.
Food, drink, and tobacco	19s. 0d.

	Women's Earnings, 1906
Cotton	18s. 8d.
Engineering, metalworking and	
shipbuilding	12s. 8d.
Paper and printing trades	12s. 2d.
Pottery, etc.	11s. 10d.
Food, etc.	11s. 5d.

Sources: For textiles, BPP, 1909, Board of Trade Earnings and Hours Enquiry, Cd.
4545, p. xxii; boots and shoes, Cd. 4844, p. xivi; building and woodworking,
Cd. 5086, p. x; public utilities, Cd. 5196, pp. xx, xxiii, xxv, xxvii; agriculture,
Cd. 5460, p. xii; pig iron, iron and steel, engineering and boilermaking, Cd.
5814, p. xiii; railways, Cd. 6053, p. xi; paper and printing, pottery, food and
drink, Cd. 6556, p. xiv.

account the 37 percent rise over twenty years, cotton's 27 percent rise in the average weekly earnings per workers between 1886 and 1906 set the pace.

"Round about a pound a week"—Edwardian Britain's rhetorical shorthand for the putative wages of adult male general laborers carried with it a penumbra of implications: slum housing, inadequate food and clothing, large numbers of ragged children, adding up to chronic poverty. Yet as we have seen, the fact of pooled cotton family earnings was cited, and the effect was to banish decisively the poverty stereotype and to substitute in its place a picture of adequacy that bordered on outright affluence.

In its broad outlines the antipoverty argument is sound enough if advanced with due respect shown for the fundamentals of socioeconomic statistical method. This contemporaries often failed to do. Writing in 1910, a journalist who wrote an ILP pamphlet entitled "Cotton and Competition," attempted to show how a family could earn seven pounds a week from working in the mills, and with the wife staying at home into the bargain. The method was simple and straightforward.[21]

	Low Estimate	High Estimate
Father, a mule spinner	45s. 0d.	60s. 0d.
Teenage boy, a big piecer	19s. 0d.	19s. 0d.
Son, a little piecer	10s. 6d.	10s. 6d.
Daughter 1, cardroom hand	18s. 0d.	18s. 0d.
Daughter 2, cardroom hand	25s. 0d.	25s. 0d.
Daughter 3, a four-loom weaver	16s. 0d.	24s. 6d.
Total	£6.13.6	£7.17.0

The figures given for the father's wages are quite unrealistic, since spinners' full-time wages in Oldham and Ashton averaged 41s. 10d. in 1906, and even in Leigh, the highest-paying district of all, the figure was 47s. 0d. for spinners.[22] (Besides, there existed a strong tendency for spinners' and weavers' wages to vary inversely within a district, so that if one selects the high end of the spectrum for spinning, one should follow with the low figure for weaving, and vice versa.) But the real difficulty is the confusion embodied in this approach between something that *could* have happened and how frequently something *actually* happened. The question is whether data and methods are available to make possible alternative approaches.

Fortunately, there are alternatives. To be sure, we have no records of surveys made with a view to ascertaining family earnings derived from mill work, and the manuscript census will not be available for many years. What can be used, however, are printed census data for 1911. They show 40,114 married women of all ages who worked in cotton mills. Now if one assumes that all of them were married to the 74,247 men aged twenty and older who also worked in the mills, the case for the typicality of multiple family earnings would be strengthened.[23] But the assumption is unfounded, since the census does not indicate the occupations of these women's husbands, and there are no compelling reasons to suppose that most, or even a majority, of the men also worked in the trade. Furthermore, one is not justified in supposing that married women cotton workers also had children working in the mills as well; on this point the census data are mute.

Even more revealing are the data relating occupation to family size in Table 10. Here the conclusion emerges that, on the average, cotton workers had fewer than two surviving children, a pattern one associates with current practices in advanced industrial society. As for the question of how many children of cotton workers went into the mills, one cannot tell. But it is clear that the vast majority of cotton worker families simply were not large enough by the twentieth century to generate incomes above five pounds a week, and it should be added that on any realistic accounting that such very high family earnings as might have existed could not have lasted for more than a few years in the history of any given family.[24] Accordingly, it strongly appears that the true impact of family earnings was to provide a margin between "making ends meet" and "doing without."

Just as the point of the argument over multiple earnings is to reconcile the prosperity thesis with the evidence, one can proceed in the same spirit regarding statistics on pauperism. As Table 11 shows, the Wigan poor law union was the only cotton district to register a pauperism rate above the average for England and Wales, a deviation that is probably best explained by the dominance of coal—rather than cotton—in the local economy. Nor should Manchester be considered a cotton town, in the sense of spinning or weaving being either the first or second largest employer.[25] But just because one finds a consistent pattern of low pauperism rates in the cotton towns, the conclusion that high wages are the cause does not necessarily follow. If the wage level in a district's staple trade is the key determinant, then one should expect to find a higher (relative to Lancashire) rate in the

Table 10

Standardized Number of Children Surviving per 100 Couples

Age of Wife at Marriage	According to Husband's Occupation		
	Workers in Spinning Processes	Workers in Weaving Processes	All Cotton Workers
15-19	316	273	296
20-24	222	196	208
25-29	144	130	136
30-34	100	100	98
35-39	51	49	48
Average	202	179	190

When Wife's Occupation Is That of Cotton Worker	
Age of Wife at Marriage	Number of Children
15-19	234
20-24	163
25-29	101
30-34	70
35-39	34
Average	147

Source: BPP, Census of England and Wales, 1911. Vol. 13, pt. 2 (1923), pp. 78, 167.

Table 11

Pauperism Rates per 1,000 Population for Selected Districts
as of January 1, 1911

Bolton	19.8	Huddersfield	16.6
Blackburn	16.8	Keighley	15.3
Clitheroe	17.1	Merthyr	31.5
Manchester	55.7	Newcastle	27.0
Oldham	17.1	Northampton	22.7
Wigan	24.8	Stoke	25.4
Dudley	29.8	Rotherham	16.4

Source: BPP, "Pauperism, England and Wales" (HC263), p. 30.

woollen towns of the West Riding of Yorkshire, since wages in the woollen and worsted trades were substantially lower than cotton (see Table 9). Yet pauperism rates in both regions were virtually identical: compare Huddersfield and Keighley, on the one hand, with Blackburn and Clitheroe, on the other. One must reject, on the grounds of there being no evidence whatever, the argument that for some reason West Riding poor law guardians cracked a meaner whip. Instead, both in the case of Lancashire and the West Riding the most plausible hypothesis appears to be the opportunity for family earnings within the context of an old, stable working population that had been around long enough to "learn the ropes." Conversely, the best explanation for towns like Merthyr might well be the influx of newcomers to the urban, industrial scene. Additionally—rather than alternatively—the structure of the labor market in northern mill towns in the late nineteenth and early twentieth centuries seems to have lacked casual and part-time jobs and consequently the "floating class" or "lumpen proletariat" that one associates with the social and occupational structure of really large, cosmopolitan cities in Western capitalism.

To sum up the argument so far, the Lancashire cotton workers were by 1910-14 as seasoned and experienced a community of workers as could be found anywhere in the industrial West up to that time. Having collectively experienced and learned much, they had also come to expect a good deal as well. And in these years the trade was delivering certain things, the most important of which were sustained growth and consequent employment prospects. However, the benefits were by no means evenly distributed among the workers. The full measure of the unevenness is the subject of Chapter 3.

The Tenacity of Sectional Differences | 3

A major question in labor history is the impact of modern industry upon socioeconomic divisions within a laboring population, or, to put matters more concretely, whether industrial capitalism creates over the long haul a working class essentially free from major sectional divisions with respect to industrial, political, and cultural experiences and outlooks. The Lancashire cotton workers provide extraordinarily rich evidence for the contention that modern large-scale industry does not automatically lead to reductions in sectionalism and that, on the contrary, differences among workers—even those in the same industry—can be deeply rooted in the workers' own experiences and lives. In this chapter we examine three large areas: wage differentials, the position of women in the cotton industry, and, finally, childrens' work and schooling.

To say that wages averaged 19s. 11d. per capita in 1906 tells one nothing about wage differentials *among* cotton operatives. Did the majority of their pay packets cluster at or near the 19s. 11d. figure? If not, which and how many workers received more, or less? Where sizable differentials are found, how are they best explained? What are the implications of wage differentials in terms of workers' behavior and consciousness?

The answer to the first question—whether or not the pattern of wage distribution looked like a bell-shaped curve—is that it did not. Instead, an image of several discontinuous points around which wages tended to cluster should be substituted. At the lowest end were children. Although it is true that a range is to be found extending from the traditional half-crown a week for beginners up to 14s. 0d. for little piecers in Oldham in 1906, nevertheless the fact remains that the average of 11s. 6d. for "lads and boys" and 10s. 1d. for girls was several shillings less than the lowest-paid jobs reserved for adults.[1] That children in the cotton industry were badly paid was of course far from unique. What was unusual was that the number of youthful workers ran into the scores of thousands and that they were regarded by almost everyone as a permanently "given" section of the work force.[2]

A second group, whose wages tended to cluster a bit below the 19s. 11d. average, consisted mainly of women workers engaged in processes preparatory and ancillary to the actual spinning of yarn and weaving of cloth. For example, frame tenters, working at machines that attenuated the carded or combed cotton into thin "rovings" in Bolton received between 17s. 2d. and 18s. 8d.[3] Workers engaged in winding and reeling processes, in which yarn from the mules was repackaged for use as warp and weft threads in power loom weaving, received even less—14s. 6d. was the average in 1906 for winders in the relatively high-wage Blackburn and Accrington district.[4] In 1914 there could have been upward of 75,000 to 80,000 of these workers.[5] To them should be added at least 20,000 big piecers. Overwhelmingly male and in their late teens and twenties, they constituted along with the half-time children a collective "problem child" of the industry by virtue of (1) low wages—averaging 19s. 4d. in Oldham, 15s. 9d. in Bolton, and 16s. 7d. in the United Kingdom as a whole—[6] and (2) the uncertainty of promotion to the much better paid job of operative mule spinner. The exact source of the downward pressure on the wage levels for these jobs is clear only in the case of the piecers, who found themselves on the receiving end of a tacit alliance between the spinners' union and the employers. As for the others, relatively low skill requirements and a certain lack of centrality in the production process could well have been the decisive factors. What is beyond doubt is that the cardroom and weavers' unions did little to "service" them. It is true that the Cardroom Workers Amalgamation organized many of the tenters, but its chief motive in doing so appears to have been to augment the bargaining power of the male carding-engine operatives, the strippers and grinders, with the result that the union was accused of failing even to negotiate the speeds at which management would be allowed to run tenting frames.[7] Likewise, there is no evidence that the Amalgamated Weavers went out of their way on behalf of winders and reelers; as a result, the latter apparently remained largely without any union organization.

The third point around which wages clustered was substantially above the 19s. 11d. industry-wide average and was made up of adult men and women weavers. They are interesting in a number of respects. First, they were the largest single occupational group in the industry, comprising about 200,000 workers.[8] Second, it was within the weaving branch that differences between men's and women's earnings came closest to being obliterated,[9] as Table 12 shows. Indeed, if one takes seriously the argument put forward by contemporaries that the women were treated like "second-class citizens" with respect to the assistance they received from the power loom mechanics (or "tacklers," as they were called) and the earning potential of the sorts of cloth they were given to weave, the evidence suggests that women weavers might have been more efficient workers than their male counterparts.[10] Third, it will be noted from Table 12 that if, on the one hand, four-loom weavers were paid better

Table 12

Wages of Men and Women Weavers, 1906

	Men		Women	
	Four-Loom Weavers	All Men Weavers	Four-Loom Weavers	All Women Weavers
Ashton-under Lyne	23s. 10d.	21s. 11d.	21s. 6d.	18s. 1d.
Oldham	—	—	21s. 33d.	17s. 11d.
Bolton	24s. 10d.	25s. 0d.	22s. 10d.	18s. 9d.
Leigh	—	—	20s. 0d.	17s. 7d.
Manchester	—	—	20s. 0d.	16s. 0d.
Stockport	23s. 3d.	22s. 11d.	22s. 2d.	21s. 0d.
Preston	24s. 10d.	23s. 9d.	23s. 1d.	20s. 5d.
Blackburn	25s. 5d.	24s. 9d.	24s. 9d.	23s. 6d.
Accrington	24s. 6d.	22s. 5d.	23s. 4d.	20s. 11d.
Burnley	25s. 11d.	27s. 7d.	25s. 3d.	24s. 11d.
Bacup	24s. 4d.	24s. 0d.	23s. 0d.	20s. 4d.
Rochdale	23s. 4d.	23s. 4d.	22s. 7d.	19s. 8d.
All Lancashire and Cheshire	25s. 1d.	25s. 4d.	23s. 6d.	20s. 10d.

Source: BPP, 1909, Cd. 4545, op. cit., p. xxxiv.

than general laborers, on the other hand they were just as far from being labor aristocrats. As such they constitute good evidence for Henry
Pelling's contention that a bipartite division of the late Victorian working class into aristocrats and laborers is an oversimplification.[11] Finally,
and most important for our purposes, is the propensity of the weavers
to strike. As will be shown, the weavers were responsible for much of
the industrial conflict between 1910 and 1914; also, the weavers' union
stood politically to the left of the other cotton unions.[12]

The fourth large cluster to be discerned was made up of well-paid
adult men, and almost unanimously labor historians have called such
workers labor aristocrats. As far as cotton is concerned, the term is largely
—but not entirely—satisfactory. The problem is not so much that cotton
aristocrats were not in fact markedly better off—especially with respect
to wages—than their "plebeian" mates, but rather that there appears to
be three distinct groups of them, each with its own characteristics as to
how its members got to be aristocrats in the first place and how they
maintained the "trappings of gentility." These three groups may be labeled
"subaristocrats," "true aristocrats," and "contrived aristocrats."

The largest and clearest example of subaristocrats was the several thou-
sand strippers and grinders, that is, carding-engine minders and technicians
in spinning mills. That the term "aristocratic" correctly applies to them
can be seen from their almost complete unionization and their favorable
working conditions—for example, they were not on piece rates, and they
performed several distinct technical operations on the carding engines as
the need arose, rather than just "minding" the machines day in and day
out. This gave them a certain degree of on-the-job autonomy. However,
their wages, averaging 29s. 3d. in 1906,[13] though good money, were not
unusually high. What is more, such aristocratic trappings as they did enjoy
were of fairly recent origin and therefore liable to attack from the employers. Indeed, the spinning lockout of 1910, which is analyzed in Chapter 7,
can be seen in terms of the strippers and grinders successfully defending
their newly acquired prestige and material gains. Accordingly, it makes
sense to introduce the qualification of subaristocracy in describing the
strippers and grinders, and it would not be surprising if research was to
show that other workers in other industries also shared these characteristics.

The second group, true aristocrats, may be considered as a paradigm
case of E. J. Hobsbawm's checklist of aristocratic features;[14] this group

was admirably represented by the tapesizers. A very small occupational group—only one man was needed for a good-sized mill of 350 looms[15]— these men straddled a real bottleneck in the production process, that of applying sizing to the warp threads. They were one of the few groups in the entire industry to enforce a real apprenticeship system.[16] Their wages were very high: 47s. 3d. in the Blackburn district in 1906.[17] They appear to have called no strikes of their own during the period 1910-14.[18]

Operative mule spinners, of whom there were at least 25,000 in the years 1910-14, comprised the trade's contrived aristocrats. The term is less than perfect in view of the social scientist's insistence that practically all significant human group activity is the result of wit, intelligence, and imagination—that is to say, is more "contrived" than "natural" or "spontaneous." Nevertheless, the usage is justifiable insofar as it allows a distinction to be drawn between work groups whose aristocratic status was achieved with relative ease as opposed to other groups that had to create, and indeed struggle for, their aristocratic position.

That the spinners definitely fall into the latter category can be shown in several ways. First, let us consider the element of skill. Although it is quite true that before the invention by Roberts of the fully self-acting mule, spinning required both physical strength and manual dexterity,[19] the self-actor itself demanded nothing at all unusual in the way of strength and a level of dexterity that although real enough hardly exceeded that of, say, a joiner or a skilled engineer. Nor was the skill factor the only plebeian feature of life in the mulegate. If many weavers had to work with condensed steam dripping onto their heads amid the deafening clatter of shuttles, spinners worked in a superheated atmosphere where temperatures ranged from 95° F. to 110°F.,[20] irrespective of the outside weather. It was thought that heat made the rovings less brittle. Accordingly, spinners and piecers wore only the lightest trousers and shirts on the job. For reasons that specialists in industrial health and medicine are not fully agreed upon, mule spinners were liable to the incurable disease of cancer of the scrotum—a ghastly way to die, by any reckoning. What is more, the problem was not even positively diagnosed until about 1900.[21]

How then did the spinners manage to achieve wage levels of two pounds and higher? Pointing to strong organization and militant tactics in the abstract will not do at all: What is needed is an analysis of the specific mechanism that the spinners adopted to stave off the fate of being treated like run-of-the-mill semiskilled hands. The answer is to be found in the union's insistence that a pair of mules be staffed by one adult man and two or more younger assistants (piecers), thus ensuring that the spinner (or minder, as he was sometimes called) would receive the lion's share of the "earnings of the mules." And as a symbolic flourish, thrown in as a reminder of who really ruled the roost, the union and the employers agreed that piecers' wages should be handed over directly and personally by the minders. This holdover from the days of true subcontracting still retained a remarkable vitality.[22]

Now in an important sense the spinners' policy cannot be faulted. Trade unions must seek the best deal possible section by section and are often justified, if other less well-off workers cry foul, in replying: "go thou and do likewise." However, one may question whether these particular tactics were not partially self-defeating. It will be noted that the spinning "team" of one adult and two or sometimes three assistants must result in a permanent oversupply relative to job openings of persons capable of running a pair of mules, save for periods of the most rapid expansion of production. This meant that a mad scramble occurred every time a pair of mules opened up—a scramble that although grueling enough from a piecer's standpoint was if anything even worse for men who were already spinners, as it made lateral mobility within the trade almost impossible.[23] Suppose, for example, that a spinner, having recovered from injury or illness, was seeking reemployment. Perforce he would be engaging in queue jumping, because in most mule rooms in Lancashire there was a more or less formal seniority system that gave piecers already employed the first crack at openings as they arose. A spinner's interloping could easily trigger off a piecers' strike, and indeed, promotion disputes accounted for the majority of piecers' strikes between 1910 and 1914. Moreover, within their own terms these strikes were often successful, with the result that the interloping spinner might well have to revert to piecing, individually negotiating with his new employer the best terms he could as regards his place in the line.[24]

The point is that the spinners' aristocratic status was a peculiarly brittle and fragile affair from an individual spinner's standpoint—lengthy and difficult to attain initially and all too easy to lose. Contemporaries were quite well aware what the problem was. No less an authority than James Mawdesley, the general secretary of the Amalgamated Spinners during the last quarter of the nineteenth century, came to the conclusion that the spinner-piecer system benefited the bosses more than the workers. As he told the Webbs:

. . . the employers [are] rather stupid in encouraging and the men in denouncing the joining system as it would certainly result in a scarcity of spinners, for where there are now two piecers to one man there would be then one piecer to two men. Of course now there are plenty of spinners as most piecers learn [to become spinners] and the masters have their pick and reject the slow and unsteady ones, but they won't be able to do this if joining is adopted everywhere, for the number of spinners will be greatly decreased.[25]

Prediction is one thing, performance another. And the thing that spinners could not but fail to notice was that in the marginal spinning districts of northeast Lancashire, where the joiner-minder system referred to by Mawdesley of two adults and one juvenile to a pair of mules had been in effect for a long time, wages showed no signs of moving upward toward those of minders in south Lancashire working under the spinner-piecer system.[26] There is no evidence in our period of attempts to follow up on Mawdesley's advice.

One final implication remains to be drawn regarding the conjunction of aristocratic status and considerable insecurity. Historians have long been puzzled by the spinners' political and social conservatism and have pointed to factors such as the spinners' supposed belief that the Tories had displayed a better record over time on factory legislation, the possibility that the spinners reacted against the crude liberalism of many cotton mill owners, and the fact of high earnings per se.[27] (In fact, spinners' Toryism was not the monolith it has sometimes been made out to be.) But is it not possible to suggest that their conservatism flowed from the tenuous and fragile protective structure they had contrived? Admittedly, it is a difficult point to prove conclusively, but at least it has the advantage of attempting to relate politics and values directly to the spinners' life and work situation, rather than resorting to an appeal to vague and undefined "traditions."[28]

Cotton workers were thus sharply divided by wage level according to one's occupation within the industry, but there were several other determinants besides. A second factor influencing wages was how heavily a branch of the trade was concentrated in a particular district—concentration here being defined as the number of spindles and looms in operation.

What is significant about Table 13 is that it shows two tendencies at work simultaneously. First is the consistency of the positive correlation

Table 13 Wage Differentials According to District

District	Looms	Spindles	Women Weavers' Wages	All Men's Wages	Spinners' Wages
Burnley	111,052	545,776	24s. 11d.	29s. 7d.	29s. 2d.
Blackburn	99,417	1,259,998	23s. 6d.	27s. 4d.	29s. 2d.
Preston	71,321	2,242,306	20s. 5d.	28s. 6d.	39s. 3d.
Accrington	40,019	727,158	20s. 11d.	28s. 1d.	34s. 1d.
Bolton	24,569	6,916,087	18s. 9d.	32s. 0d.	45s. 9d.
Manchester	23,796	3,725,092	16s. 0d.	32s. 3d.	47s. 0d.
Rochdale	20,726	3,718,566	19s. 8d.	27s. 9d.	41s. 1d.
Oldham	16,728	17,193,544	17s. 11d.	31s. 8d.	41s. 10d.
Ashton	19,782	1,983,448	18s. 1d.	31s. 3d.	41s. 10d.
Stockport	9,887	2,305,890	21s. 0d.	29s. 11d.	41s. 3d.
Bacup	9,135	325,442	20s. 4d.	26s. 0d.	30s. 9d.
Leigh	7,766	2,500,526	17s. 7d.	34s. 10d.	47s. 6d.

Sources: Looms and Spindles, J. Worral, Ltd., *Cotton Spinners' and Manufacturers' Directory for 1914*, Oldham: 1915, p. 11; Wages, BPP, 1909, "Earnings and Hours Enquiry," Cd. 4545, p. xxx.

for both spinning and weaving between concentration and pay. In north-east Lancashire, where a handful of mule spinners were lost in a crowd of weavers and others, their wages were the lowest of all the spinners. Similarly, Manchester weavers, also overwhelmed by other trades, were the lowest paid of all the weavers. Secondly, one notes an equally consistent inverse relationship such that in districts where spinning predominated, weaving tended to be weakly concentrated and vice versa. Whatever the precise causes, the result in spinning centers was to accentuate even more sharply the skewed and discontinuous wage structure that already existed between spinning aristocrats and the rest.

Wage differentials between districts are of course common enough in industries that are nationwide in location, but for differentials to be so marked within an industry as geographically compressed as cotton is perhaps surprising. In the case of northeast Lancashire mule spinners, the reason for their relatively low wages has already been given: that is, the joiner-minder system of staffing a pair of mules was in effect, meaning that two adults had to share the piece rate earnings of the mules between them. However, in other places, the reasons are not all that clear. In explaining, for example, why women weavers in the Burnley district earned 41 percent more than women weavers in Leigh—24s. 11d. versus 17s. 7d. —one should take into account: (1) technological modernization, (2) the profitability of firms, (3) the kinds of cloth woven, (4) the labor supply, (5) trade union penetration, and (6) the sexual composition of the labor force. These six factors are often mutually interactive so that beyond a certain point attempts to rank-order them become impossible and therefore misleading.

Difficulties notwithstanding, the unusual distribution of occupations within the industry by sex demands separate attention as a factor determining wages. Indeed, for most occupations sexual segregation was close to 100 percent—a state of affairs for which the unions must share historical responsibility along with the employers. A particularly vivid example of the lengths to which the unions would go to enforce segregation is provided by the spinners. In 1911 they learned to their consternation that an employer in Wigan had taken on women as mule spinners. The union's response was not to organize them, which if done would have raised their pay considerably, but rather to complain to the factory inspector and lobby for an amendment to the factory acts barring women from the mule room altogether.[29] By the same token, the spinners refused to organize ring spinners, all of whom were women, preferring to leave the task to the cardroom union.[30] In addition to ring spinners the Cardroom Workers Amalgamation had already organized women frame tenters, and in fact women formed a sizable majority of the total membership.[31] However, for our period it appears that all appointed officials and elected rank-and-file branch committee members were men. In addition, there were a number of winding and reeling processes that were considered strictly "women's work."[32]

The one great exception to strict occupational segregation was power loom weaving, and, as we have already seen, weavers were the most highly paid women workers in the entire economy. It is difficult to resist the conclusion that the facts of occupational integration and high women's wages are causally related. The explanation is not so much that the all-male officials of the weavers' union pressed for high wages for women per se, but rather that precisely because there was a large and permanent minority of men weavers,[33] a "living-wage" trade policy became the order of the day, which in practice meant the demand for equal pay for equal work. On the other hand, where rigid occupational segregation was the pattern, as in the cardroom, the union was under no such constraints.

Nevertheless, wage differentials between men and women weavers still existed—ranging from 5.3 percent in Blackburn (24s. 9d. vs. 23.s. 6d.) to 33.3 percent in Bolton (25s. 0d. vs. 18s. 9d.), with Ashton somewhere in between with a differential of 14.5 percent (21s. 11d. vs 18s. 11d.). Both the spread of the differential and the level of women's earnings appear intimately related to the number of men weavers expressed as a percentage of men cotton workers in a given locality. Fifty-three percent of Blackburn's cotton men were weavers. In the Burnley district, which had the highest wages for both men and women weavers, 65 percent of the cotton men were weavers and the male-female differential was a relatively small 10.7 percent. Conversely, in the three districts where the percentage of men weavers was statistically insignificant—Oldham, Leigh, and Manchester—the wages of women weavers were the lowest in all Lancashire—17s. 11d., 17s. 7d., and 16s. 0d., respectively.[34]

A final determinant of wages to be considered is the degree of trade union organization. Or is it begging the question to put the matter in this form, in light of the possibility that trade union successes in bargaining merely reflect an industry's ability to pay? Unfortunately, the data available for the Lancashire cotton industry are inadequate. Particularly intractable is the problem of accurately designating the catchment area for many cotton union branches; and if this cannot be done, it becomes impossible to derive accurately the proportion of unionized workers, except in the aggregate. What can positively be said is that the Lancashire experience provided the strongest *circumstantial* evidence that unions could and did raise wages. Firms that withheld union recognition almost always paid less than the union scale. The most strongly organized sections were also the ones that paid the highest wages. Conversely, poorly organized sections—for example, winders, frame tenters, piecers—were all badly paid. A final and hardly original observation on the question is that the mill owners also operated on the assumption that union strength and pressure made a difference. Thus evidence that decisively refutes the ability of unions to raise the level of real wages will have to be drawn from sources other than that of the Lancashire cotton industry in the early twentieth century.

On the narrow economic criterion of wages, then, cotton workers were deeply divided among themselves. Nor was it simply a matter of skill and wage levels differentiating workers who were otherwise socially homogeneous. As has been noted, women and children constituted two social groupings that between them made up a majority of the total work force. It is their problems as workers and the unions' responses to those problems that the next two sections examine.

WOMEN

The full history of women in the cotton industry cannot be attempted in this book. However, we can probe along two lines: (1) How did women in the cotton industry in Britain differ from women elsewhere in the country? (2) To the extent that women cotton workers had distinctive needs and interests, how well were they fulfilled? A quantitative, statistical approach is indicated for the first question; an analysis of written, "literary" sources is indicated for the latter.

A first important way in which women cotton workers differed from their sisters in the manual-labor force has already been mentioned: Women in cotton factories were the best-paid manual workers in the country.[35] To this should be added the Factory Acts, which had been extended and improved throughout the nineteenth century, although it may be said that if the Factory Acts were comprehensive, there were many abuses in cotton mills for which they had to be comprehensive. However this may be, when one considers the types of occupations open to early twentieth-century British working-class women—domestic service with its low pay and even lower status (or is it the other way around?); work in match factories; garment making, often under sweated conditions; retail shop work with its long hours; other textile trades; and a seemingly endless "tail" of often unskilled occupations in and about practically every trade in the economy[36] —the distinctiveness of cotton workers stands out all the more clearly.[37]

In theory many of the 129,021 women cotton workers aged twenty and older who were unmarried at the time of the 1911 census—and especially the 59,953 weavers—were paid well enough to set up housekeeping on their own, or with other similarly situated women. How many women did in fact live this way? According to a Board of Trade Labor Department inquiry conducted in 1909 and 1910, out of 30 cotton factory workers, 23 lived at home with either one or both parents, 2 lived with sisters who also worked, 1 shared rooms with a friend, and 2 lived alone.[38] Most unfortunately, the inquiry did not ascertain the age of the respondents, so that for all one knows every one of them was under the age of, say, twenty-five years. In any event the sample is too small to bear much analytical weight, revealing once more the usefulness of the manuscript census.[39]

If one cannot draw firm conclusions about the life styles of unmarried cotton women, comparative data about their propensity to marry vis-à-vis other groups of women are ample. As Table 14 shows, the institution of marriage was as popular with women in the cotton towns as it was for Lancashire and the rest of the country as a whole. But the country was not homogeneous in this respect. In solidly middle-class areas like Hampstead, in northwest London, compared with the national average a markedly smaller percentage of women were married. On the other hand, in the steel and heavy-engineering districts of South Yorkshire over three women out of five between the ages of fourteen and forty-five were married. Accordingly, one cannot advance a single explanation for marriage rates in early twentieth-century Britain. As far as the women in the cotton towns are concerned, there are two a priori hypotheses, each of which is diametrically opposed to the empirical evidence in Table 12. The first is that, because the occupational and wage structure of the cotton industry gave many women the opportunity to earn a living wage, women

Table 14

Marriage Rates for Selected Regions, 1911

Place	Married Women (%)	Married Women Aged 15-45[a] (%)
England and Wales	38.4	48.6
All Lancashire	38.2	48.7
Ashton	40.0	49.6
Blackburn	39.7	47.4
Burnley	41.2	50.7
Clitheroe	38.5	57.2
Bolton	38.0	46.9
Oldham	40.6	50.6
Preston	36.6	44.9
Rochdale	41.1	49.9
Manchester	36.8	50.4
Salford	37.8	50.9
Liverpool	35.9	49.6
All London	36.9	45.6
Paddington	33.3	36.2
Hampstead	28.4	27.5
Islington	39.1	48.7
Bethnal Green	36.7	51.5
Stepney	36.9	53.0
Poplar	38.4	53.3
Southwark	39.6	54.1
Lambeth	39.0	48.9
Camberwell	38.6	48.3
Surrey	37.0	44.5
Kent	38.6	47.5
Sheffield	41.7	60.3
Rotherham	41.6	63.3
Doncaster	41.7	60.9
Bradford	40.8	46.5
Leeds	47.8	46.0
Huddersfield	39.6	46.5

[a]The 1911 census does not appear to contain data regarding the age at which women married.

Source: BPP, 1913, Census of England and Wales, Cd. 6610, percentages calculated from pp. 382, 392.

in fact took the option of remaining single; and there one should find relatively low marriage rates. The other hypothesis is that insofar as the cotton men and women were "mature industrial workers," one should expect them to have been in the vanguard of the twentieth-century marriage upswing. However, the data seem to fall between the two extremes. Perhaps both tendencies were at work together in the cotton towns with the result that the two contradictory tendencies canceled one another out.

Indeed, the evidence suggests that the mills did not radically transform the life cycle of Lancashire women compared with women elsewhere. In industrial society the overwhelming majority of working-class women perform paid manual labor before they get married, and in the cotton districts the largest source of employment happened to be the factories. But as Table 15 shows, women tended to drop rapidly out of the labor force after age thirty-five. Whereas men over thirty-five made up 32.9 percent of the male work force, women over thirty-five accounted for only 19.1 percent of female workers. To be sure, the data do not exclude the possibility that some of the older married women who had dropped out of the labor force to have children returned to full-time work after the children had grown old enough to care for themselves. But the dominant tendency appears to be that once most women left the trade, they left for good. Accordingly, the biggest impact of women working seems to have been more economic than social. As discussed in Chapter 2, work in the mills afforded the opportunity for thousands of Lancashire families to supplement earnings by the wife's working before children were born.

In the case of marriage, then, one finds that relatively good wages and job opportunities did not cause women in the cotton towns to differ much from women in the rest of the country. However, if one looks at the number of domestic servants in the cotton towns, significant differences are found. Table 16 shows that although the cotton districts were not absolutely uniform, nevertheless even Wigan, with the highest ratio of indoor domestic servants per 1,000 household-families, is substantially lower than all the other noncotton towns except Stoke. On the face of it, employment in the mills appears to have been preferred to doing other (and usually wealthier) women's housework. The only objection is whether in practical terms the alternatives were posed in this way for women: In other words, did opportunities for becoming a domestic servant actually exist? It could be argued that the social structure of places like Oldham, Nelson, and other cotton towns were so truncated at the top that servant-employ-

Table 15

Men and Women in the Labor Force by Age (Percentages)

			Men			
Less than 20	20-24	25-34	35-44	45-54	55-64	65 and over
30.4	15.6	21.1	17.1	11.2	5.1	1.7
			Women			
35.8	20.6	24.5	12.4	5.4	1.5	0.3

Source: BPP, 1913, vol. 79, "Census of England and Wales," Cd. 7019, p. 205.
Percentages are computed to slide-rule accuracy.

Table 16

Domestic Indoor Servants per 1,000 Separate Occupiers or Families

District	No. of Servants
Blackburn[a]	51
Bolton	60
Bury	60
Burnley	45
Little Lever	
(urban district near Bolton)	22
Nelson	29
Oldham	51
Chadderton	
(urban district near Oldham)	24
Wigan	77
Manchester	93
Liverpool	135
London	194
Northampton	99
Newcastle upon Tyne	137
Sunderland	128
Jarrow	90
Barrow in Furness	96
Wolverhampton	128
Stoke on Trent	75

[a]Italics indicate selected spinning and weaving districts.
Source: BPP, 1913, Census of England and Wales, Cd. 7018, pp. 436-39.

ing strata were simply not to be found in anything like the proportions of, say, Manchester, Liverpool, or London. Against this one can point out that towns like Barrow, Sunderland, and Jarrow had as high a percentage of manual working people as did the cotton towns, but that even so the servant-to-household ratio was higher. Therefore, since the possibility of becoming a servant appears to have been ubiquitous, the conclusion is justified that where industrial occupations existed for women, they would choose them over domestic service, a conclusion reinforced by the figures for Stoke, where women's jobs in the potteries did not pay nearly so well as in cotton. Nonetheless, the servant-to-household ratio is only slightly above that of the cotton towns.

A third way in which women cotton workers differed from women elsewhere in Britain was in the number of children they had. As has been shown earlier, the families of cotton workers were not all that large in absolute terms; but what basis of comparison should we use? According to Table 17, male cotton workers fall roughly midway between middle-class professionals—whose families were smaller yet—and labor aristocrats, like engine drivers and metal machinists—whose families except for watch- and clockmakers were somewhat larger. The coincidental figure of 86 percent for cotton workers and insurance agents, the latter being typically lower middle class, neatly summarizes the picture. In view of the general uncertainty among historical demographers regarding the determinants of

Table 17

Children Born and Children Surviving, per 100 of the Corresponding Numbers for the Total Population of England and Wales

Occupation	Children Born	Children Surviving
Cotton workers: men	86	81
Cotton workers: women	74	63
Army officers	59	66
Accountants	69	75
Commercial travelers	76	81
Woollen and worsted: men	84	82
Watch- and clockmakers	84	88
Insurance agents	86	90
Railway engine drivers	98	100
Metal machinists	100	98

Source: BPP, 1923, Census of England and Wales for 1911, Cd. 8678, pp. 84 ff.

family size in advanced industrial and other societies, one is most reluctant to stress any one single hypothesis to explain why cotton workers chose to limit the size of their families.[40] What the Webbs wrote in 1902—

> We attribute family planning chiefly to the spread of education among working-class women, to their discontent with a life of constant ill-health and domestic worry under narrow circumstances, and to the growth among them of aspirations for a fuller and more independent existence of their own. . . .[41]

—still appears to be a viable formulation of the question.

Theoretically, one should expect to find that birth rates and infant mortality rates decline together, and this was certainly the case with the cotton workers. But Table 17 also shows that despite this decline the infant mortality rate for cotton workers remained comparatively high. When, for example, the statistics tell us that the wives of army officers brought children into the world at a rate that was 59 percent that of all occupied and unoccupied couples and that the percentage surviving was 66, this means that infant mortality among the offspring of army officers was less than the infant mortality rate for all couples. (If the infant mortality rates were identical, the identity would be expressed by a 59 percent entry in the "children surviving" column of Table 17.) For cotton workers' families, though, the statistics are reversed. Where the husband is listed as a cotton operative and the wife's occupation is not given, one notes that the mortality is 5 percent higher—that is, a differential of 5 percent between children born and children surviving—than for the whole population. The tendency is even more pronounced when the woman is a cotton operative: Seventy-four percent are born compared with 63 percent surviving.

It has long been known to social historians that one cannot explain differential infant mortality rates by an appeal to poverty in general, and the case of women cotton workers is no exception.[42] Besides, one cannot make a good case for widespread poverty in the cotton towns.[43] What does, however, stand out in the Lancashire experience is a social nonorganization—there appears to be no other expression for it—of childbirth and child care that in its own way was every bit as perverse as the mid-Victorian practice of sending middle- and upper-class women off to bed at the end of the seventh month of pregnancy. We are referring to the all but total absence of social services such as maternity leaves, crèches, well-baby clinics, visiting nurses, and preschool education. Of course, the cotton towns were not alone in this respect; the problem was nationwide. The point is that Lancashire working women stood in special need of these services.

We may attempt to reconstruct the sequence of concrete problems faced by a woman cotton worker about to have a baby. In the first place, since maternity leaves did not exist, a woman was "free" to continue at work right up to the onset of labor. If she wanted her job back after the baby's birth, arrangements would have to be made for a minimum of four weeks, if the letter of the Factory Acts was followed, though it was asserted that evasion of this proviso was widespread.[44] No doubt there were cases in which a woman's skill and efficiency were highly regarded by the (male) overlooker, who might then promise orally to give her her old job upon her return to the workplace, trade conditions permitting. In other cases, however, it is likely that the woman would herself find a substitute; this was the common practice for minor illness. After the baby had been born, someone would have to be found to care for it when the mother returned to work. That someone could range from the husband[45] or another family member, particularly older children, to women in the neighborhood who took care of babies for a living: Five shillings a week for a three-to-six month old is one figure cited.[46] One can only guess as to which methods of child care were most frequently used, or on the average length of the post-partum convalescence period.

More specifically, one would like to be able to know how many women temporarily dropped out of the labor force for the years of childbirth and infant care, which is one inference that can be drawn from the data in Table 18. These figures show progressive upward jumps in the proportion of married women workers as age increases. But even if this happened to a limited extent, it could at best be called a private response to a public problem. In retrospect one cannot see how anything less than either a mass exodus of married women from the trade or a radically new approach to the social services could have decisively broken the factory-high infant mortality axis; before 1914 neither was forthcoming.[47]

The analysis indicates that many of the women were in a sense "part-time" workers. In the case of young, unmarried women, millwork was a short phase in their life cycle, a preface to marriage and child rearing. In the case of married women with children, domestic commitments took up much of their time spent off the job. Two questions present themselves. First, how did these factors influence men's perceptions of women's

Table 18

Unmarried and Married Women Cotton Factory Workers,
Aged 15-44

Occupation	15-19	20-24	25-34	35-44
Card and Blowing-Room Processes				
Unmarried	14,009	8,691	4,993	1,724
Married	98	1,848	5,128	2,711
Percent of married women	0.1	17.7	52.6	69.6
Spinning Processes				
Unmarried	13,245	7,304	3,730	1,013
Married	123	1,848	3,862	1,510
Percent of married women	0.1	20.4	52.1	63.5
Winding and Warping Processes				
Unmarried	9,776	8,378	7,445	3,052
Married	48	1,447	5,429	3,860
Percent of married women	0.5	15.1	43.2	59.3
Weaving Processes				
Unmarried	38,135	27,466	20,254	7,653
Married	235	5,707	22,288	13,141
Percent of married women	0.1	17.4	53.0	65.6
Other Processes				
Unmarried	917	559	392	169
Married	2	71	279	168
Percent of married women	0	12.0	42.8	57.6
Undefined				
Unmarried	1,577	420	214	75
Married	4	60	106	126
Percent of married women	0	14.3	49.9	70.4

Source: BPP, 1913, Census of England and Wales, Cd. 7018, p. 108.

"proper" role in industrial life? And, second, to what extent and with what success did women participate in the "public" life of the labor movement—particularly in the unions?

It has already been shown that the cotton unions had fully articulated policies regarding occupational equality: The Spinners excluded women altogether, as did the craft unions in cloth manufacturing such as the Twisters and the Tapesizers; the Cardroom Workers, even though their union admitted women to membership, went along with 100 percent occupational segregation; and the Weavers Amalgamation, though formally integrated with respect to the occupation of power loom weaving, acquiesced in and possibly even connived at preserving the best-paying kinds of jobs for men only.[48] Indeed, the three policies were not all that separate and distinct from each other when one considers that each union was accepting situations that already existed and were not of their own original making. There is every reason to suppose that if, for example, the history of power loom weaving had been one in which all weavers were men and all reelers and winders were women, the Weavers Amalgamation would have accepted the status quo, just as the cardroom workers' union made no attempt to create opportunities for women to become strippers and grinders.

On the surface it would appear that the consistent policy of retaining sexual inequalities with regard to occupation is best explained by attributing to the unions' leadership the same sexist values that pervaded the larger society. Evidence to this effect can certainly be found; perhaps as graphic an example as any is the president of the Bolton Spinners speaking as one of a minority of four against women's suffrage at the 1913 annual conference[49] of the Trades Union Congress. But it may be questioned whether the male union leaders' antifeminist stance in fact did not flow from different social and historical pressures. After all, the employers had exploited women workers to the combined detriment of women and men alike at the beginning of the factory system; at least so it must have appeared from the standpoint of intelligent male trade unionists. Since the functioning of trade unions has historically been primarily defensive, it is not surprising that the men's attitude was to "make the best of a bad job," that is, to accept as given the women already employed, and adopt the defensive measures of: (1) unionizing women who had obtained a sizable or exclusive foothold in an occupation and (2) freezing the occupational structure at that point of development.

Hence the antifeminist stand of the union leadership had specific sources in that leadership's experiences and own reading of history. What is more, Fabian Socialist trade union theory, as expounded by the Webbs in *Industrial Democracy,* powerfully endorsed what the cotton men were already doing. The Webbs begin their remarkable analysis of women in industry by noting that the ordinary urban middle-class citizen is already so accustomed to seeing women in the professions that he is usually unaware that in manual industry, occupational demarcation by sex is the general practice.[50] Male "artisans" object to women on the grounds that their presence invariably undercuts the Standard Rate.[51] As for management, "it has never occurred to the most economical employer to substitute women for men,"[52] and they provide evidence as to why management adopts this policy so consistently by citing one counterexample in which a cotton-weaving firm tried to teach women twisting and drawing but abandoned the scheme when it became clear that the women were not catching on to the intricacies of the work.[53] Nevertheless, in those cases in which management is really determined "to bring women into any trade within their capacity,"[54] management invariably succeeds in doing so, despite the union's equally invariable opposition. An occasional consequence of the employers' insistence is spatial as well as occupational segregation by sex, whereby, as in the case of London-based printing firms, a company might operate an inner-city shop that was fully male and fully unionized, and also a shop in the outlying Home Counties that employed women.[55]

The Webbs' account bristles with difficulties. Since on their own showing women did hold down the same white-collar jobs as men, the question of whether there were manual jobs that women could perform and in fact did perform just as capably as men, cannot be sloughed over. Yet this *ignoratio elenchi* is precisely what the Webbs resort to. From their discussion of the London printing trades one simply cannot tell whether women did the exact same work as the men in the Metropolis, or whether physically easier, less technically complex work was expressly set aside for them. In a slightly different context they observe that in the light of the ways the spinners treat their male piecers, "no one . . . can doubt the wisdom of women being excluded from the mule room"[56]—a formulation that once again does not directly address itself to the possibility that women piecers might have been just as efficient as men, but at the same time does not explicitly deny the possibility either. Since they do not take a straightforward position on whether women could do "men's" work in any given occupation, they end up justifying occupational segregation by sex on the grounds that women have different "faculties, needs, and expectations" from the men for which reasons it would be "unfair and even cruel to uphold the fiction of the equality of the sexes in the industrial world."[57] What empirical content one is to assign to these different faculties, needs, and expectations, they do not suggest.

One gets the feeling that the Webbs regarded women in industry as more of a headache than a challenge to trade union leaders. But they point out that most of the unions underwent a change of attitudes in the 1880s (the Spinners being an important exception) whereby instead of simply excluding women from membership and thereafter not bothering with them at all, modern trade union practice is to accept them as members but to insist upon occupational segregation. The problem for the (from the context, male) trade union leader is to ensure women workers

> the utmost possible freedom to earn an independent livelihood
> [and] to devise such arrangements as shall prevent that freedom
> being made use of by the employers to undermine the Standard
> of Life of the whole wage-earning class. . . . Once competition is
> eliminated the fact that women sell their labor at a low price
> does not endanger the Standard Rate. . . . In the very small num-
> ber of cases in which men and women compete directly with each
> other for employment, in precisely the same operation, in one
> and the same process, there can, we believe, be no effective Trade
> Unionism until definite Standard Rates are settled for men's work
> and women's work respectively.[58]

What "the problem" is for the woman trade unionist, they do not say.

It would be no exaggeration to say, then, that the women were hemmed in from all sides. The employers took no interest in the needs of women workers, nor did the male union leadership, and the two most influential upper-middle-class prolabor publicists could not find anything objectionable in current practices. Whether or not one can speak of a causal relationship, the evidence for 1910-14 shows no public, articulated protest by women cotton workers against their systematic exclusion from occupational specialties in the industry. The most one finds is several wildcat strikes by weavers in which the issue was the accuracy of piece rate calculations. Conceivably, any number of these strikes might have been triggered by women discovering that they were being paid at a lower rate than men engaged in identical work; however, none of the reports explicitly indicates a sexual dimension, so that the only legitimate inference allowed is, "cannot tell."[59]

Yet the overall absence of unrest regarding occupational segregation does not mean that in these years there was no movement at all. Turning to the question of women's participation in trade union governance, one finds evidence that suggests that participation was on the upswing. In the Cardroom Workers Amalgamation male domination appears to have gone unchecked. But according to a survey of weavers' branches made by B. L. Hutchins of the London School of Economics in 1914, Glossop had four women on the branch committee, Blackburn had two, Oldham had "several," in addition to sending a woman delegate to the 1910 and 1912 annual conferences, of the Trade Union Congress (TUC) and Preston had just elected its first women, number unspecified.[60] Furthermore, the *Factory Times* claimed that "there are Weavers Committees with not a single man,"[61] an assertion whose force might be greater had the paper indicated which branches and if they had turned up in the Hutchins survey, which they did not. Indeed, if one places the matter in perspective, it is almost certain that an absolute majority of weavers' branches had no women serving in the union, including radical Nelson, where women did participate actively in the town's 800-member ILP branch.[62]

But it is in Manchester that one must look for the most advanced instance of women initiating and governing their trade union affairs and for the full measure of the Weavers Amalgamation's response. In 1902 the Salford and District Power Loom Weavers was founded, consisting wholly of women members and officials. Membership fluctuated dramatically—starting with 700 in 1902, falling to 320 in 1904, rising again to a peak of 1,107 in 1907, and thereafter declining year by year until by 1910, 300 members were claimed.[63] In 1907 the Amalgamated Weavers Association also formed a branch, calling it the Manchester, Salford, and Pendleton Weavers, and reported a membership of 270 in 1908, 350 in 1909, and 100 in 1910. In the same three years the Salford and District Power Loom Weavers reported a drop in membership from 500 to 300.[64]

By late 1909, friction between the two unions had reached the point that the Manchester and Salford Trades and Labor Council was called upon to make an adjudication. Their recommendation was that "the ladies put the question of amalgamation [that is, federating into the

Weavers Amalgamation] before their members and not merely to put it before them but to recommend amalgamation to them."[65] This the women refused to do. In a letter to the general secretary of the amalgamation the secretary of the women's union wrote:

> The members . . . met on Wednesday last and duly considered the proposal made at the joint conference held on November 10th. The women were of the opinion that their interests would be best secured by remaining as they are and unanimously decided against joining the Northern Counties Weavers Amalgamation.
>
> YOURS FAITHFULLY,
>
> *Nellie Keenan*[66]

The reason for the unanimous rejection was not given, though it is as likely as not that the amalgamation demanded newly appointed officers as a condition of affiliation. However this may be, S. J. Bardsley, the amalgamation's Manchester organizer, claimed that the women's union did not increase wages or improve working conditions, and he promised to agitate and to recruit members in Manchester just as soon as trade improved. The women counterattacked in a leaflet a year later:

> Fellow women workers—Don't be patronized today by the men who refused to organize you when there was no society in existence to look after your interests.
>
> Fellow women workers—Show to these men that you have the administrative and organizing abilities to manage your own affairs and are able to look after your own interests. . . .
>
> Sisters—Don't be misled by specious promises, but turn up at the above meeting on Tuesday next, and join with your sisters, who have worked side by side with you, who understand your wants and aspirations, and, above all, understand every detail of your occupations, and who have been successful in removing innumerable grievances that your sisters in other factories have suffered from. . . .[67]

Toward the end of 1911 rivalry between the two unions had reached the point that a *Factory Times* columnist was moved to review the history of the dispute, assuming throughout that the women indeed had organized a bona fide trade union and suggesting that this time the Manchester and Salford Trades and Labor Council and the editor of the *Factory Times* arbitrate.[68] Again, Bardsley threatened to "organize them out of existence," on the grounds of dual unionism rather than his original assertion of the women's ineffectualness.[69] But still the women refused to roll over and die. In December 1912 they were still strong enough to threaten to strike a mill because of six nonunionists, which was averted by the nonunionists joining the amalgamation's branch.[70] Nevertheless, the internecine rivalry took its toll. The amalgamation admitted by its own figures its inability to organize Manchester permanently.[71] Neither did the women's union make a decisive breakthrough, and both branches apparently folded during the war.

One would like to know far more about the policies and personalities involved than the sources disclose. But several points stand out. The first is the women's real skill in keeping a one-branch union afloat for more than a decade. The second is the determination, indeed the fury, that the amalgamation showed in attacking the women. Why? One cannot be positive, owing to the paucity of the sources, and besides in such a sensitive area one would not expect the men to divulge their true feelings. But had the amalgamation permitted the women to join on their own terms, it would have been the first time a branch built and staffed exclusively by women had been admitted. It is hard to imagine that the men of the amalgamation overlooked the unique circumstances.

The rather sordid business of the Weavers Amalgamation smashing the Manchester women might be regarded as a limiting case, and an exceptional one at that. For the most part the leadership's practice toward its women members was one of neglect, its rhetoric a mixture of subborn defense against the charge that the unions overtly discriminated against women holding office[72] and a defense of the manners and morals of mill girls.[73] One might have thought that a public stance in favor of votes for women would have been something of a "hardy annual" with the cotton unions, but in fact the United Textile Factory Workers Association, the political-action arm of the cotton unions, took no steps on the matter during 1910-14. However, the Nelson weavers did in 1913 pass a resolution in favor of women's suffrage, apparently at the request of the Nelson ILP,[74] and the *Factory Times* reported a women's suffrage agitation in the weaving towns of northeast Lancashire, again in 1913.[75] In the last analysis, though, it is the insensitivity and unresponsiveness of the men that must be stressed. Perhaps the creation of militant women's caucuses within the branches might have made a dent. But there were none of these, and the example of what happened in Manchester stood as a grim reminder to any women who chose to take the lesson. Like Alderman Bauler's Chicago, the women cotton workers might not have been ready for reform. But ready or not, they were not getting any.[76]

CHILDREN AND THE HALF-TIME QUESTION

The tenacity with which cotton workers and their spokesmen defended the practice of twelve-year-old children working half-time in the mills is one of the better-known facts of British labor history. A recent study of the half-time system refers to the cotton workers' "blind spot" on the question.[77] Phelps Brown relates the story of how David Shackleton, leader of the Weavers Amalgamation and member of Parliament (M.P.) for Clitheroe from 1902 to 1910, attempted to disarm opponents by standing up in Parliament to his full and considerable height and girth and rhetorically asking how the half-time system did him any harm.[78] Perhaps as a first approximation the conventional wisdom is serviceable enough; however, the historical reality was a great deal more complex.

In the first place, recent historians of the question have been imprecise in specifying whose children went into the mills, apparently assuming that most of them were the children of cotton operatives. In 1898 the factory inspector for the Bolton district made an inquiry, the results of which are presented in Table 19.

The data show a consistent pattern for the subregion stretching from Bolton to Wigan of cotton workers' children constituting a minority of the half-timers. This means, among other things, that when the cotton workers balloted on the retention of half-time, many of them were talking about other people's children. But one must not run ahead of the analysis. Since the 1898 inquiry provides the best hard data, the question remains as to how representative are its findings with respect to (1) who the half-timers were more than a decade later, and (2) other cotton-manufacturing districts.

In the case of the first question, there are grounds for assuming that the patterns shown in 1898 were still visible a decade and a half later. By 1910-14 fewer half-timers were employed than in 1898,[79] and this

Table 19

Occupations of Fathers of Children Employed in Cotton Factories

Town	Boys	Girls	Boys & Girls Over 12 Years of Age	Boys & Girls Under 12 Years of Age	All Children Cotton Operative	All Children Collier	All Children Other	Children Under 12 Years of Age Cotton Operative	Children Under 12 Years of Age Collier	Children Under 12 Years of Age Other	All Employees	Children Without Father	Children Without Mother	Children Without Father or Mother
Bolton	594	765	954	405	269	99	814	73	29	240	30,290	162	41	15
Wigan	59	155	146	68	9	130	43	3	38	16	9,883	30	12	2
Farnworth	336	433	530	239	65	319	292	17	114	85	10,647	83	12	10
Leigh, Tyldesley, and Atherton	281	302	416	167	75	298	175	18	90	47	9,124	35	32	—
West Houghton, Horwich, and Golborne	45	104	103	46	12	88	28	3	21	12	2,650	20	6	1

Source: Factory Inspector's Annual Report Pt. II for 1898, p. 70.

suggests that the secular decline of a practice would result in an intensification of tendencies already existing rather than any abrupt new departure from past practice. As for the second question, Bolton can be accepted as being typical enough of southeast Lancashire spinning districts,
leaving a question mark hanging over those weaving centers of northeast
Lancashire, where, in contrast to places like Wigan, cloth manufacturing
was practically the only large-scale industry.[80] Here it is very likely that
a higher percentage of half-time children of cotton workers should turn
up, because so great a proportion of parents were cotton workers in the
first place.

A second complexity that has received insufficient attention is that
support for the continuance of the half-time system was not limited solely
to the operatives and those employers who hired half-time labor. Giving
testimony in 1902, Richmond, the chief inspector of factories for the
northwest, showed himself quite willing to defend the system in the face
of sustained hostile questioning:

Q. Is there any opinion in the neighborhood about the effect of
this work upon their education?

A. My experience has rather been that they are the sharpest
children.

Q. Is not that possibly because they are children who have passed
certain standards?

A. Yes; but even before the days of the School Boards, they were
looked upon as the sharpest children. I think their work sharp-
ened their wits.

Q. In what way would the work of the textile industries sharpen
a child?

A. It is education.

Q. But a very low form, is it not?

A. Not altogether.

Q. What sort of work do they do—is it divided into different em-
ployments?

A. They may work in different parts of the mill. . . .

Q. And is the feeling of the operatives as strong as it used to be
about half-time?

A. Quite.

Q. What are the average wages?

A. I should say about half-a-crown a week.

Q. That is half-a-crown for about 26 hours work, or about a penny an hour?

A. At first. . . .

Q. You have no evils to point out with regard to textile half-time or full time?

A. No. . . .

Q. You consider that 11 was too low?

A. I think it ought to be raised by degrees.

Q. Would you stop now or go on raising it?

A. I would stop at 12.[81]

This is not to say that Richmond represented the views of all factory inspectors. In fact the principal lady inspector spoke out against half-time on the grounds that the work strained the youngsters' eyes and that the double load of millwork and schoolwork constituted a heavy burden.[82] The point is rather that those cotton workers who favored the system's retention had support in high and unexpected places.[83]

What about the unions? It is true that at the 1901 TUC annual conference the cotton men put on an extraordinary performance:

D. Shackleton (Weavers): "The children were treated as well as could possibly be expected."

J. Cross (Weavers): "A lot of sentimental bosh was being uttered. . . ."

T. Ashton (Spinners): "We can get legislation for our children by our own efforts."[84]

But even as early as 1898 and 1899 the Spinners had opted for what might be called an "evolutionary" solution to half-time:

With the gradual improvement in the position of the workers and the tendency amongst the more enlightened of them to keep their children out of the mills so long as they can afford, the half-time question is gradually settling itself in the best of all ways, viz., by the pressure of public opinion making itself felt in the direction of leaving half-time work to those children who, on account of their position and surroundings, are more likely to grow into better men and women as half-timers than would otherwise be the case.

. . . We believe that in the long run they [the parents] will come to recognize that the raising of the age at which children should go to work has its advantages as well as the reverse.[85]

On a cynical reading, this is no more than a position of benign neglect that committed the union to nothing in the way of positive measures like agitating and educating the membership. It can also be interpreted as an unexceptional stance of "enlightened" union officials who, being well aware of rank-and-file "backwardness," had decided to proceed slowly and cautiously. But however this may be, the leadership had, a decade later on, swung around to a position of opposing half-time working at age twelve. At the 1908 conference of the United Textile Factory Workers Association a resolution was approved, by a vote of 186 to 27, to raise the minimum age of half-time employment to thirteen; and in 1914 another resolution was unanimously carried that instead of another membership ballot the officials should go and educate the workers.[86] The new majority and minority feelings can be seen from the following *Factory Times* interview:

Thomas Ashton [secretary of the Oldham Spinners and a trade union official since the late 1860s] : Formerly, Mr. Ashton was opposed to the abolition of half-time, but in recent years his opinion has changed. The system did not affect the Oldham operative spinners much. "I don't think the abolition of half-time is a question we need trouble our heads very much about. The half-time system is dying."

James Bell [b. 1872, committee member of the Nelson Weavers at age twenty-two, sacked three times for union activity, secretary of the Oldham Weavers from 1905,[87] three-time Labour candidate for Oldham Council] "My experience in the mill has made me desirous of keeping children at school as long as possible. Unhesitatingly, I say that the half-time system is educationally unfair to the child, and is a serious handicap on its future life. To drag a child out of bed at 5 or 5:30 in the morning and turn it into the streets, especially in the cold winter months, cannot, no one can contend,

be good for it. I think there are more crooked legs or cripples of
one kind or another in Oldham than in any other town in the
world, and conditions of labor that produce such effects are not
fit for children!"

But how were people of Bell's opinion to win over the rank and file, which
in 1908 had voted, 150,723 to 33,968 for the retention of the status quo?
It is difficult to see how resolutions like the one passed at the 1910 conference of the United Textile Factory Workers Association, instructing
delegates to be bound by the 1908 poll at the TUC annual conference,
could have helped to "educate" anybody.[89] By the same token the *Factory Times,* despite its stated opposition to half-time, must have muddied
the issue with its shrill denunciations of "meddlesome outsiders" who
attacked the half-time system—although one can perhaps understand the
paper's annoyance over items such as London magazine articles entitled,
"The Child Slaves of Lancashire and Yorkshire."[90] In any event, in the
last prewar ballot held on the question late in 1911, the vote was 116,573
for retention, 29,933 for raising the age to thirteen, and 11,468 neutral.
The 1911 ballot saw over 35,000 fewer workers voting than in the previous ballot, a drop in the turnout that cannot be explained fully by the
fact that the officials of the Burnley and Clayton Weavers refused to issue
ballot papers.[91] (They argued that the results were a foregone conclusion.) The second notable point is that there were two small groups of
workers who bucked the landslide by actually voting against half-time.
In Hyde, Cheshire, where the employers had already ended the system,
the weavers voted 1,453 for raising the age, 1,450 against, and 49 neutral. In the adjoining and otherwise similar town of Stalybridge, the weavers' vote was a lopsided 54 to 342, with 7 remaining neutral. At the other
end of the cotton region, in Preston, the spinners also voted against the
half-time system as it stood, 122 to 88 with 597 remaining neutral.[92]
This turnout, in the context of the aggregate results, would be utterly
inexplicable if one did not know that the secretary of the Preston Spinners was a vocal critic of life and conditions in cotton mills. For reasons
unknown, he angrily asserted that "parents who have spent their lives in
the spinning room or weaving shed, when asked about their own children,
often reply, 'I'll drown them before they shall go in a factory.' "[93]
Few of the other union officials talked this way. Among the Preston Spinners, support for the half-time system was effectively neutralized. Also,

the Oldham weavers' support for retention, by a vote of 2,557 to 1,993 with 11 remaining neutral, was far narrower than in Lancashire as a whole.

Nevertheless, as with women, the older attitudes continued to influence many workers' and leaders' attitudes toward children, work, and school. The connection between what children are taught in school and their subsequent accomplishments in advanced industrial society is not clear. As for the cotton workers and their spokesmen in the early twentieth century, the evidence suggests that they were highly skeptical of either education for the sake of personal development and fulfillment, or of education with a view to providing social mobility, neither of which their children were receiving to begin with. The consensus was that education should be "practical." Thus the author of *How to Become a Successful Operative Cotton Mule Spinner* complained that

> It is all very well for a spinner, while studying cotton spinning, to learn the different varieties of cotton, the countries and localities in which they are grown, how picked, ginned, and baled. . . . But how much do these things assist him as an operative spinner? Technical knowledge as now taught does not necessarily make good spinners. We should come down with our teaching, be more practical, point out the pitfalls, and direct to the straight and easy way . . .
>
> May the time not be far distant when we shall teach in our public schools the young and rising generation more about the trades by which they have to earn a livelihood. This ought to be the object of all education. . . .[94]

The *Factory Times* implied on occasion that schoolteachers were little better than clergymen—the chief complaint against both being their studied ignorance of the world of industry and labor.[95] And this takes us close to the heart of the matter: If a working-class child was certain also to become a worker, then the outstanding criterion of both schools' and children's success was the ability of a youngster to obtain and hold down a job. This comes across clearly in a case that the Oldham Education Committee brought before the magistrates in 1914. John Boardman, age fourteen, had been certified under the terms of the Epileptic and Defective Children's Act of 1889 as having to attend a special school until sixteen. But his father, a cotton operative, had sent him into the mill as a piecer instead. The magistrates wanted to know one thing: Was young Boardman holding his own on the job? He was? Case dismissed. But the King's Bench Divisional Court overruled the magistrates and instructed them to bring in a conviction for disobeying the statute.[96] Boardman, Senior, was duly found guilty and fined one shilling without costs.[97] Later on in the month three more cases were brought before the magistrates concerning not keeping "defective" children in school. When the deputy town clerk, prosecuting on behalf of the Oldham Education Committee, argued that Oldham had the "proud position of pioneering special schools," William Mullin, Justice of the Peace (J.P.), and general secretary of the Cardroom Workers Amalgamation, interrupted: ". . . don't say the 'proud' position!"[98]

Our conclusions must be tentative. On the one hand, the half-time system *was* dying on its feet, from reasons ranging from employers' findings that child labor was no longer economically attractive, to workers' outrage over the employers exploiting "our" children who had better things to do with their lives than to be broken in and turned into "good hands." But what was to become of the children if they did not learn to become "good hands"? This was the dilemma, and most of the concerned parties in prewar Lancashire showed the signs of having been impaled on its horns.[99]

The Decline of Workers' Mobility and Shareholding 4

Observers of the later nineteenth- and early twentieth-century Lancashire cotton industry have on the whole agreed that the trade was marked by a great deal of operative shareholding and upward mobility into ownership, directorial, and managerial positions. Chapter 2 was concerned with taking socioeconomic measurements of the cotton workers and proceeded as though they were a closed group whose members displayed no tendencies toward upward mobility into the managerial and property-owning classes. In fact, only in the cases of marriage, infant mortality, and family size were any comparisons made with social groups outside the working class. In this chapter we explicitly redress the balance and consider two related phenomena: (1) changes over time in the numbers of the cotton workers entering managerial strata; and (2) the propensity, again measured over time, of workers to buy shares in cotton mills.

The Webbs appear to have regarded these features of the industry as the realization of a highly desirable form of social and industrial organization in which several roles—for example, those of trade union official and employers' federation secretary—were practically interchangeable and in which the personnel interchanges actually took place.[1] Other Socialists of the time took a dimmer view, either lamenting what would today be called corporate rather than hegemonic consciousness on the part of the workers or suggesting that in some cases—notably that of operative mule spinners—an element of duress was present in a worker's taking shares.

In turn, these evaluations can easily be integrated into an analytical framework that places emphasis on technological simplicity and the (relatively) small size of firms and amount of capital required, archaism rather than ultramodernity being the keynote. But whatever the explanation, the facts go unquestioned.

This is odd. In the case of shareholding, discussion has rarely been buttressed by quantitative data; rather, the argument appears to be based more on folklore than on anything else.[2] The case for upward mobility on the other hand was apparently clinched in a 1912 article by S. J. Chapman and F. J. Marquis in which the authors presented the results of a questionnaire. Each mill owner, director, or manager was asked whether he started out in the world of industry "either as an operative or clerk, and got on through his own efforts and not through inheriting position or capital."[3] The replies ran heavily in the direction of self-help. Of those who responded, 73 percent of the spinning-mill directors, 76 percent of the cloth manufacturers, and 84 percent of the spinning-mill managers claimed that they had "got on through their own efforts."[4] Evidently aware of the need to verify independently these remarkably high figures, Chapman and Marquis proceeded to conduct their own "minute inquiries," but unfortunately they did not specify the investigative methods employed. Here the percentages were somewhat lower: 63 percent first-generation employers in cloth manufacturing; in spinning 13 percent directors, 42 percent managers, and 67 percent assistant managers.[5] Even on Chapman and Marquis's own showings the spirit of Mr. Bounderby was not altogether dead in Lancashire in the early twentieth century.

With the help of Public Record Office documents of limited-liability firms that went out of business before 1948,[6] it is possible to reopen the question, this time on a more substantial quantitative basis.[7] Because these sources reveal the stated occupations of shareholders, directors and original subscribers, one can answer three sets of questions. First, who were the directors and original subscribers of new mills? Second, how many operative held what percentage of shares in mills for which data are available? Third, what changes took place over time? To anticipate the argument, it will be shown that cotton operatives did indeed invest in cotton mills, but that investment was quite selective and that operatives holding 6.97 percent of the shares in a mill represented the high-water mark. With regard to social mobility, a marked shift in the stated occupation of initial subscribers and directors took place between the period 1873-96 and

1900-14, with the result that recruitment was increasingly confined to the trade itself—but that the manual work force did not provide the bulk of the new recruits. Finally, the findings will be related to labor-management relations, in particular the labor unrest of 1910-14.

Although cotton spinners[8] and mill managers account for 60 out of 178 directors and original subscribers enumerated in Table 20, nevertheless quite a wide breadth of occupations and strata is revealed. Merchants

Table 20

Stated Occupations of 178 Directors and/or Original Subscribers of 25 Spinning Mills Formed Between 1865 and 1896

Cotton spinner	41
Mill manager	19
Merchant and dealer, cloth and waste	13
Agent, salesman	12
Tradesman, innkeeper, shopkeeper	11
Bookkeeper, clerk, timekeeper	8
Merchant, noncotton or unspecified	7
Engineer, machinist	7
Builder, contractor	6
Director, mill owner, capitalist	5
Manufacturer, nontextile or unspecified	5
Loom overlooker	4
Building trades craftsman	4
Draftsman and mechanic	4
Auctioneer and valuer	4
Accountant	3
Mule overlooker	3
Attorney, solicitor	3
Architect	2
Carder	2
Estate agent	2
Roller coverer	2
Twiner, doubler	2
Gentleman	1
Cotton cloth manufacturer	1
Secretary	1
Warehouseman	1
Miscellaneous	5

and dealers in cotton products and cotton waste (i.e., the fluff created in the process of spinning rovings into yarn) form the third largest category, which suggests that it was far from impossible for persons connected with the trade but not directly engaged in production to move upward. This should not be regarded as merely lateral mobility, particularly in the case of waste dealers, which occupation consists essentially of scavenging. The fifth largest category—tradesmen, innkeepers, and shopkeepers—points to the same conclusions and provides reinforcement for arguments asserting the trade's "openness," since so far as one can tell from the evidence, these persons had no previous direct connection with either the productive or distributive side of the trade. Indeed, this can be said for 49 of the 178 persons.

Labor too is represented. As far as cotton operatives are concerned, it is significant that even in the brisk early days of the "Oldham Limiteds" boom of the early 1870s, none is recorded, although it is safe to assume that some of the three mule overlookers and four loom overlookers were at one time in their lives "hands." But there were four draftsmen and mechanics and four more building-trades artisans (as opposed to builders), again suggesting the ability of outsiders to break in. As for the two "twiners and doublers," one cannot tell whether they were owners or workers.

Table 21 refers to 22 of the same mills for which data after 1896 are available. The first major difference is the 23 persons describing themselves as "gentlemen";[9] only 1 turns up in Table 20. Other newcomers include 7 sharebrokers (compared with none in Table 20) and 21 directors and others whom we may suppose to be first cousins (socially speaking) of gentlemen.

Further comparison reveals that the changes extend much more deeply. The connection between dealing and directing appears to have shriveled— 3 out of 135 as opposed to 13 out of 178. Tradesmen and others have declined but not disappeared—4 out of 135 as opposed to 11 out of 178. No mule or loom overlookers can be found, and there is only 1 non-cotton-skilled craftsman. As regards "openness," the ratio has declined from 49 out of 178, or 27.5 percent, to 29 out of 135, or 21.5 percent.

The results of the comparison between Tables 20 and 21 are not very surprising. It is altogether plausible that once a firm has been successfully established, the social distance between workers and employers should widen, and that there be no compelling reasons for replenishing the top ranks by recruiting from outside the trade. However, the presence of nine

Table 21

Stated Occupations of 135 Directors of 22 of the Mills
in Table 20, 1896-1913

Mill manager	28
Gentleman	23
Director, mill owner, capitalist	15
Manufacturer, nontextile or unspecified	9
Cotton spinner	7
Sharebroker	7
Secretary	6
Agent, salesman	5
Insurance agent, manager	5
Tradesman, innkeeper, shopkeeper	4
Cotton merchant and dealer, cloth and waste	3
Bookkeeper, clerk, timekeeper	3
Commercial traveler	3
Engineer, machinist	2
Merchant, noncotton or unspecified	2
Auctioneer, valuer	2
Accountant	2
Cotton cloth manufacturer	1
Builder, contractor	1
Attorney, solicitor	1
Draftsman, mechanic	1
Estate agent	1
Miscellaneous	2
Cannot tell	2

accountants and seven builders and contractors toward the top of Table 21 suggests the continuing infusion of new blood and requires an explanation. Accountants can be regarded as an instance of functional differentiation within the managerial infrastructure, stemming from the conviction that up-to-date firms required the full-time services of an accountant. Builders and contractors turn up for less "functional" reasons. Given the relatively stable and accessible technology of the industry, there were few obstacles to prevent a speculation-minded contractor from taking a flyer. It is not surprising that in periods of depressed trade the practice was roundly denounced in terms of "reckless expansion," to the point of George Harwood, M.P., a Bolton mill owner, introducing a bill in the House of Commons providing that newly created firms be adequately capitalized.

But however this may be, the important thing to note about Table 22 is its similarity to Table 21. Only one waste dealer and one tradesman are to be found. There are no overlookers or noncotton artisans. As for the slight rise in the proportion of "outsiders, " that is more than accounted for by the peculiar relationship of builders and architects to the process of erecting new mills in the early twentieth century.

Our overall conclusions for the whole period may now be stated. An upward shift in the social status of directors definitely took place between the introduction of the limited-liability form of business organization and the last pre-World War I mill-building boom. At the same time, such mobility as did take place was increasingly restricted to those already inside the trade. A columnist in the *Cotton Factory Times*, the quasi-official journal of the cotton unions, noted in 1911 how

Table 22

Stated Occupations of 110 Directors and/or Original Subscribers of 16 Mills Formed 1900-08

Mill manager	21
Gentleman	15
Cotton spinner	12
Accountant	9
Builder, contractor	7
Engineer, machinist	6
Agent, salesman	6
Secretary	6
Merchant, noncotton or unspecified	5
Bookkeeper, clerk, timekeeper	5
Architect	3
Manufacturer, nontextile	3
Attorney, solicitor	2
Cotton merchant and dealer	1
Insurance manager	1
Tradesman	1
Miscellaneous	7

years ago men held directorial positions while possessing only a few
shares. Now the qualification is fixed at anywhere between 200
and 500 shares, and in a few instances as high as 1000. . . . For
some years there has been a gradual move in this direction, plain-
ly indicating that the control of the mills founded on the principle
of limited liability are [sic] more and more being controlled and
falling into the hands of men possessing capital, and are gradually
drifting away from the control of small capitalists. . . .[10]

The same source also claimed that in the past the practice obtained of
dividing the mule rooms of spinning mills into compartments, with indi-
viduals "running" a few pairs of mules each[11] —an arrangement similar
to the room and power system in the weaving trade and the "little master"
system in the Sheffield light trades. But by the twentieth century only
in twining was this found any more, amounting to far less than 5 percent
of the spindles in Lancashire.

Do the conclusions presented here decisively refute the contentions of
Chapman and Marquis? This is not so straightforward a question as it
might first appear, since our findings have been reached by methods very
different from those used in the earlier survey. As has been noted, the
accuracy of the 1912 data depends heavily upon whether the respondents
were telling the truth. By contrast, the data we have used are virtually immune from subjective and ideological bias, for what reason would anybody have for misstating his occupation on official forms? Furthermore,
even if one grants that many directors had working-class backgrounds, our
findings show positively that by the twentieth century a worker in Lancashire had to climb higher up the socioeconomic ladder in order to break
into the directorial ranks than he had to do in the nineteenth century.
Accordingly, whatever other forces there were in the years 1910-14 making
for an ideology of harmony between cotton workers and management,
easy access for workers to enter the higher levels of management was not
one of them.

In the early twentieth century a favorite example of "property-owning
democracy" was the large number of cotton workers who assertedly held
shares in cotton mills. However, a rather different picture emerges from
Tables 23, 24, and 25.

Table 23

Mills for Which Only One Set of Figures Is Available or in Which No
Operatives Held Shares Throughout

	(1)	(2)	(3)	(4)	(5)	(6)	(7)	(8)
Oak 1874	1914	20,000	369	1.84%	45	70	12.2%	32.9%
Rugby 1907	1913	15,300	655	4.3%	250	225	38.2%	72.5%
Grange 1904	1904	5,000	0	0	0	0	0	0
Laurel 1905	1905	16,000	0	0	0	0	0	0
Scot 1905	1914	14,000	0	0	0	0	0	0
Cecil St. 1906	1907	4,250	0	0	0	0	0	0
Royd 1906	1906	10,000	0	0	0	0	0	0

Note: Column numbers stand for the following:
   (1) Year for which data are available
   (2) Number of shares taken up
   (3) Number of shares held by cotton operatives and foremen
   (4) (3) divided by (2)
   (5) Number of shares held by operative spinners
   (6) Number of shares held by foremen
   (7) (5) divided by (3)
   (8) (5) plus (6) divided by (3).

On three questions the data give straightforward answers. First, a small
minority of cotton workers held a small minority of outstanding shares.
Second, what shares they did hold were distributed most unevenly from
mill to mill. Third, operative spinners constituted some two-thirds of all
worker-shareholders. A fairly obvious hypothesis as to the unevenness is
that worker-shareholders behaved like any other investors: Dividends
and rising share values attracted; falling (or no) dividends repelled. Such a
test falls outside the scope of this essay; but if the hypothesis is correct,
then Table 25 would represent those mills for which initially high hopes
of profitability were not fulfilled, and Table 24 mills with proven records
of profitability and high dividends.

There is a second aspect of operative shareholding that requires examination. It was frequently charged in labor circles that in order to obtain
promotion to operative spinner, piecers were compelled to buy up shares.
The same practice was said to hold with regard to operative spinners seeking jobs in brand new mills. On this point the figures are enlightening only
insofar as they establish that spinners *did* own shares. (No spinner-share-

Table 24

Mills in Which the Number of Operative Shareholders Increased

	(1)	(2)	(3)	(4)	(5)	(6)	(7)	(8)
Athens 1905	1906	14,485	0	0	0	0	0	0
	1911	16,000	270	1.69%	100	120	37.1%	81.5%
Briar 1906	1906	15,700	250	1.47%	250	0	100%	100%
	1911	16,000	1,115	6.97%	285	650	25.6%	84.3%
Fernhurst 1905	1905	13,045	0	0	0	0	0	0
	1915	20,000	540	2.7%	410	80	75.9%	90.7%
Manor 1905	1906	14,450	95	0.66%	40	55	42.0%	100%
	1911	16,000	125	0.78%	75	50	60%	100%
Orb 1907	1907	15,692	270	1.72%	20	250	7.4%	100%
	1912	16,000	706	4.4%	220	400	31.1%	87.8%
Ram 1907	1907	24,000	0	0	0	0	0	0
	1913	24,000	55	0.2%	0	55	0	100%
Swan 1880	1880	12,000	170	1.42%	54	30	31.8%	49.5%
	1911	12,000	259	2.16%	5	161	1.9%	64.2%

Note: Column numbers stand for the following:

(1) Year for which data are available
(2) Number of shares taken up
(3) Number of shares held by cotton operatives and foremen
(4) (3) divided by (2)
(5) Number of shares held by operative spinners
(6) Number of shares held by foremen
(7) (5) divided by (3)
(8) (5) plus (6) divided by (3).

Table 25

Mills in Which the Number of Shareholders Decreased

	(1)	(2)	(3)	(4)	(5)	(6)	(7)	(8)
Grape 1905	1906	14,000	450	3.21%	250	150	55.5%	88.8%
	1909	14,000	350	2.5%	250	100	71.4%	100%
Hartford 1906	1907	11,860	120	1.0%	20	100	16.7%	100%
	1911	15,970	20	0.01%	20	0	100%	100%
Honeywell 1875	1875	8,000	213	2.7%	20	50	9.4%	32.9%
	1910	10,000	24	0.25%	14	10	41.7%	100%
Rose 1865	1876	200	14	7.0%	1	4	7.1%	35.7%
	1910	16,950	210	1.2%	0	0	0	0

Note: Column numbers stand for the following:
  (1) Year for which data are available
  (2) Number of shares taken up
  (3) Number of shares held by cotton operatives and foremen
  (4) (3) divided by (2)
  (5) Number of shares held by operative spinners
  (6) Number of shares held by foremen
  (7) (5) divided by (3)
  (8) (5) plus (6) divided by (3).

holders would, it is safe to say, constitute a prima facie rebuttal.) But neither would evidence that workers invested in their own workplaces definitely settle the question even if it could be established that they invested exclusively in their own mills, which they almost certainly did not. Purely statistical data thus are something of a cul-de-sac, but certain pieces of qualitative evidence point toward the conclusion that some operative spinners were forced to take shares. What is important here is not merely the fact that the charge was made, nor the number of times it was made, but the quality of the responses. Replying to the assertion that operative spinners had to pay up to 200 pounds for a pair of mules, that is, to work at a pair of mules,[12] a writer in the correspondence columns of the *Factory Times* conceded the facts of the matter and defended the practice on the grounds that "this was done only at new mills by directors who were in difficulties as to how to finance their mushroom companies. . . ."[13] However, the precise extent of such practices—and related items like the average number of shares that promotion "cost" and the proportion of workers who invested in their own workplace vis-à-vis those who invested in other mills—remains practically insoluble.

What conclusions may be drawn from our findings that neither upward mobility nor shareholding by workers was widespread in the early twentieth century? The first is that the data reinforce the assertion made in Chapter 1 that the prewar cotton workers—far from being a race apart from workers in other industries—shared most of the socioeconomic characteristics of their colleagues elsewhere. This is all the more so when one remembers that workers' shareholding was limited to the spinning side of the industry. In cloth manufacturing, by contrast, individual shares tended to be priced high and held by the directors or original subscribers. A Blackburn weaving company established in 1897 with a nominal capital of 2,000 pounds divided into 200 10-pound shares, all of which were held by the original subscribers, may be taken as typical.[14] The norm for spinning mills established in this period was a nominal capital of 75,000-80,000 pounds divided into 15,000-16,000 5-pound shares.

A second conclusion would appear to follow that the fact of a few workers owning shares in mills had no discernible moderating influence upon trade union militancy and broader ideological perspectives. The only serious counterevidence is the timidity and conservatism of the spinning unions compared with those in the weaving side of the industry; and as will be seen in the next chapter, the Spinners Amalgamation and the Cardroom Workers Amalgamation proved far more willing to tone down their demands upon the employers on the wages question than were the cloth-manufacturing unions. However, one has little need to rely heavily on the single factor of shareholding to explain the conservatism of the spinners, which as has already been argued was deeply rooted in the occupational structure of the trade. More important yet, the spinners participated vigorously in the prewar labor unrest. Accordingly, one may conclude that the small amount of shareholding that did occur was at most a latent factor in the shaping of the leaders' and workers' outlook. Finally, when one notes that by wise or lucky investments, dividends of 15 percent and upward could be realized, it is perhaps surprising that the incidence of workers' "taking a flyer" was not more widespread than the data indicate. But precisely because the cotton operatives were workers in a mature industrial setting, concern with wages, hours, conditions, and security—rather than the opportunity to make a killing by investing in mills—claimed top priority. As the *Factory Times* put it, "the worker has preferred a free hand—being a shareholder was thought to limit his freedom—and to have notices to strike when fighting for his rights with the owners of the mills."[15]

Attempts to Routinize Conflict: 5
The Unions' Industrial Policies, 1900-10

In this chapter the emphasis shifts from the cotton workers' exposure to influences originating outside the labor movement to a consideration of the policies of their own trade unions. As observed in Chapter 1, we shall not deal with all aspects of the cotton unions. Instead, the goal is to examine the unions' industrial-relations policies in order to understand their role in preparing the way for the labor unrest of 1910-14. Stated briefly, the argument is that the unions, although strong and (except for the Spinners) growing, had not done especially well in the first decade of the twentieth century. Collective bargaining was supposed to routinize conflict and deliver tangible gains to the workers. The actual record, however, was one of deteriorating working conditions and a disastrous lockout of spinning-mill workers in 1908 followed by two more years of depressed trade, bringing with it short-time working and reduced pay packets. The Spinners' union, groping for a way out, entered into serious negotiations with the employers with a view to concluding a sliding-scale wages agreement, which if consummated, would have meant a throwback, in terms of wages determination, to the days before genuine collective bargaining. However, a sliding-scale agreement acceptable to both sides could not be reached. The employers made it plain that they would accept a sliding scale only on their own terms, so that instead of abrogating collective bargaining altogether, it was suspended by freezing wage rates in the spinning trade for a period of five years, starting in July 1910. A lockout was thus avoided; however, subsequent labor unrest was not.

By 1900 the cotton unions were large, established institutions when compared with the trade union movement's organizing successes in most other sectors of the economy and work force. In 1910, 44 percent of the cotton workers were organized, a figure exceeded only by miners and quarrymen (60 percent) and shipbuilding workers (46 percent).[1] Rather than there being one big union of all mill workers, unionization in the cotton industry had evolved along the lines of loose federations of sectional unions, of which the three largest were the Amalgamated Association of Operative Spinners, the Cardroom Workers Amalgamation, and the Amalgamated Weavers Association. There were also unions of twisters and drawers, tapesizers, weaving overlookers, warpdressers, and warehousemen. These smaller federations, numbering some 16,000 members in 1910,[2] hardly participated in the labor unrest and are not dealt with at length in this book.

The big three cotton amalgamations differed markedly from one another with respect to size, strength, and the socioeconomic characteristics of their respective memberships. The Amalgamated Spinners was the oldest of the big three by virtue of having essentially completed its modern structure by the early 1870s. Recognized throughout the industry, by 1910 it had enrolled close to 100 percent of the male operative spinners, about 22,000 workers.[3] Following craft union traditions, the Spinners did not seek to organize workers outside of the mule room, a policy that set strict limits on the union's size and at the same time made for homogeneity of membership. As has already been noted, the Spinners had succeeded over the years in contriving a fragile but nonetheless real aristocratic status for their members.

By sharp contrast, the other union catering to spinning mill operatives, the Cardroom Workers Amalgamation (CWA), was the newest of the big three, founded as recently as 1886.[4] It was considerably larger than the Spinners—over 52,000 in 1910[5]—and was far more heterogeneous. Carding-engine mechanics called strippers and grinders made up the adult male core of the union; and by 1910 these men were perhaps almost as well organized as the Spinners, though exact figures are lacking. In addition, the CWA organized female ring spinners, women who minded the tenting

frames, and men and boys who worked in the opening, blowing, and mixing rooms of spinning mills. By 1910 full organization of these latter sections was far from complete, particularly among the women workers, who
perhaps even more than in weaving tended to be young and unmarried.
Unlike the Spinners, the CWA was expansionist in outlook, looking for
members as far afield as the lace mills in Derbyshire.[6]

The largest cotton union in the 1910-14 period was the Amalgamated
Weavers Association, with 114,000 members in 1910 (rising to 179,000
by 1914)[7] and branches in all of the cotton towns, since weaving was
ubiquitous to all parts of the Lancashire cotton region whereas spinning
was not. Power loom weavers—both male and female—constituted the
bulk of the membership, though the union also served women workers
engaged in winding, reeling and warping, which were ancillary processes
to actual weaving. These latter women, like their counterparts in spinning
mills, also tended to be organized incompletely, again, owing to low wages
and the fact that most of them did not plan to spend their entire lives in
the mills. Although unionization among power loom weavers dated back
at least to the early 1820s, the present amalgamation had only been founded in 1884.[8] Notwithstanding the apparent similarity of both the Weavers
and the Cardroom Workers serving various occupational groupings of
workers, there was in fact a major difference between the two. In the
weavers' union, power loom weavers, who made up the predominant majority of the membership, controlled the union as well, whereas the strippers and grinders who led and controlled the CWA were a small minority
of the total membership. A parallel can be seen in the International
Brotherhood of Teamsters, in which a fairly small minority of over-the-
road drivers control the union and set its policies. In short, the Weavers
were the one cotton union most closely resembling a modern industrial
union.[9]

Like all trade unions, the big three cotton unions shared the programmatic goals of raising wages and improving working conditions for their
members. But in concrete terms this did not imply uniformity of tactics
and policies. For the Spinners, *maintenance* of high wages and working
conditions already achieved took precedence. An example previously
noted of their complacency was their refusal to organize female mule
spinners in the Wigan district. The CWA, by contrast, appears to have
embarked upon a long-term campaign to achieve *parity* with the other
cotton unions in general and the Spinners in particular: first, in terms

of winning the same high wages for their male members as the Spinners had won for theirs, and, second, in terms of institutional prestige and rewards within the labor movement. To be attained, these goals required a high degree of aggressiveness on the part of the leadership, and, as will be shown, the CWA proved quite willing in the period 1910-14 to match forces against both the employers and the other cotton unions. For the AWA, priorities and policies were ordered in yet another way. Being larger than all of the other cotton unions combined, the Weavers were neither forced to cooperate nor to compete with other unions in order to achieve their overriding goal of transforming power loom weaving into a "high-wage" industry. Their strategy was consistently one of "collectivist laissez faire"—implying on the one hand an unwillingness to collaborate with management and on the other hand a policy of tolerant, if at times distant, relations toward the other unions, which was made possible by their own strength and consequent autonomy. Not by accident was it the Weavers—and not one of the spinning amalgamations—who unilaterally raised the issue of the industry-wide closed shop and who proved willing to take industrial action on the subject.[10]

We may agree with the Webbs that the historical success of the cotton unions was due in large measure to their perfecting the techniques of collective bargaining. As they wrote:

> Unconsciously and, as it were, instinctively, the cotton workers have felt their way to a form of machinery for Collective Bargaining which uses the representative element where the representative element is needed, whilst on the other hand it employs the professional expert for work at which the mere representative would be out of place.[11]

And again: " . . . the whole machinery appears admirably contrived to bring about the maximum deliberation, security, stability, and promptitude of application."[12] The "professional expert" was, of course, a reference to the salaried cotton union officials whose main job was to ensure that the operatives received full payment for their work as determined by the amazingly complex piece rate lists that governed wages in the industry.[13] However, if the officials had been "mere calculators," this in itself would hardly have sufficed to kindle the Webbs' enthusiasm and admiration. Equally important from their standpoint were the officials' commitment to and skill at the "routinization of conflict"—that is, the maintenance of an industrial-relations system in which both sides strove, first, to confine conflict to technical rather than ideological issues wherever possible and, second, to seek ultimate accommodation with the other side as opposed to one-sided victory.

Nowhere is the desire of the cotton men to bring about the routinization of conflict more clearly spelled out than in the Brooklands Agreement of 1893, which ended a twenty-five-week spinning lockout in southeast Lancashire. The first clause pledged both sides to the proposition that "it is expedient and desirable that some means should be adopted for the future whereby . . . disputes and differences may be expeditiously and amicably settled, and strikes and lockouts avoided."[14] The second clause laid down the settlement terms of the dispute in the form of a 2.9 percent wage reduction, an "honorable compromise" between the employers' original demand for a 5 percent reduction and the unions' demand for no reduction at all. Clause four spoke directly to the question of routinizing conflict:

> . . . with the view of preventing the . . . trade from being in an unsettled state too frequently . . . to the disadvantage of all parties concerned, no advance or reduction . . . shall in future be sought . . . until after the expiration of at least one year . . . nor shall any such advance or reduction be more or less than 5 percent upon the then current standard of wages being paid.[15]

Clauses six and seven went beyond the question of regulating wage rates by setting up machinery to deal with on-the-job grievances. Both sides were bound by the agreement to use the machinery before strikes or lockouts could be called. Technically, these clauses were less than perfect, and their defects were a major cause of the lockout of 1910, which will be examined in Chapter 7. But in the context of the present discussion the point to be stressed is the intent of the framers of the Brooklands Agreement, which was to ensure that expert negotiators were to remain in full charge of handling day-to-day industrial relations. A final clause of substantive importance directed unions and management to form a committee to deal with matters "in respect to the opening of new markets abroad, the alteration of restrictive foreign tariffs, and other similar matters which may benefit or injure the Cotton Trade. . . ."[16] All in all, it may be suggested that in substance and spirit, the Brooklands Agreement reads like a model agreement drafted by industrial-relations professors in the third quarter of the twentieth century.

In their treatment of the cotton unions' contribution to perfecting the method of collective bargaining, the Webbs did not speculate whether possible new developments might occur in the future; indeed, the implication throughout is that the cotton industry provided an ideal example that the rest of British industry would take considerable time in duplicating. But the cotton men, and particularly the spinners' union, did not let matters rest with the Brooklands Agreement. Around 1900 the Spinners became increasingly interested in an automatically sliding wage-regulation scheme, or, as it was called at the time, "conciliation." This was an especially ironic development when one considers that the Spinners, whom the Webbs had praised so highly in *Industrial Democracy,* were fishing in a backwater of political economy that the Webbs had unequivocally rejected in the very same book.[17]

Talk of the desirability and need for a conciliation scheme might have even antedated the Brooklands Agreement.[18] By 1906 the Executive Council of the spinners' union had drawn up a detailed proposal of its own, which was presented at a meeting with the masters held on March 16, 1906.[19] A short and straightforward document, it provided that current wage rates be taken as the standard and that for every increase (or decrease) of 1s. 8d. in the margin—that is, the difference between the cost per pound of middling American cotton and the selling price of a pound of common types of yarn—wages would rise (or fall) 2½ percent. The ceiling would be plus 7½ percent, the floor minus 7½ percent. As margins were practically a matter of public knowledge, no cumbersome procedural apparatus would be required. Wages would be adjusted as required every twenty-six weeks.

One cannot say whether the Spinners entertained serious hopes that their proposal would be accepted. But even if they intentionally aimed high for bargaining purposes, the upper limit, from the vantage point of hindsight, still erred markedly on the side of caution. Had their proposal been adopted, wage movements for the next eight years would have been as follows:

1907	plus 12½%
1908	plus 7½%
1909	list

1910   plus   7½%
1911   plus 12½%
1912   plus 12½%
1913   plus 12½%
1914   plus   7½%

With no upper ceiling at all, the figures would have been:

1907   plus 27½%
1908   plus   7½%
1909   list
1910   plus   7½%
1911   plus 15%
1912   plus 17½%
1913   plus 20%
1914   plus   7½%[20]

How would the employers have made out under the proposal? It is not possible to give as precise an answer as for the workers, because mills differed in their ability to pay. This of course was well known to the Spinners' officials, who were always at pains to show how their political economy penalized inefficient producers, and for that matter inefficient workers also. In any event the only evidence available indicates that the trade showed profits for every year except 1909 and 1910, and that even in these two years mills paid dividends, as shown in Table 26.

Table 26

Spinning Mill Profits, 1907-14

Year	Number of Companies	Average Profit	Average Loss	Average Dividend
1907	100	£13,211		15 7/8%
1908	100	£5,865		11 3/4%
1909	100		£2,720	7 7/8%
1910	100		£3,680	5 3/5%
1911	100	£288		4 3/5%
1912	100	£5,584		7 1/5%
1913	100	£5,366		7 4/5%
1914	100	£531		6 7/8%

The employers, as might be expected, were less willing to leave things to efficiency. They countered with a scheme of their own that centered on the proposition that "the rate of wages paid before the last five per cent advance is taken to be the standard rate, and that it is based upon the assumption that a profit at the rate of five per cent per annum was obtained on the whole of the capital employed, which is to be deemed the standard rate of profit,"[21] and that wage rate movements were to be related not to margins but to profits. The proposal called for a 2½ percent shift in wages for each 2 percent shift in profits within a range of plus or minus 5 percent. Clauses were included in the proposal stipulating that cost figures be obtained from a wide range of mills—large and small, new and old—and laying down guidelines for computing costs: original cost of mill and machinery, 27s. 9d. per spindle; depreciation, 1s. 4½d. per spindle; working capital, 5s. 0d. per spindle.

Given the wide gap separating the substance of the union's proposal from that of the Employers Federation, it is not surprising that no agreement was reached. Instead, the employers' proposals were adopted as the basis for experiment, neither side to be bound by the results. Moreover, from the union's standpoint there was little cause for urgency. Owing to brisk trade and large profit margins, the weavers had won a 2½ percent wage increase in January 1906 followed by a 5 percent increase for spinners and cardroom hands in April of the same year and yet another 5 percent increase for spinning and cardroom workers in April 1907. In 1908 bad trade set in, and the employers demanded a 5 percent reduction, offering to defer it until January 1909. The Executive Council of the Spinners recommended that their members accept the employers' proposal. Although a ballot showed 74 percent of the working spinners opposed, an 80 percent vote was required to approve strike action. However, the Cardroom Workers Amalgamation held out, with the result that both the cardroom workers and spinners were locked out for six weeks, with nothing to show for their struggles, except that the 5 percent reduction was now deferred until March 1909.[22] Into this context, Winston Churchill, then president of the Board of Trade, intervened with a view to reopening negotiations on a sliding-scale agreement. In a letter he invited the three largest cotton unions and the Employers Federation to a conference in London, at which the name of Sir Edward Clarke, King's Counselor (K.C.), was mentioned as independent chairman for future meetings and was ultimately chosen.[23]

Several meetings in 1909 failed to budge the employers from their contention that wages were already 5 percent above an acceptable standard. In a somewhat exasperated tone Clarke wrote to the president of the Employers Federation, Charles Macara, following a meeting in Manchester held on October 11, 1909, complaining that although the union officials had come down from a suggestion that the standard be 10 to 20 percent above present rates to an acceptance of the present rates,[24] the employers continued to maintain a position that was

> impracticable and . . . either useless or unfair in its application. It is impracticable because the two parties to the negotiations can never consent to it. It would be a declaration that the wages at present paid are too high, or that they are too low. It would be impossible for the representatives of the workmen to admit the former, and unreasonable to expect the employers to endorse the latter . . .

Macara countered with the classic Lancastrian retort: "I pointed out the extreme difficulty of anyone occupying such a position as you have accepted without a knowledge of the intricacies of the cotton industry, or of the subtleties of the controversies between the representatives of capital and labour."[25] He reiterated the demand that a wage scheme must enable the owners a fair shot at 5 percent profits. This was followed up by another letter a fortnight later, which, in addition to standing firm on their main contention that current wages were 5 percent above standard and that no more preferential leveling up of wages to lower paid workers would be forthcoming, lectured Clarke on the text that "it must not be forgotten that cotton spinning is a commercial undertaking, and the employers have to consider what wages they can afford to pay, having regard to the competition of other countries, and to the market price of the article produced as measured by the purchasing power of the consumer."[26]

Clearly, the employers were in no mood for a conciliation scheme on anything other than their own terms. Clarke made one final effort before turning the correspondence that had passed between him and the employers over to the unions for their inspection.[27] They proved equally cool to conciliation at any price and stated that "under the circumstances our executives are convinced that the position taken up by the operatives in regard to the basis or standard they proposed should be maintained. We are instructed to convey to you a warm appreciation of your services as chairman of the Conference."[28] The *Factory Times* endorsed the unions' position to the point of knocking the props out from under all conciliation schemes: ". . . the employers' proposal that a rate below the present standard should be accepted as the standard carries with it the assumption that wages and the standard of employment are practically at their zenith, and this is a position the workpeople can never accept."[29]

Thus any reasonable hope for a conciliation scheme lay in ruins. But even had the outcome been otherwise,[30] it is highly unlikely that labor relations or rank-and-file-leadership relations would have been more stable than the actual sequel. If anything, the introduction of such a scheme at a time when most unions strong enough to do so had decisively abandoned them might well have had the effect of radicalizing large sections of the work force. In any event, the unions now were confronted with the formidable task of protecting wage levels in the face of surplus productive capacity brought about by the 1905-7 mill construction boom and the near-famine price of American cotton—averaging 8d. per pound in 1910 and brought about by a crop shortfall and subsequent attempts by American speculators to corner the market.

Specifically, the problem was how to avoid being locked out. To a generation used to governments' never sanctioning and management's seldom attempting cuts in nominal wage rates, it is difficult to appreciate the efficacy of the lockout as a tactic in industrial warfare and the consequent fear it aroused in workers and their unions. The fact was that although strikes could (and often did) utterly fail to achieve their intended aims, lockouts (at least in the cotton industry) were always partially successful. That their repeated use might in the long run prove to be counterproductive is an important question whose implications cannot be explored here. Accordingly, the unions were in a state of apparent desperation when the last agreement, providing for a 5 percent wage reduction, expired on the first payday in March 1910. The Employers Federation was also initially quiet, more perhaps out of complacency than timidity.

Under the circumstances a demand for another 5 percent cut seemed only a matter of time. Before the employers formally presented it, the *Factory Times* observed that the workers would be justified in offering resistance, "but a period of respite, provided it is not too long, could do them [the workers] no harm. There is, indeed, a growing feeling that the twelve months' period specified in the Brooklands Agreement might with advantage be permanently extended."[31] However, the general committee of the Employers Federation evidently felt it possessed knowledge enough, and on the following day unanimously adopted a resolution calling for a 5 percent cut. As soon as this was approved by the employers at the district level, it was formally presented to the unions on May 2, with the further stipulation that it was to take effect the first payday in September. At the same meeting the unions offered a counterproposal for a twelve-month freeze. No agreement was reached, and no date was set for future meetings.

In light of the facts that the initiative still lay with the employers and that trade had not yet improved, it is somewhat puzzling that they chose to proceed as lowly as they did. Indeed, the death of the king was used as the occasion to put off the demand for a reduction for another three months, which delay evoked the response that "an employers' association that can postpone the question . . . should also have the power to withdraw the demand altogether or come to any other agreement that may be found satisfactory."[32]

No doubt the influence of public opinion counted for something. The *Manchester Guardian* took a very dim view of lockouts, and unseemly haste and militancy on the employers' part would have meant having to repudiate publicly a behind-the-scenes proposal to mediate the deadlock.[33] Furthermore, it appears that Macara (who was a merchant and not a mill owner) was genuinely seeking a way out. His suggestion that the state of trade be examined more closely has already been noted.

But the crisis was a real one for all that, as indicated by both the form and substance of the denouement. In a meeting held in Manchester on July 15, which was a secret to all but the top executives of both sides (the last precedent for secrecy being the all-night conference in 1893 that concluded the Brooklands Agreement), the representatives agreed to a totally unprecedented five-year wage freeze. Only one final hurdle remained: that of winning over the unions' rank-and-file members, who up to now with the excepiton of a few protest meetings called early in May[34] had not been invited to play any role in the negotiations. With a view to molding opinion, the *Factory Times* declared not to "recollect to have seen terms of settlement in any cotton trade dispute which we could more unreservedly recommend the operatives to adopt. . . ."[35] The Executive Council of the Spinners defended its handiwork in a circular to district officials and committees: "we . . .are firmly of opinion that there is nothing [about the freeze] that will be detrimental to the interests of our members. *Your E.C. therefore strongly recommends its adoption at the representatives' meeting on Saturday next.*"[36] The recommendation was adopted with no recorded opposition. As for the Amalgamated Weavers, there is no record that the winders, reelers, and warpers whom they represented were given formal opportunity to express their opinion; instead, the executive "endorsed" the agreement.[37]

This left the Cardroom Workers Amalgamation, which, as has already been argued, had reasons of its own for being reluctant about a long-term wage freeze. For reasons that the sources do not make clear, the president of the CWA did not attend the secret meeting of July 15. When asked his opinion on the settlement, he replied that the main question was, "[W]ill the agreement be acceptable to those whom we are supposed to represent?"[38] This, it turned out, was not just idle speculation. A few delegates to the quarterly representatives meeting of July 20 had been instructed to oppose ratification, the main objections being that the agreement froze the status quo regarding wage differentials between spinning and cardroom workers, that five years was too long, and that the rank and file should have been consulted beforehand. Rather than vote on the agreement—which would have had the effect, if the agreement had been repudiated, of forcing the CWA to reopen negotiations alone as had happened in 1908—the executive made a virtue of necessity and referred the matter back to the sixteen local branches for an open vote by members.[39] It is not possible to trace the steps that either the executive or the opponents of ratification took in the ensuing fortnight to round up support for their respective positions, but only one local in the Oldham province appears to have offered stiff resistance.[40] Once it had been brought into line—verbal persuasion seems to have been the means employed—the struggle for acceptance of the five-year freeze was over.

It is easy to understand the alacrity with which the union leaders settled for a five-year standstill. Even if it is true that absolutely nothing had been gained for the workers, neither had the principle of collective bargaining been breached: Instead, collective bargaining had been put into cold storage. Seen in this light, the freeze was more favorable to labor than a scheme to regulate wage movements automatically, even one with no upper limit. Nevertheless, one cannot retrospectively endorse it as the most that could have been obtained under the circumstances. As has been shown, the employers had already in effect revoked the demand for another 5 percent reduction until September 1910. Had the unions played for time instead of seeking a once-for-all settlement as quickly as possible, they might well have come away with a pact for far fewer than five years, which would have gained the workers more of a share in the boom of 1911-13 than merely full employment. A second line of criticism is that although the freeze by definition removed wage rates as an issue over which there might be potential conflict, the result was not a net reduction, but an intensification, of conflict within those spheres of mill life in which the status quo had not been frozen. It is therefore accurate to attribute the militancy that the spinners displayed in the strikes over bad materials in 1913-14 to the feeling that as real earnings could not be raised through negotiations, one had to make sure that production and earnings were easy and continuous. By the same token the cardroom union's determination to hold the line on the duties of strippers and grinders must be seen in the context of their already perceiving themselves to be on the defensive. In the *Factory Times* a correspondent correctly predicted a revolt of big piecers as a result, noting that they were essentially unrepresented at the negotiations.[41] Thus, judged from the standpoint of the union leaders' stated aims of seeking long-term harmony (leaving aside the question of whether this ought to be a desideratum for a trade union), the freeze was a failure.

The ease with which the union leadership gained the rank and file's approval points up the correctness of the Webbs' argument in *Industrial Democracy* that in getting its way on major questions of policy, the leadership almost invariably held the top cards. However much one might sympathize with the sentiments of "A Mule Spinner," who wrote that "our trade unions are, or ought to be, fighting organizations; when they cease to be that, it is time they went under. . . . It [the freeze] may suit our leaders, but I call in [sic?] the rank and file to reject this argument,"[42] the fact remains that neither he nor anyone else had in 1910 a program for pressuring the leadership from below, much less for replacing them. On the eve of the labor unrest the officials had every reason to believe that they were firmly in the driver's seat.

It is presently the fashion in writing social history to carry out sociometric research largely for its own sake as part of a larger conceptual strategy to write "event-free" history. This, however, has not been our intention in Chapters 1-5. Our goal has been to set the stage for the cotton workers' participation in the labor unrest of 1910-14, not in order to dispense with the description and analysis of events, but rather to make the events more intelligible. Unlike traditional narratives, which present the events first and all too frequently deal with social and economic factors in a cursory and impressionistic way, we have reversed the process by starting with a systematic presentation of the socioeconomic context.

How can our findings best be summarized? On the one hand we have shown that real economic pressures were affecting the cotton workers. The main source of pressure was not so much the eroding of real earnings; as shown in Chapter 2, these held up surprisingly well, particularly after the recession of 1908-10. Rather, the workers found themselves persistently exposed to difficult working conditions with no signs of either short- or long-term amelioration, either through technological or other changes. Interestingly, onerous working conditions were no respecter of persons: It was the relatively skilled mule spinners and weavers who bore the brunt of having to make do with imperfect materials.

Around this "hard economic core" of deteriorating working conditions we have also specified satellite "sore spots." Chief among these were grievances of the underpaid and superexploited mule piecers, to whom should also be added groups of underpaid women workers. Also, as has been noted in Chapter 3, whether or not upward mobility always works as a soothing influence upon industrial relations, there was very little of it in the immediate prewar years. Finally, the two main spinning unions had by 1910 evolved an industrial policy of *sauve qui peut,* rather than one that aimed at the mitigation of grievances along a broad front. And even if the Weavers Amalgamation saw matters differently, it did nothing to oppose actively the spinning unions' policy as it affected those unions' rank and file.

On the other hand, however, there existed against these pressures durable structures of long standing that historically served to keep industrial action in check. The most important was the sectional differences among the workers—skilled versus unskilled, men versus women, adults versus children. These sectional differences showed few signs of diminishing in our period, with the slight exception of the decline of child labor. In a word, it was extremely difficult for any one section of cotton workers, however militant, to speak and act for *all* cotton workers. A second factor making for stability, though difficult to quantify, was the absence of disruptive technological change. A mill in 1914 was recognizably the same place as a mill in 1870—noisy and cramped everywhere, stiflingly hot in the mule rooms, wet in the weaving sheds, and dusty in the blowing and mixing rooms of spinning mills. Equally stable was the degree of industrial safety in the mills, which fluctuated mildly around a level trend in the early twentieth century.

Was the cotton industry sitting atop a volcano ready to erupt? In a sense, the question is misplaced, since by definition history is what has been shown actually to have happened and not prophecies or predictions. Accordingly, the answer, which is presented in Chapter 6, is that the cotton workers indeed engaged in almost 250 strikes and lockouts between 1910 and 1914. But the question is not altogether pointless. In Chapters 1-5 we have established only the existence of discomforts and potential grievances for the workers to strike and agitate over, but we did not establish whether and to what extent they actually did so. The description, measurement, and analysis of the unrest are the subject of the rest of the book.

The Strikes of 1910-14 _____ 6

Say, lads and lasses, strike against
This unofficial striking!
It's naught to your advantage, and
It can't be to your liking
When you have troubles, grievances
Your officers are ready
To thresh out matters duly put
And all your evils storm 'em
If you will only kindly but inform 'em!

. . .

Why, lads and lasses, men who drive
The tram or train you're riding,
You do not seek to shove aside
And try your hand at guiding.
You know they're trained unto their work
And best know how to do it—
'Tis so with your official band
Don't flout 'em 'cos you pay 'em.
Accept their rules, their counsels, and obey 'em![1]

According to the Board of Trade's statistics, between the years 1900
and 1908 there was only one year, 1908, in which more than 800,000
working days were lost in textile strikes. The year 1909 was particularly
quiescent: Only 177,912 days were lost. However, in 1910 the figure
jumped to 917,558 working days for 1910, the year 1911 was higher yet,
with 1,434,068, and the year 1912 was the highest of all, with 3,698,376

working days lost.[2] But the aggregate number of working days lost is only one measurement—and a crude one at that—of industrial conflict. In Appendixes 1-5 a "data bank" has been compiled containing information on all of the industrial disputes in the cotton industry from January 1, 1910, to the outbreak of World War I for which data could be found. Since the Lancashire cotton industry witnessed no strikes in this period involving all workers in yarn spinning and cloth manufacturing walking out as a body, and since, furthermore, each occupational section of workers displayed its own distinctive style of waging industrial conflict with respect to the issues in dispute, the duration of strikes, and the propensity to wildcat, analysis of the data will proceed section by section. At the outset, however, a number of generalizations applicable to all of the strikes can be made. First, none of them can be attributed either to direct syndicalist agitation or to an articulated acceptance of a syndicalist perspective by cotton workers themselves. Second, all of the strikes were industrial rather than political, in the sense that in every instance it was the employers—and not the state or agents of the state—upon whom demands were being made and who, it was believed, had the power to set matters right. Third, in only one strike during the entire period did workers other than cotton mill operatives physically participate in strike action. Despite the numbers of strikers and of workers involved, the labor unrest in the cotton industry stayed closely within the confines of limited warfare.

THE WEAVERS' UNREST

Table 27 and Appendix 1 lend support to H. A. Turner's description of "general unrest" among weaving workers during the years 1910-14 and especially the three-year period 1911-13.[3] Almost all of the industrial issues over which workers have been known to go on strike are included—ranging from broad demands of principle like union recognition and the closed shop to quite narrow and specific demands involving "human relations." In addition to the wide spectrum of demands and grievances, strikes occurred in almost every locality—large and small—in which cloth manufacturing was found: from Bollington in Cheshire to Hebden Bridge and Skipton in the northern reaches of the West Riding of Yorkshire.

Broadness did not imply uniformity; some districts were far more strike prone than others. One can speak of a northeast Lancashire strike belt extending from Blackburn to Colne with Padiham and Nelson leading the

Table 27   Strikes Initiated by Weavers and Winders

Place

A. Industrywide	1	E. Irwell Valley	
		Radcliffe	1
B. Northeast Lancashire		Bury	3
		Haslingden	13
Blackburn	9	Heywood	1
Accrington	8	Ramsbottom	4
Church	3	Whitworth	1
Oswaldtwistle	2		23
Burnley	11		
Padiham	9	F. Rossendale Valley	
Brierfield	3		
Nelson	13	Bacup	2
Colne and district	4	Rawtenstall	1
Skipton	1	Todmorden	6
Darwen	2	Littleborough	2
Unspecified northeast			11
Lancashire	3		
	69	G. Other places	
C. West Lancashire		Bollington	1
		Hebden Bridge	1
Preston	5	Glossop	2
Bamber Bridge	1	Hadfield	1
Chorley	1	Macclesfield	1
Leyland	2		6
Wigan	2		
Leigh and district	2	Duration of Strikes	
Westhoughton	1		
	14	A. One day or less	62
D. Bolton and southeast		B. Two days—one week	20
Lancashire		C. Eight days—one month	10
		D. More than one month	26
Bolton	5	E. Data not available	21
Eccles	1		139
Manchester	1		
Oldham	3		
Rochdale	1		
Shaw	1		
Ashton under Lyne	2		
Stockport	2		
	16		

Table 27 continued

Status of Strikes

A. Official	32	C. Wages and working conditions	
B. Unofficial	94	Bad materials	24
C. Data not available	8	Reduced earnings	4
		Fines for bad work	1
D. Lockout	5	Irregular employment	1
	139	"Playing" for warps	1
		Disputed piece rates	5
Cause of Strikes		Payment for additional/	
		unusual work	5
A. Disrespectful treatment		Unspecified conditions	24
Dismissal	11	Unspecified grievances	11
Favoritism	2	Unusual heat	3
Nepotism	1		
Abusive treatment	6	D. Other causes	
"Driving"	3		
Overexact clothlooking	2	Works reorganization	2
		Feuding among workers	1
B. Trade union goals		Data not available	1
Union recognition	10	Unclassifiable	6
Management claim of			
local disadvantage	2		
General underpayment	6		
Refusal to work with			
nonunionists	7		

charge. Conversely, southeast Lancashire towns experienced few strikes in proportion to the number of weavers employed, and in the flannel-weaving town of Rochdale only one strike was recorded. The pattern of strike activity is closely correlated with wage levels and the proportion of male weavers. As was shown in Chapter 3, northeast Lancashire had the highest wages and the most men, whereas lower wages and a very high proportion of women workers were the rule in southeast Lancashire.[4] It is, however, significant that by 1913 and 1914 low-paid female workers showed signs of asserting their claims—see in particular the strikes at Horwich (number 106) and Heywood (number 129).

Strikes fought over union recognition were among the least problematical in terms of issues involved, since the goals were clearly defined and the "rules of the game" were well understood. At the same time, they were difficult and protracted contests of strength in which defeat was more likely than victory. A good example is Wigan (number 38), where a four months' strike punctuated by a couple of riots by supportive miners,[5] ended with the workers' drifting back, lured by a promised wage increase far smaller than the union had demanded. Even in Skipton (number 30), where a strike of weavers in all of the town's mills for recognition was both solid and peaceable, the workers had to settle for the Colne Colored Goods piece rate list, minus a 2½ percent reduction for "local disadvantages," which meant compromising the important point in the political economy of trade unionism that employers must not be allowed to get away with differential poor-mouthing. These strikes over recognition also indicate the expansionary thrust of the weavers' union during the period 1910-14.

Eight strikes were fought over the refusal of union members to work alongside persons who for whatever reason would not join the union. This area of contention led to the only cloth-weaving-industry-side lockout to occur between 1910 and 1914. As with strikes over recognition, it was a drawn-out affair, lasting four weeks, and it ended in failure from the union's standpoint. Because the demand for the closed shop reveals much about the values and working assumptions of the weavers and their union officials, the lockout of 1911-12 receives extended treatment in Chapter 8.

But the majority of disputes in our period broke out over wages and working conditions. In a few cases the distinction is analytically and empirically clear, as in the disputes over the correct payment for a certain kind of cloth: for example, the strikes at Westhoughton and Ashton (numbers 37 and 75). However, it was far more frequently the case that wages and working conditions were inseparably linked. In the twenty-four strikes in which the principal grievance was bad material, the problem was that snarled or brittle yarn—in addition to making the weaver's job more difficult—invariably reduced the weaver's pay packet as well, since the looms had to be stopped in order to make the necessary repairs. It is probable that many of the thirty-five strikes listed under the headings of unspecified grievances and conditions were also directly related to the quality of materials. In one sense the "Workers Revolt" in the weaving industry was a protest against what must have struck weavers as unnecessarily difficult, nerve-racking and eyestraining work, and as such was eminently "modern" insofar as workers were demanding that management toe the line and maintain production standards. Labor economists point to this kind of evidence when they argue that unions can, under certain conditions, provide an important stimulus to industrial efficiency.

In strikes waged over bad materials, monetary compensation was demanded to make up for lost earnings. The forms in which the outcomes were recorded—a lump sum of money or a percentage added on to piece lists for a stated length of time—make them extremely difficult to interpret; for this reason, among others, the standard categories of victory, defeat, and compromise have been sparingly employed. In at least two cases, Foulridge and Whittle (numbers 70 and 99), the employers insisted as a matter of principle on their right not to pay compensation. But most of the others were willing to come across with an offer, however minimal. The workers would lodge an initial claim, firms would respond with a counteroffer, and a final settlement would be negotiated. In one instance, Whittle (number 99) it seems clear that the firm would not be budged from its initial offer; in Haslingden (number 119), on the other hand, the union's full demand was conceded. Although it is impossible to tell whether the typical settlement was closer to the labor or management figure, most of them seem to have been judged by the workers to be satisfactory, since strikes tended to be settled fairly quickly—Oldham, Rawtenstall, and Whittle (numbers 7, 70, and 99) were unusual in that the former occurred during a period of bad trade and in the latter ones the principle of compensation was itself at stake. Nor was it a policy of union branches to allow a backlog of ongoing strikes to pile up with a view to forcing a breakthrough on the issue. At the same time, though, one cannot say that the weavers definitively solved the problem of bad materials, as strikes continued sporadically, following the peak years of 1912-13, right up to the outbreak of the war—see Haslingden and Saddleworth (numbers 119 and 124).

By contrast to bad-material disputes, strikes over what workers felt to be unfair treatment by management were short and explosive (Hadfield, number 123, is a puzzling exception). On the whole, these strikes seem to have succeeded (but see Hadfield again) and constituted an impressive display of workers' solidarity—especially in those cases in which entire mills struck in the defense of single individuals. One can object that disrespectful treatment should fall under the heading of working conditions, but since it usually involved specific workers rather than all workers at once, the distinction seems justified. The frequency of these strikes is easily attributable to buoyant employment prospects and the ease of lateral mobility for weavers—even if a weaver was sacked for wildcatting he could usually find work elsewhere, since weaving jobs were not generally filled by internal promotion. On the other hand, these strikes raise the question of whether ill will between workers and managers in fact increased between 1910 and 1914. Workers and union spokesmen did not publicly assert that management in the years 1910-14 had become surlier than usual. But however the bosses were carrying on, what our quantitative analysis of these strikes shows is that many workers seized the opportunity to keep management's behavior in line.

The majority of weavers strikes were unofficial—that is, workers walked off the job on their own initiative and not on the union's instructions to hand in notices and present demands prior to striking. But how important is the distinction between official and unofficial? At one end of the interpretive spectrum one may contend that in most cases the distinction is an essentially meaningless formality, except perhaps when union officials explicitly instruct members not to strike but are ignored. A second approach to wildcats is that a large percentage of unofficial strikes argues either a badly functioning system of industrial relations or, more specifically, unions' loss of control over the actions of the rank and file, but are by themselves indicative of little else. A third hypothesis maintains that wildcatting implies trade union rank-and-file militancy, and by extension the propensity of a given group of workers to wildcat is held to be an accurate indicator of heightened class consciousness. Industrial relations is seen as a zero-sum game, in which losses suffered by struck employers confer automatic gains to the workers.

Each of these three hypotheses has a measeure of applicability in analyzing specific strikes by weavers. When unorganized workers struck—see, for example, Patricroft and Horwich (numbers 53 and 106)—the label "unofficial" is clearly more formal than real. The other side of the same coin is that strikes for union recognition could hardly be anything else but official. However, the overwhelming majority of the unofficial strikes were undertaken by unionized weavers. Here analysis is complicated by the fact that class-conscious workers are most likely, given the opportunity, to battle employers than workers who ideologically accept existing social and power relations. Nevertheless, a distinction between unofficial strikes caused by a faulty or sluggish grievance machinery and wildcats triggered by committed radicals is justified by the evidence. For example, the spate of unofficial actions in Accrington, Bury, and Haslingden appears to have grown out of the local unions' reluctance to call any official strikes in our period, rather than a strong penchant for industrial militancy or political radicalism on the part of weavers in those districts, which, in political terms, seem to have been rather somnolent places.[6]   By contrast one notes a high incidence of both official and unofficial strikes around Burnley and Padiham. It would be arbitrary to suppose that the wildcats were the "really" militant strikes whereas officially called strikes must imply moderation. Rather, the coincidence of official and unofficial strikes suggests a dynamic at work whereby union officials responded to the mood of workers by officially calling strikes that might have been proceeded with anyway. Admittedly, hard data are lacking on this point. Finally, one observes in Nelson (number 84) an instance of prolonged unofficial action organized by militants that would indeed have been impossible in the absence of radical leadership. The wildcat-radical hypothesis receives close examination in Chapter 9.

The effects of the weavers' strikes can be grouped under four headings. Taking their economic impact first, we have already observed that where money was the issue, workers bold enough to strike stood a good chance of maintaining or augmenting their earnings. The internal logic closely resembled the decentralized shop-floor wage bargaining whose consequences in the form of a "wage drift" were to bedevil post-World War II planners and politicians. However, as has been shown in Chapter 2, no drift can be statistically ascertained, a reminder that even under optimal conditions labor's impact upon the economy was far less than it was to become as the twentieth century progressed.[7]

The second effect takes the form of a question: Did the militancy of the weavers trigger an employers' counteroffensive aimed at "disciplining" the workers? In Chapter 8 we shall see that the employers proved that they could be as hard as nails when principles like the closed shop were involved. Also, signs of slackening trade in 1914 aroused fears that the employers would drag their feet on the question of instituting organized short-time working.[8] But there is evidence on the other side as well. In June 1912 a 5 percent wage increase was conceded, and the employers agreed to increase the length of the summer holidays by two days beginning in 1914—a revealing incident, as the cotton unions appear not even to have entertained, much less demanded, vacations with pay.[9] It is safe to say that the record boom years of 1912-13 seriously deterred the employers from mounting concerted action even if they had desired to do so, as they certainly must have in Nelson when the weavers struck mill after mill in 1913 in order to rid the town of nonunionist and dual-unionist weavers.

A third question is whether the weavers revolt led to new perspectives on the part of workers and increasing pressure from below upon union officials to implement them. Normally, the kinds of evidence labor historians look for in establishing the presence and strength of such movements are articulated rank-and-file discontent, unofficial organization, the voicing and spread of new ideas, and changes in union leadership, with the new leaders claiming to be more closely in step with their constituents than their predecessors. Some evidence along these lines does exist. Rank-and-file weavers in northeast Lancashire booed and hissed their own officials during the lockout of 1911-12, insisting that they had been sold out. In Burnley and Nelson, the British Socialist Party and the Independent Labour Party respectively functioned as ongoing caucuses for militant weavers, and in Burnley they helped contribute to the retirement of Fred Thomas, the branch secretary and an old-school Lib-Lab who appears to have devoted much time to fighting the Socialists, in addition to fighting the employers.[10] Most interestingly, W. H. Aughton, a member of the Nelson ILP who had at one time been a member of the weavers' local executive committee and who had achieved standing in the town as an excellent theoretician, began plumping vigorously for guild socialism—in 1914. His arguments in favor of guild socialism were drawn directly from the industrial struggles of the weavers.[11]

But new discontents and new ideas were articulated only by a small minority, and undue stress on them can easily divert attention from the true nature of the unrest. What the majority of striking weavers were most interested in doing was achieving improvements in earnings, conditions, and the behavior of management by the most direct and efficacious means. This meant the uninhibited use of the strike weapon. The years 1910-14 gave the weavers just this opportunity. On the whole they seem to have had no regrets.

THE "PIECER PROBLEM"

> And so the "Piecers' Problem"
> Will always be on the hob,
> Because it's not a "calling,"
> But a temporary job![12]

Thanks to the Webbs, students of British labor history are aware that mule piecers—that is, the assistants to operative spinners—were hardly a privileged section of the British working class in the late nineteenth and early twentieth centuries; and as as has been indicated, the taproot of the piecer problem was the spinners' union's insistence that a pair of mules be staffed by an adult male. It is also widely documented that piecers occasionally went on strike and attempted to organize their own union.[13] The data in Table 28 enable one to form a clearer picture of the frequency of piecers' strikes and their outcomes.

Using the crude index of the number of strikes per worker, one notes that the approximately 50,000 piecers were, after the spinners, the most strike-prone section of the cotton industry work force. It is also safe to suggest that because none of the strikes was officially called by any union, they were the most likely class of strikes to be undercounted. The propensity of piecers to go on strike is not surprising when one considers just how high the stakes were. Except for a really rapid expansion of mule-spinning productive capacity, a piecer's chance of landing his own "pair of wheels" depended almost wholly upon an equitable promotion arrangement. (Here one obviously excludes those piecers who by kinship or other influences exercised "pull.") Accordingly, when a firm appeared to have no agreed-upon promotional ladder or when it appeared that the ladder was not being used fairly, piecers had every reason to conclude that they had nothing to lose by walking out.

Indeed, piecers' strikes in the period 1911-14 (none was called for 1910) were not foredoomed to failure. In eight out of forty-six cases they succeeded outright in their stated goals. In at least one instance (number 27) the piecers received mass support from both the spinners and the community. Whether this was an unusually blatant case of unfairness by the standards of the day one cannot tell. There is no a priori reason to suppose that all of the unspecified settlements of piecers' strikes consisted of ultimatums to get back to work or of unkept promises. If the evidence is given a fine combing, only seven strikes were utter losses. However, one must not lose sight of the length to which firms and spinners would go in order to discipline the piecers: In at least four cases the piecers were brought to court and fined. One spinner even sued a striking piecer for a half-day's lost wages because the piecer had turned off the gas valve and plunged the mule room into darkness. In the ensuing commotion the spinner tripped and twisted his ankle.[14]

Table 28

Strikes Initiated by Piecers

District			
A.	Oldham		21
B.	Bolton		13
C.	Other places		
	Glossop		3
	Blackburn		1
	Bollington		1
	Manchester		4
	Heywood		1
	Hadfield		1
	Rochdale		1
	Burnley		1
Cause			
A.	Out-of-town promotion, nepotism, etc.		31
B.	Wages		6
C.	Other causes		
	Working conditions		4
	Unspecified grievances		4
	Unfair sacking		1
	Not available		1
Outcome			
A.	Demands of piecers conceded or status quo ante		10
B.	Demands of piecers refused or promise to make changes in the future		9
C.	Unspecified settlement arrived at or not available		28
Duration			
A.	One week or less		29
B.	More than one week		3
C.	Not available		15

Source: Calculated from Appendix 2.

Of course, nobody suggested that spontaneous strikes by themselves constituted a definitive solution to the piecer problem. Leaving aside the top officials of the spinners' union, who in their printed reports never once acknowledged that a problem existed,[15] and commentators outside the cotton unions who suggested that operative spinners pay their piecers more out of their own pockets, one can divide proposals into two categories: (1) reforms of existing practices and (2) an autonomous trade union for piecers. Regarding the first set of proposals, throughout our period the editorial and correspondence columns of the *Factory Times* overflowed with suggestions. Piecers should be elevated to first-class citizenship in the spinners' union to the point even of guaranteed piecer representation on the executive, and the piecers' associations set up by the Spinners should be disbanded.[16] Wages should be related to age and experience, so that piecers in their early twenties would earn enough to support a family.[17] All mills should follow a strict policy of promotion by seniority, because even if a man proved to be inefficient upon promotion to a pair of mules, management still retained the right to give him the sack.[18] In view of machinery speedups and stricter enforcement of machinery being stopped during mealtimes, a period of the working week ought to be set aside for systematic instruction of piecers in belt splicing and other operations necessary to ensure good spinning and top production.[19] The difficulty with these proposals was not that, taken individually or together, they would have done nothing at all to mitigate the piecer problem. Rather, the trouble was that they were all utopian in the strict sense of the term, for, except for strict seniority, their implementation in the absence of a strong, trade-wide piecers' union depended upon the willingness of the spinners' union to provide leadership. But, as we have seen, the Spinners were in no mood to do so.

Accordingly, the idea of a separate piecers' union was not too unrealistic. Attempts had been made in 1889[20] and again in 1908,[21] only to be snuffed out both times by recessions. Possibly because the last failure was so recent, it was not until October 1913 that the resolution to try again was made by piecers from two mills in Kearsley,[22] a small fine-spinning center near Bolton. The new effort appears to have generated a great degree of enthusiasm. In December 1913 the piecers from two more mills in Bollington (near Macclesfield), which was also a somewhat isolated town, formed a branch of the new association.[23] By June 1914 the union claimed 1,000 members, most of whom apparently worked in and around Bolton, and lodged a claim with the Spinners for a farthing per hour more for little piecers and a minimum wage of from twenty to twenty-four shillings for big piecers, depending on the length of the mules.[24] A strike vote of 89 percent in favor was reported, and "a large number" of the 1,000 members handed in a week's notice.[25]

No strike followed. Having apparently lost his nerve, the president of the United Piecers Association argued that because the spinners' union had not replied to the demands, notices should be withdrawn "for the time being."[26] In turn, the decision to designate the spinners rather than the firms as the real employer was neither courageous nor realistic, since the minders were every bit as unlikely as the firms to grant an increase, and to go straight to management would have helped to dispel the historic confusion over just who the piecers' employer really was. The questions of how badly the United Piecers' credibility was damaged as a result of its backing down and whether it might eventually have succeeded in calling a strike are unanswerable, since the war came and among the first casualties was the United Piecers Association itself.

The piecer problem is often implicitly treated as an anomaly—the one great failure in an otherwise well-organized trade. One can agree, in the sense that it was the most refractory problem in a period when other abuses were on the way out. The employment of children was declining;[27] the dehumanizing "slate and board system," under which weavers' wages were prominently displayed in the shed, was being suppressed by the aggresive action of the weavers' union;[28] and the Cardroom Workers were beginning to agitate for exhaust equipment in cardrooms in order to keep cotton dust and byssinosis down to "tolerable" levels.[29] But in another sense the piecer problem reflected in miniature the insecurity and tensions that beset most workers in the industry. A *Factory Times* correspondent made the suggestion that, rather than ensuring survival of the fittest, the piecer system objectively rewarded dogged mediocrity and that really ambitious and talented lads rejected mule spinning as a career in favor of trades in which promotion by merit and seniority was speedier and more equitable.[30] It is impossible to put this hypothesis to a practical test, though one notes that in Manchester, where spinners' wages were quite as high as in other, larger spinning centers, piecing was by 1914 rapidly becoming women's work.[31] In Bolton, where women had been evicted from the mule room in the late 1880s, an influx of women being taken on as piecers was also reported.[32] The full employment—by pre-Keynesian standards—of these years might be a sufficient explanation of why teenage lads were not to be found beating a path to the mule room. However, we might also be dealing with the first stirrings of higher expectations, of the idea that years of low pay and uncertainty over the prospects of promotion were simply not worth putting up with. In 1936, hardly a good year for Lancashire yarn, or cotton town employment prospects, it was reported, again from Bolton, that male piecers were not to be had.[33] By the late 1940s piecers had been upgraded to assistant spinners, with a rise in wages as well as title.[34] Ironically, the secular decline of the industry seems to have been an important precondition for the solution of the piecer problem.

THE SPINNERS

At their best, working conditions for mule spinners were a model of industrial elegance, but several factors had to operate concurrently. Cotton of the proper staple length for given yarn counts had to be carefully carded, combed, and attenuated preparatory to actual spinning. The belts and straps that transmitted motive power to the mules and the mules themselves had to be perfectly "tuned" in order for the mule carriage to make its inward and outward journeys smoothly. Under optimal conditions spinners and piecers could—calmly and unhurriedly—piece up occasional broken ends, make adjustments to the machinery, unload spun yarn and replenish rovings, and be assured of maximum earnings. When, however, spinners and piecers had to contend with continually breaking ends, the mule room could turn into a madhouse of feverish scrambling up and down the length of the carriages; if matters got totally out of hand, the mules would have to be stopped in order to catch up. Aside from the extra work involved, bad spinning—which was what an unacceptably large number of broken ends per draw was called—necessarily reduced the spinners' earnings, which were determined by piece rates.[35]

As has been argued in Chapter 2, the period 1910-14 was not characterized by the spinners' work becoming easier or more highly paid. Perversely, the fact of good trade appears to have contributed to deteriorating conditions. The spinners frequently asserted that when the demand for yarn was brisk, customers tended to be less demanding about quality, thus inviting manufacturers to use cotton of a shorter staple length than was required for good spinning.[36] The spinners' response can be seen from Appendix 3. Bad spinning was the most frequent, though not the only, cause of strikes initiated by the Spinners Amalgamation. One notes further that bad-spinning strikes were confined to the sectors of the trade using American—that is, short and medium staple—cotton, which was clustered around Oldham and other spinning towns of southeast Lancashire and northeast Cheshire.

Spinning strikes were thus similar in their motivation to weavers' strikes over bad material: In both cases extra exertion and reduced earnings were the target under attack. However, when all spinning and all weaving strikes are compared, it is the differences that stand out. First, officially called spinning strikes frequently lasted for months (see numbers 6, 12-16, 19, 27, 32, and 33). In the cloth-manufacturing sector of the industry, only strikes called over union recognition showed such a marked tendency to drag on. The reasons for this difference are not altogether clear. Part of the explanation may be found in the Spinners' strike pay scale of a pound per week, a luxury made possible by union dues of a shilling a week (as against sixpence for the weavers). Also significant in influencing the duration of strikes was the union's policy of carefully selecting mills to be hit, particularly when bad spinning was the complaint, which in addition to allowing the union to claim that they penalized only bad employers, also helped to conserve the strike fund. Still another aspect is the (undocumented) possibility that the employers themselves were content to let a vanguard of managerial militants "fight the battles of the trade."

A second difference is that only 8 of the 34 spinners' strikes were definitely unofficial, whereas for weaving strikes the figures are practically reversed: 94 out of 139. This reluctance to engage in wildcat strikes is best explained by the spinners' status as contrived aristocrats. The difficulty of lateral mobility within the trade almost surely acted as a deterrent: If spinners were fired for wildcatting, they had little chance of finding work elsewhere. Moreover, it was inherent in the spinner-piecer relationship that the piecers could not be fully trusted in an enterprise as risky as unofficial strikes, since scabbing could, from the piecers' standpoint, provide an easy shortcut to promotion on the job. A third area of difference is the relative infrequency with which spinners walked off the job over "human relations," though on occasion official support for workers' demanding fair treatment was given—see in particular numbers 6 and 20.

Because they did not bring about an industry-wide stoppage, the bad-spinning strikes of 1911-14 have received little attention. Yet they were fought just as seriously as any other industrial conflict, not the least important reason for their urgency being that in 1910 the union had closed off the option of making the employers pay for bad working conditions by a rise in money wages. As in weaving, the area of contention was not the principle of compensation for bad material as such, but rather improving the speed with which a determination was made, increasing the amount of compensation paid, and tightening up the criteria for what constituted bad spinning.

By June 1912 the union, pressed forward by the Oldham Province, center of the coarse-spinning trade, had resolved to tackle bad spinning on a trade-wide basis. Proposals submitted to the employers asked:

1. That bad Spinning Inspectors be appointed by both Associations [i.e., the Union and the Employers Federation] so that complaints can be quickly attended to.

2. That an agreed test should be applied for ascertaining the breakage of ends so as to prevent differences of opinion amongst bad spinning investigators as to whether bad spinning complaints are justifiable or otherwise.

3. In case of loss of wages arising from bad spinning, that full compensation must be allowed to such of the minders who suffer a loss in their wages from the cause before named.

4. That in case of the average breakage being in excess of the standard breakage agreed upon, each spinner affected by the bad spinning complaints shall be allowed an advance of wages, varying from 5% to 10% on the total earnings in normal times, the same being for the extra labor and anxiety to which he is subjected in having to contend with inferior materials and bad spinning, and that it be left to the decision of the investigators which of the percentages must be allowed in accordance with the degree of bad spinning they find to exist when inspecting the work.[37]

Each of the new proposals constituted a departure from the leisurely provisions of the Brooklands Agreement, which had heretofore laid down the procedure for all grievances including bad-spinning complaints, and which stipulated a three-week period of negotiations before the workers could take strike action. It is significant that the new proposals made no attempt to offer anything to the employers. As the Oldham Employers Federation noted:

The employers' chief objections to a standard breakage test are:

1. That present methods on the facts adduced have proved satisfactory.

2. It seems that all breakages are due to the fault of the material or of the firm.

3. There are many indirect ways by which minders can affect the spinning in such a way as to bring about a breakage of any number of ends desired.

4. The idea of a subsidy beyond loss of wages would be a direct incentive for the encouragement of bad spinning complaints, and is the very last thing that our committee will agree to.[38]

Accordingly, the proposals were rejected outright, save for a concession that the time taken to investigate bad-spinning complaints be shortened to ten working days. If no agreement was reached, workers could then "constitutionally" strike.

Clearly, the spinners' complaints over bad spinning were not to be resolved by peaceful negotiation alone. In August 1912 several mills were struck—numbers 12-15. These also failed to rouse the employers from their lethargy in dealing with bad spinning. As a response, in January 1913 the spinners' union took the unprecedented step of unilaterally withdrawing from the Brooklands Agreement[39]—and in addition announced its intention to strike thirteen more firms running twenty-one mills. With a flourish all strikes in progress were settled, and the new round began (see number 16.)[40] A ballot taken beforehand showed an enormous majority in favor of strike action—581 to 32.[41]

One might have thought that in Lancashire's all-time record year for yarn production the firms would have settled at practically any cost. But this did not happen, despite the offer of the mayors of Oldham and Mossley to bring the two sides together,[42] and the strikes dragged on through the spring and summer of 1913. In June the employers, for no readily apparent reason, reiterated their proposal of the previous year to speed up the grievance machinery on bad-spinning complaints and again the amalgamation turned it down on the grounds of being one-sided without even going through the trouble of submitting a new offer of its own.[43] Agreement was finally reached in October whose substance if not form was close to the union's original proposal. The Employers Federation took the unusual step of hiring two spinners' union officials (who of course gave up their union posts) to investigate conditions at the struck mills.[44] This went more than half way toward meeting the union's demand for bad-spinning inspectors. Compensation awards of various sizes were concluded for each of the struck mills.[45] Rather than restoring the status quo ante with respect to grievance procedure, the union and employers resolved:

> 1. That notices shall not be tendered at any mill in connection with a bad spinning complaint until the representatives of the two organizations (local and central) have jointly enquired into the dispute.

> 2. That this Agreement shall remain in operation two months from this date.[46]

Whatever hopes the amalgamation officials might have entertained that the agreement would satisfy the spinners and that employers would pay closer attention to quality were dispelled early in 1914. Strikes called by local spinners' branches continued to break out (numbers 26, 27, 30-34), and do not appear to have differed in their essentials from earlier bad-spinning strikes. Another equally significant indicator of discontent, which does not show up in the strike data, was the conversion of the Middleton branch of the spinners to industrial unionism and their subsequent attempts to continue the attack against bad spinning by going over the heads of the official amalgamation leadership. This was the only instance between 1910 and 1914 of organized cotton workers agitating to challenge directly the trade policy as laid down by the official union leadership. Because the revolt of the Middleton branch did not take the form of strike activity, extended analysis is deferred until Chapter 9.

One need not accept the proposition that the British government, economy, and society faced a general crisis during the years 1910-14. But the evidence we have reviewed in this section does suggest that for spinners in the American section of the trade, a crisis did exist—even if its precise dimensions were obscured by the record production of 1913 and by the ability of Bolton-made Egyptian yarns to continue to compete successfully in world markets until 1929. At stake was the ability of Lancashire coarse and medium yarns to compete internationally, and the burden of competition fell most heavily upon the experienced and usually patient shoulders of the spinners. It is not surprising then that the spinners of southeast Lancashire should have taken their place in the militancy of the prewar years. Still less surprising is that no solution was found.

THE CARDROOM WORKERS

Strikes by cardroom workers must be analyzed in light of the fact that they comprised several distinct occupational groups, including male carding-engine mechanics called strippers and grinders, female operatives called tenters who minded the slubbing, intermediate and roving machinery, female ring spinners, and the men and boys who operated the opening, blowing, and mixing equipment. Predictably these different subsections displayed propensities to strike that grew out of different working conditions.

As Appendix 4 shows, the one trade-wide lockout involved strippers and grinders or, more precisely, one of their number. This turned out to be their only strike, predominantly because of the skill and dogged persistence with which the Cardroom Workers Amalgamation conducted the struggle. Their strategy and tactics are more fully examined in Chapter 7.

The union's careful handling of the 1910 strike and lockout appears to have characterized its overall strike policy. Strikes number 2, 3, and 4 of 1911—all involving wages paid to ring spinners—seem to have been carefully selected as test cases preparatory to negotiations with the Employers Federation for a trade-wide ring-spinning piecework list. Previously, the ring spinners had been the lowest-paid adult workers in the entire industry;[47] and it is evident that in waging these strikes the union was pursuing a two-fold goal of attempting to show: (1) that the employers could indeed afford to pay their ring spinners more, and (2) that the union was serious in seeing through the demand for a ring-spinning list. On both counts the union was successful. Moreover, these strikes are significant for being the only instance in the years 1910-14 of a cotton union calling strikes directly affecting a group of workers, all of whom were women. Strike number 9 also shows the CWA's concern for establishing a precedent—or, more precisely, preventing the employers from setting a precedent. The firm had fired and refused to pay out a workman's compensation claim on the grounds that a woman operative had sustained injury while cleaning moving machinery in contravention of notices posted in the mill. When the union called a strike, demanding that the established grievance procedure be used, the management responded by closing the mill—that is, locking out all the workers—and suing the union. Although the outcome was a compromise by which both sides agreed to bring the case to court, the union should be credited for tackling a vexed area of industrial relations. It was a common Lancashire practice for management to put up signs but concurrently frown upon the machines being stopped for cleaning, which in any case cut into earnings. As a weavers' union official put it: ". . . if the operatives clean the machinery during the meal hours, they run the risk of prosecution under the Factory Acts; if they clean with the machinery in motion and are injured, they get no compensation; if they stop the machinery to clean it, they usually get the sack. What are they to do?"[48]

About the eight strikes that can be definitely ascertained as unofficial it is difficult to generalize, because there were not enough of them to form a clear pattern, and the information is scanty. It does appear, however, that complaints about working conditions figured prominently; in this respect they resembled weavers' strikes. Also, the fact that the strikes were scattered over the entire spinning region suggests that they stemmed from practices and conditions in individual firms, rather than from local pockets of cardroom worker militancy. Finally, a tendency should be noted for unofficial strikes by cardroom workers to become more numerous over time, which again runs parallel to the trend in weavers' strikes.

But the overriding fact to be explained about cardroom strikes is their infrequency compared with those of other sections. Relatively good wages and working conditions and a successful defense of their on-the-job autonomy accounts for the complacency of the strippers and grinders, but an explanation along these lines does not fit the facts of industrial life for workers like tenters and blowing-room hands, who, in addition to being badly paid, performed some of the most repetitive, boring, and alienating tasks in textiles and, for that matter, modern industry—jobs that mostly consisted of watching seemingly endless amounts of cotton being processed and sent on its way. These workers had hardly any control over the quality of the material being sent through.[49] Thus even though workers like mule spinners and power loom weavers might to the layman appear to be engaged in mere machine tending, the content of these latter jobs was actually far richer. Conflict could and did arise over the question, "how do you expect us to make yarn or cloth from this junk?"[50] But for many cardroom workers the question did not apply. Because it did not, strikes were few and far between. It is therefore accurate to conclude, at least for the Lancashire cotton workers, that alienation and monotony do not by themselves breed strikes and conflict. On the contrary, partial freedom from total powerlessness and nonresponsibility for the quality of the end product was an important precondition for industrial conflict. For the cardroom workers this meant that they would not be counted among the leading activists in the prewar labor unrest.

Starting from quite different theoretical perspectives, Neil Smelser, in *Social Change in the Industrial Revolution*,[51] and E. J. Hobsbawm, in "Customs, Wages, and Work-load in Nineteenth Century Industry,"[52] reached the conclusion that workers in mature industrial societies acquire the skills and values to cope with the challenges of industrial life. How right they both are can be seen from the analysis of the almost 250 strikes presented in this chapter. By the twentieth century the Lancashire cotton workers had indeed learned what Hobsbawm has called the "rules of the game."[53] First, they demanded that payment must be made promptly and in full. Second, they insisted that organizational and technological procedures must be fully mobilized to make the working day tolerable. Third, management was informed that workers were to be treated like citizens and not chattels. The penalty for unsatisfactory performance by management in these three areas was that management would be confronted with strikes.

The industrial militancy of the cotton workers has often been overlooked and misunderstood. In a slightly different context the Webbs remarked that "absorbed in chapels and cooperative stores, eager by individual thrift to rise out of the wage-earning class, the Cotton Operatives, as a class, are not remarkable for their political capacity.[54] However accurate this assessment may have been in 1896 when it was first published, our findings indicate that by 1910-14, the cotton workers in their industrially oriented activities behaved neither like hustling, would-be *petits bourgeois* on the one hand, nor like "cheerful robots" on the other. Rather than passively waiting on either management or union officials to remedy grievances, they walked out. In this context the frequency of wildcatting, far from constituting a primitive or archaic means of protest, appears to have been a most efficacious means of communicating with the union officials that there was work, in the form of negotiations with management, to be done.

There remains, however, an elusive question mark hanging over the analysis of the strike data as it has been presented so far. Merely to show that there was quantitatively more strike activity among the cotton workers than has been recognized is no substitute for analysis of the strikes' significance. Specifically, we have not yet shown in which ways the strike of 1910-14 affected and altered the history of the workers. In order to accomplish this, a shift in method is required from the static manipulation of statistics to the dynamics of actual conflict. These dynamics are examined in the following three chapters.

Limited Industrial War: The Spinning Lockout of 1910   7

A consideration of the spinning-trade lockout of 1910 must begin with
G. R. Askwith's account in *Industrial Problems and Disputes* (1920), as
it contains the only tolerably complete account of the dispute that has
appeared, and upon which subsequent treatments have been based.[1]
Without saying so directly, Askwith seems to have regarded the affair as
a monumental instance of Lancastrian stubbornness and very little else.
The dispute began when the foreman of the Fern Mill, located at Shaw,
near Oldham, demanded that one of the strippers and grinders, George
Howe, clean the flats of his carding engines with a pick or an awl. Howe,
backed by the local branch of the Cardroom Workers Amalgamation,
refused. Howe was fired, and a strike of 269 workers at the Fern Mill
began on June 7. Negotiations between the CWA and the employers became bogged down at the outset in a squabble over the meaning of the
Brooklands Agreement, which as has been shown in Chapter 5 was the
collective-bargaining Magna Carta of the spinning trade. The union claimed
that management had broken one clause of the agreement, while management claimed that the union had broken another clause.[2]

There matters stood until September 19, when the employers met and
decided upon a general lockout of the spinning trade as a means of breaking the impasse. On the same date the CWA also met and agreed to accept
Askwith as arbitrator, but demanded that the Fern Mill remain out on
strike until Askwith brought in his award. Arriving in Manchester, Askwith

found that "both sides were very determined, there was strong and bitter feeling; the question of George Howe was discussed up hill and down dale. ..."[3] The employers' position was that the mill must be restarted without Howe and that only then would they agree to arbitration. The union insisted that "either the mill must stop until arbitration is over, or George Howe must start with the other workpeople at the Fern Mill."[4] On the day before the lockout was scheduled to begin, the CWA made a final proposal that if the employers found Howe a job in another mill, the union would call off the strike. But the employers claimed that they had only the power to recommend to the firms in Shaw that Howe be taken on when the first vacancy arose. This the CWA did not accept, and the lockout began on October 3.

Askwith's original mediation strategy had been to get the two sides away from the idea that one or the other must have broken the Brooklands Agreement, and to concentrate instead on rights and powers allowed by the agreement and how best to utilize them. But the union continued to insist that the question of what to do about Howe took precedence over all other issues. Fortunately, an agreement was reached whereby Howe would swap places with a stripper and grinder in a nearby mill. This compromise ended the lockout. Some months afterward Askwith delivered his judgment that there was a gap in the Brooklands Agreement to ensure that:

> No provision was made in it, where there was a difference of opinion about a particular change of work, to that it must be dealt with before a stoppage of work, in the spirit of the Brooklands Agreement, and that the Secretaries ought to meet, and if they differed on procedure, the matter should come before the Associations for discussion on merits.[5]

The gap was duly plugged, and another victory had been recorded for the theory and practice of mediation.

Although accurate enough in factual details, Askwith's account of the lockout of 1910 does not go far enough. As perhaps befits someone in his line of work,[6] Askwith tended to view faulty grievance machinery and incompetent negotiating as major causes of industrial conflict. This judgment neatly complemented his beliefs that strikes and lockouts did the community more harm than good and that public opinion favored industrial peace.[7] However, the assumptions that informed Askwith's approach to the lockout can, if followed slavishly, divert the student from a whole range of other questions.

Were the union's instructions to Howe not to pick flats with an awl a hasty overreaction, or were they part of a developed and ongoing strategy to maintain improvements already won for strippers and grinders? Was the union's insistence that the Fern Mill had broken the Brooklands Agreement really the kernel of the dispute or a diversion? Did insistence on this strengthen or weaken their bargaining position? To what extent did the union's tactics make a lockout inevitable, and to the extent that it was within their power, should they have sought to prevent a lockout? Finally, is the outcome best regarded as victory, defeat, or honorable compromise? The answers to these questions are mixed, as befits a highly complex situation. At the same time, there was a substantive rationality to the proceedings. If, as Askwith thought, the outcome was a victory for conciliation, it was also a victory for militant trade union tactics.

THE RISE AND PROGRESS OF STRIPPERS AND GRINDERS

As Table 29 shows, strippers and grinders, whose job it was to keep the carding engines of a spinning mill operating at peak efficiency so as to maximize both the output and the quality of carded cotton, were among the better-paid male cotton workers. By 1906 their earnings (excluding foremen) were second only to those of mule spinners. In addition, Table 29 shows that this had not always been the case: Their average wages in 1870 were little better than those of general laborers. It appears that a technological shift from roller and clearer cards to revolving flat cards in

Table 29

Wage Movements of Strippers and Grinders, Compared with Selected Occupational Groups, 1886-1906

	1886	1906	Increase (%)
Strippers and grinders	20s. 4d.	29s. 5d.	44.7
All male operatives	23s. 3d.	27s. 3d.	17.2
Mule spinners	31s. 3d.	41s. 5d.	32.6

Source: Wood, *History of Wages*, pp. 149-51.

the 1880s[8] was a factor of some importance, for although one effect of
this change was a significant reduction in the number of men working
round and about carding engines, another effect was that those who remained now had a more sharply defined and delineated occupational
status. The Cardroom Workers Amalgamation can itself be seen as a further consequence of the change.

If, as H. A. Turner notes, the Weavers Amalgamation of 1884 was the
first of the "new unions," the CWA was the most successful—the wages
of strippers and grinders rising some 44.7 percent over a twenty-year
period.[9] Although there is no documentary evidence, it may be conjec-
tured that the long-term goal of the union was the attainment of wage
levels for strippers and grinders equal to or above those of the mule spinners.[10] At the same time, a number of tendencies converged around 1910
that appeared to throw into jeopardy the union's hopes of future progress. First and most immediate was the dispute over which the Fern Mill
was originally struck: that is, management's insistence that a certain task
be performed and that it be performed in a specific manner. Important
though the procedural side of the dispute was to become, the union's
sensitivity to changes in working conditions must not be overlooked.
Over the years the union's main bargaining objective was the definition
of tasks to be performed and the demand that all work was to be paid
for according to the Universal List, which was recognized by the employers
only in 1902, thus making strippers and grinders the most recent major
section of operatives to achieve effective recognition. Precisely because
of the direct link between task and payment[11] the union's officials were
predisposed to regard tampering with explicitly codified procedures as
smacking of a return to the "bad old days." As the *Factory Times* commented:

The introduction of extra duties . . . is but the thin end of the
wedge, and very soon the stripper and grinder would go back to
the days when he was known as a "jobber"—a term that stank in
his nostrils—and when he was at the beck and call of everyone.
In many quarters the subject of the dispute has been made light
of, but it is through lack of a knowledge of the real facts. The
strippers and grinders are fighting to retain their position as work-
men—not to go back to the days of promiscuous drudgery.[12]

All in all, the circumstances surrounding the outbreak of the dispute at the Fern Mill suggest little in the way of a qualitatively new consciousness, but rather a marked continuity of traditional concerns.

A second cloud on the strippers and grinders' horizon concerned an economic trend that took the form of a technological snag. Cardroom workers found themselves working a lot of short time following 1908, not only because of the trade depression of 1908-10 but also because the balance between the amount of cotton that could be carded and the amount of yarn that was spun from a given amount of cotton had gotten out of phase in many spinning mills. The result was that it took cardroom workers roughly forty-eight hours to keep the mule rooms busy for a full workweek. This was not due to mismanagement on the part of the employers. Faced by foreign competitors whose stock in trade was coarse goods produced by badly paid workers and a relatively backward technology, Lancashire had responded with a slow but steady tendency toward the production of finer yarn and cloth, an option made possible by up-to-date technology and an experienced, skilled workforce. Necessarily, a given amount of carded cotton yields more feet of fine yarn than of coarser yarn. Inasmuch as equilibrium could be restored only by future expansion of the forces of production (leaving aside the expediency of cutting back on the number of cardroom operatives, which it was not in the union's interest to propose), this problem was not raised as an issue during the Fern Mill strike. Nonetheless, it was clearly a part of the context within which the strike took place and as such must be counted among the factors contributing to the unease of the period.[13]

A third setback was the five-year freeze on spinning-mill operatives' wages, which meant a five-year moratorium on the already indicated goal of catching up with the mule spinners. Ironically, the only documentary evidence suggesting that the freeze had an impact upon the union's motivation comes not from within the labor movement, but from a source hostile to organized labor, the *Times*. According to the paper's Lancashire correspondent,

> Among the employers the opinion is growing that the officials of the Cardroom Amalgamation are afraid that their position will become less important than when it was before a five years' truce on the wages question was arranged, and that they are raising questions on details of working to show that their services are still ur-

gently needed by their members. Questions arising out of the
amendment of the Universal List have previously been settled in
an amicable way. . . .[14]

This line of reasoning was vigorously contested by the *Manchester
Guardian* on the grounds that anyone familiar with the past practice of
the Cardroom leaders knew that they were not the type of men who would
foment disputes out of personal spite or ambition.[15] The union itself maintained a discreet silence. Whom, then, should we believe? The *Times*'s
charge does not constitute a proof, being badly lacking in hard evidence.
On the other hand, though, the *Manchester Guardian*'s line was eminently
appropriate for a self-appointed friend and adviser to the community. As
for the union, even if it were true that the five-year freeze stiffened its
will to fight, there was under the circumstances no tactical advantage to
be gained from proclaiming the fact. So that the most that can be done is
to exercise the historian's right to admit circumstantial evidence, which
at the very least suggests that though the *Times*'s argument might have
been made out of whole cloth, nevertheless the texture and pattern were
quite plausible.

WHO BROKE THE BROOKLANDS AGREEMENT?

The strippers and grinders were subjected in 1910 to a set of industrial
and economic pressures that were both complex and real—indeed, real
enough to explain why the strike occurred without recourse to exogenous
factors. Yet both at the time and afterward, observers have sought the
cause in the grievance machinery provided by the Brooklands Agreement
of 1893. The union was at pains to base its case upon its probity in adher-
ing to the letter and spirit of the agreement. As has already been noted,
Askwith tended to approach industrial conflict in terms of procedural
forms, a line apparently justified by his claim to have located a flaw in
the agreement itself. Three lines of inquiry are indicated. First, before one
can evaluate Askwith's claim as to the defectiveness of the Brooklands
Agreement, one must sketch out the major characteristics of grievance
procedures in general. Only by reference to a "well-wrought" model can
"defects" be spotted. Second, the Brooklands Agreement itself must be
examined and Askwith's charge against it assessed. Third, if Askwith was
correct, it must be explained why the principal disputants could not locate
the defect for themselves.

An important first point about grievance procedures in modern industry is that the relationship in which labor and management stand to them is essentially asymmetrical. In actual practice the impact of the decisions reached through the machinery is felt more quickly and more concretely by workers than by managers. This is true because the effects of management-proposed changes in work rules are found out and evaluated by reference to medium- to long-term changes in overall productivity, quality, and profit, rather than by reference to gain or loss, comfort or discomfort experienced by individual managers on a day-to-day basis. By contrast, a proposal on labor's part for a change in established work methods means that workers are dissatisfied, in an immediate and concrete way, over something that management does not directly experience, since managers do not perform physical labor. To be sure, the question in the case of the Fern Mill strike was who initiated a proposal for change. But this does not alter the lines of the argument.

A second characteristic of grievance procedures is that their very existence represents a working compromise between management and labor. From time to time employers have seen fit to do without any form of grievance machinery. The vast majority of trade unions, on the other hand, have regarded the establishment of such machinery as central to the successful functioning of trade unionism. It would thus seem that the notion of compromise is misplaced and that grievance machinery won through union recognition is a clear union gain and corresponding management loss. Such a conclusion, however, is wrong. For just as an employer who feels strong enough insists upon being "master of his own house," a union bent upon maximizing workers' control of production also seeks to maximize flexibility and freedom of action. Taken to a logical conclusion, this would mean in practice no fixed time period between the lodging of a complaint and the right to down tools, which latter tactic would be viewed as a first not last resort. Now it is evident that grievance procedures are designed and in fact work so as to fend off such "syndicalist" practices. The most important substantive provisions lay down the inherently time-consuming channels through which the grievances are to run. Accordingly, grievance procedures are a cornerstone of any scheme that seeks to routinize conflict.

Seen in this light, the Brooklands Agreement represented a comprehensive, concrete set of machinery to implement the goals and purposes of collective bargaining. In addition to stipulating time periods between and increments for increases and decreases in wage rates,[16] a two-stage

procedure for adjudicating on-the-job grievances was also laid down. How
the machinery was supposed to function was indicated in Clause 6:

> That in future strikes or lockouts may be initiated only after the
> following procedure has been followed. 1. all grievances must be
> submitted in writing by the secretary of the local employers as-
> sociation to the local union secretary or vice versa, depending on
> which side is lodging the complaint. A local joint committee con-
> sisting of the secretaries and three representatives from each side
> has seven days to arrange a settlement. 2. If they are unsuccessful,
> the dispute moves upward to another joint committee, this time
> consisting of the general secretaries and four representatives from
> each side. They have up to 14 days to arrive at a settlement.
> *Should either the local Employers' Association or the local Oper-*
> *atives Association fail to call such a meeting within seven days*
> *(unless by consent of the other side), then the party which has*
> *asked for the meeting shall have the right to at once carry the*
> *question before the Joint Committee of the Employers' Federa-*
> *tion and Operatives' Amalgamation without further reference to*
> *the local Association, and should either the Employers' Federa-*
> *tion or the Operatives' Amalgamation fail to deal with the matter*
> *in dispute within a further seven days, then either side shall be at*
> *liberty to take such action as they may think fit.*

The keynote is one of symmetry. Should a dispute arise, each side is
equally bound to use the machinery; and each side has equal representation at the factory, local, and amalgamation levels. But, as has been argued previously, the authority structure in which disputes actually arise
does not allow symmetry. Workers and their union cannot initiate changes
on their own. They must avail themselves of the grievance machinery, for
any attempts to the contrary would constitute a prima facie breach of
factory discipline. Clause 7 of the agreement extended the restriction on
initiating unilateral changes to management as well:

> Should any firm make any change which when completed involves
> an alteration in the work or rate of wages of the Operative which
> is considered not satisfactory by them, the firm shall at once place
> the matter in the hands of their Association, who shall immediate-
> ly take action as per Clause 6, failing which the Operatives involved

shall have the right to tender notices to cease work without further notice to the Employers' Association.[17]

As befits an instrument drawn up with the help of lawyers, the Brooklands Agreement implicitly assumes that every dispute has a plaintiff and a defendant and that the plaintiff, who defines himself as such, by definition begins the proceedings. But what if each side steadfastly refused to answer to the name of plaintiff? Far from being a hypothetical question, this is precisely what happened in the Fern Mill dispute. The carder—that is, the overseer of the carding department—told Howe to clean out his flats with an awl. Howe, backed by the union, refused on the grounds that the work was not customary. The management replied that it indeed was customary and that failure to comply would result in dismissal. The upshot was a welter of charges and countercharges[18] as to who was plaintiff and who was defendant. Replying to a reporter's question whether the union could not have set the machinery of the Brooklands Agreement in motion, the secretary of the union bluntly replied, "yes we could, but we are not going to be the plaintiff in every case. In this case the onus was clearly on the masters. . . ."[19] The refusal of either side to adopt the plaintiff's role meant in effect that there was no way in which the grievance machinery could be turned on and that a search for an answer to the question, who broke the Brooklands Agreement, as each side accused the other of doing,[20] must amount to an exercise in chasing one's tail. It was Askwith who saw this and was thus correct in his argument that the agreement was defective. As he wrote,

> No provision was made in it, where there was a difference of opinion about a particular change of work, to ensure that it must be dealt with before a stoppage of work, in the spirit of the Brooklands Agreement, by mutual understanding or agreement, and that the secretaries ought to meet, and if they differed on procedure, the matter should come before the Associations for discussion on merits.[21]

A close reading of the text of Clauses 6 and 7 (not provided by Askwith in his account) enables one to see that he was indeed correct.

Why was it not possible for the officials of the union and employers to notice for themselves that a gap existed in the machinery? On this question contemporaries were silent, and it is tempting to dismiss it as just one instance of engaged combatants so close to the action that a clear focus was impossible. But in view of both sides of the cotton trade's demonstrated ability to manage their own affairs, it is perhaps advisable to take a more contextual approach. As has been noted, the union officials' attitude was that the time had come to put their foot down.[22] In actually shutting down the Fern Mill they had created for themselves a tactical advantage of no small efficacy. For them to notice and make public the fact that the Brooklands Agreement was not "self-acting" would have meant calling off the strike and starting all over again at the first move. However, there is no evidence that they noticed the defect. On the other hand, the managers of the Fern Mill and their fellow employers had quite a bit to gain by exposing the inadequacy of the Brooklands Agreement on this point. Two possible answers may be suggested. First, the apparent willingness of the unions in the past to start up the machinery without cavil may have had a dulling effect upon the employers: To the extent that the Fern Mill impasse was genuinely novel (though in theory possible all the while), they might have been disoriented and taken aback. Second, just as the union possessed and implemented ready-to-hand tactics, the employers also possessed a powerful deterrent of their own, a general lockout. And in the final analysis they proved willing to impose a lockout.

A summing up is in order. The Brooklands Agreement, on the whole an unexceptional specimen of its kind for the period, was incomplete in its provisions. This fact, coupled with the inability of the principals to make the correction on their own, in large measure shaped the form of the dispute, but was by no means the sole cause, the others, as has been shown, flowing from economics and technology. Hence it would be unjustified to infer that had the gap not existed, a strike and lockout would not have occurred. One simply cannot tell. But even if the procedural side is assigned preponderant importance, there remains the question of the outcome—who won, who lost, and how well each side played its hand.

HONORABLE COMPROMISE VIA MILITANCY

An industry-wide lockout appears to have been a peculiarly frightening and explosive tactic to workers and their unions in the early twentieth century. Indeed, the fear it aroused may have been exceeded only by the use of violence against strikers. It is therefore necessary to examine the motivations on both sides that led to the lockout.

Cotton union spokesmen saw the employers' decision in the darkest terms. In addition to complaining about the general inequity that would result from "a lockout which will bring destitution on the poor people, who are already half-starved due to short time,"[23] it was also alleged that the employers were taking cynical advantage of the Fern Mill dispute in the hope that during a prolonged lockout trading conditions would improve: ". . . they are in a position to recoup themselves when this is over, but the operatives will have to lose both their trade union funds and their wages. . . ."[24] Although this line of speculation cannot be positively dismissed—among other reasons lockouts have a tendency to occur during bad trade periods rather than during booms—it nevertheless appears that the employers' motivations were informed by a diametrically opposed consideration, that of getting production started again. Especially in view of the employers' misunderstanding of the impasse, it is probable, if impossible to prove since documentation is lacking, that they regarded the lockout as a way out, a tactic whose efficacy and cheapness (given the fact of narrow margins) stood the test of time.

A far more complex question than why the employers locked out the trade is why the CWA officials and rank-and-file representatives stopped short of doing everything in their power to make sure that a lockout did not happen. There is no evidence to suggest that the union men's basic attitude toward lockouts had changed: They had always represented a grim challenge to be avoided in all but the most desperate circumstances. Neither is it the case that the lockout was the inevitable result of rigidity, a once-for-all position that the union adopted at the outset and from which it subsequently refused to budge. The very reason Askwith was asked to mediate was that both the employers and the CWA agreed to mediation. To be sure, the employers first proposed it, and the union initially demurred, on the grounds that there was nothing to mediate, since it had been the employers who broke the Brooklands Agreement.[25] However, once the employers' executive council voted for a lockout to take effect on October 1, 1910, the union changed its stance, deciding not only that Askwith would be acceptable as a mediator but also that the strike would be called off provided that the status quo ante was restored at the Fern Mill.[26] In other words, the union proved itself flexible to the point of offering to give up its position of strength and rely exclusively on a favorable award from Askwith. But as the union's position softened, the employers' position hardened. They now made it plain that Howe had been

irreversibly sacked, even though earlier in the dispute an informal management offer was made that the mill be restarted with the exception of
Howe, who was to be put on wages—that is, a fixed amount not determined by work actually performed—until joint agreement could be reached
reached.[27] High principles were at stake:

> The employers have unanimously reaffirmed their resolution of
> the 26th inst., viz., that on the acceptance of arbitration, the Fern
> Spinning Company's workpeople who left work on June 14th
> must return to work.
>
> In relation thereto, I am desired to say that George Howe was
> discharged for an act of insubordination, after having been given
> seven days' notice, and the right to do this my committee, as rep-
> resenting employers responsible for the maintenance of discipline
> in our mills, cannot lightly give up.
>
> As, however, we have no feeling against George Howe, we shall
> be prepared, in the event of arbitration going against us, to com-
> pensate him.[28]

It is quite unclear why the employers chose to take such a hard line.
But whatever the reasons, the reaction was one of unalloyed anger. The
general secretary of the CWA replied:

> It is unfortunate you persist in your statement that Howe was
> guilty of insubordination. This is the point in dispute, and the
> one we are prepared to put to arbitration.
>
> Insubordination, as we understand it, is to set all authority
> at defiance.
>
> In this case extra work was demanded, and the man, acting
> on advice, declined to do it. This fact was made known to both
> carder and manager. Later the manager had two conferences with
> the man, who still persisted in declining to do the work. . . .
>
> Your committee, evidently with a view of cloaking a crass,
> stupid blunder of your official in this case, persisted in putting
> the blame on Howe, and this we decline to accept.
>
> Nor do we desire to interfere with the internal management of
> your mills, but we must and shall take not of legitimate complaints
> of our members whenever such are made. . . .

Your letter carries with it an unnecessary sting, for we know our duties, and shall not come to your association to be taught them. . . .[29]

It is likely that Mullin's anger was shared by the rank and file. Reports of CWA representatives' meetings indicated unanimity of opinion and tactics. During the lockout, it was reported that in Bolton people on the streets booed and hissed when news arrived that the employers' negotiators had not yet yielded.[30] There appears to have been only the interunion meeting between the executives of the Oldham Spinners and the Oldham Cardroom which took place immediately after the lockout was announced. No public statement was issued, but it was thought that a difference of opinion existed regarding arbitration.[31] Once again the *Times* was on the lookout for interunion rivalry, quoting a spinners' union official that he could not "forget that the cardroom workers' officials issued from the lockout of 1908 with very little credit to themselves. . . . There is yet time for the Cardroom leaders to move successfully towards a settlement."[32] The *Factory Times* countered that "the spinners are at one with the cardroom workers and recognize the injustice of the employers. The ruse to secure a division in the ranks of the two associations will not succeed."[33] Neither assertion accurately describes the actual behavior of the spinners and other cotton unions: Something like benevolent neutrality would be closer to the mark.

By refusing to capitulate before the threat of a lockout, the union in effect placed the employers in the uncomfortable position of having to explain why some 100,000 working people had been thrown "onto the cobbles" when the employers by their own admission harbored no personal feelings against Howe. Furthermore, the union persisted, evidently against the wishes of Askwith,[34] in demanding that equity for Howe be given top priority—a logically unassailable position once Askwith demonstrated the flaw in the Brooklands Agreement. For why should Howe be penalized for other persons' oversights? Precisely because the union's formulation of the problem was sound, a substantive proposal regarding Howe had to be brought in; and the suggestion that he move to a neighboring mill was accepted by the union. In all, the mills were closed for exactly one week, and both sides were able to claim victory.

What were the consequences of the dispute, lockout, and its settlement upon subsequent events? If keeping memories green is an important criterion, then one might be tempted to conclude that they were minimal.[35] But in the context of the cotton workers' history from 1910 to the outbreak of the war, the possibility of real consequences cannot be ignored. First, no further disputes are recorded with respect to the job duties of strippers and grinders in spinning mills, although the return of good trade must also be a consideration. A second possible consequence concerns the marked policy of independence and fractiousness displayed by the CWA leadership vis-à-vis the other cotton unions in the ensuing years. Having successfully "gone it alone" and having emerged victorious, the leadership may well have concluded that interunion harmony and cooperation were unimportant, to judge from their policy of nonsupport for the United Textile Factory Workers Association candidate in the Oldham by-election of 1911 and their walking out of the UTFWA a year later. Third, the success of the CWA might have inspired other sections to challenge the employers. In particular the Amalgamated Weavers appeared to conclude that if the historically least militant and strike-prone of the major cotton unions had held off what looked like an employers' offensive—and this during a patch of bad trade—then the employers would think twice before resorting to the tactic of a lockout to avert the weavers' demand for a closed shop. But, as has been argued throughout, the Cardroom's victory did not drop out of the laps of the gods: Intelligent tactics were a crucial precondition. As the Weavers were to find out, in the absence of sound tactics the lockout weapon still retained all of its potency.

The Weavers' Lockout of 1911-12: Trade Union Principles Versus Managerial Prerogatives | 8

Although both the cardroom workers' lockout of 1910 and the weavers lockout of 1911-12 were trade-wide disputes which at the time attracted nationwide attention, the contrasts between the two struggles far outweigh the similarities. In the first place, the weavers lockout involved far more workers (165,000 as against 102,000) and lasted four weeks (as against one fairly calm week). A second contrast is that although the Cardroom Workers Amalgamation managed to conduct the struggle with a minimum of rank-and-file involvement, the operative weavers were actively involved at crucial points in the conflict, and their presence was an important determinant in setting boundaries on the leadership's freedom of action. Thirdly, while the dispute in 1910 turned on the interpretation of an existing collective-bargaining agreement, the weavers raised the unprecedented (for the weaving industry) demand for the closed shop; that is, they were demanding the right of unionized workers to insist that all workers in the trade join the union as a condition of employment. Fourthly, the outcomes of the two disputes were utterly different. Because the cardroom workers were (justifiably) satisfied with the outcome, relations between workers and management remained calm following the settlement of the Fern Mill dispute right down to the outbreak of World War I. The weavers, on the other hand, were utterly outmaneuvered and defeated, which, far from resulting in industrial peace, triggered a series of angry aftershocks in certain districts of northeast Lancashire that acquired an intensely bitter ideological form and reverberated for years to come.

There are two more reasons why the weavers lockout deserves close analysis. The first is that more documentary material exists for the weavers lockout than for any other strike by cotton workers in our period, especially in the crucial area of relations between leaders and rank-and-file members. The second is that in 1911-12 the weavers were close to the zenith of their collective power as organized workers, and thus allow the historian to assess the limits of their strength and endurance and their ability to enforce their principles of political and moral economy upon the community in the last years of "Liberal England."

The problem then is one of analyzing how the weavers exercised (or failed to exercise) the strength at their command. It will be argued that the leaders had compelling reasons to seek the closed shop and that it was easy for the rank and file and leadership to agree on the desirability of achieving the closed shop. Next, the reasons are given why the leadership thought that 1911 was a good time to force the issue, *despite* their advance knowledge that the employers bitterly opposed granting the closed shop. Thirdly, the tactics used by both sides and the reasons for the union's defeat are examined. Finally, the short- and long-term consequences of the union's defeat are evaluated.

THE CLOSED SHOP: THEORY AND PROMISE

In modern industry the demand by a union for the closed shop where it has not yet been attained is an offensive action in the double sense that (1) the trade unionists themselves usually originate the demand and (2) it is always the case that new rights are being claimed[1] (unlike, for example, a wage claim, which even if unprecedented in magnitude is nevertheless simply the implementation of rights already won). Precisely because principles and initiatives were involved, it is necessary to look at the related questions of why the weavers felt the closed shop was justified, what the closed shop was supposed to accomplish, and why they chose to raise the demand in the time and manner that they did.

The argument in favor of the closed shop is apparently as old as trade unionism itself; historically, the keystone of the argument is an appeal to

a common obligation. The case for the closed shop begins with the assertion that in general it is unfair for anyone to receive something for nothing. Next, the claim is made that gains won by trade union action and
organization are conferred equally upon union members (who pay dues)
and nonunionists (who do not.) The conclusion follows that all workers
ought therefore to join their appropriate union; and since unions operate
in the real world, a further conclusion is drawn that an efficient form of
compulsion—over and above attempts at verbal persuasion—is legitimate
if found to be necessary. During their propaganda and recruiting campaign
that took place in 1911, the weavers repeated the "good old argument,"
which is not surprising in view of the fact that the staple argument cannot
easily be improved upon.[2]

What did the weavers expect to gain from the closed shop, aside from
having an abstract right recognized by the employers? It must be remembered that that world of labor was a different mental habitat from that
of the generation following World War II. In the first place, although industrial unions, under which heading the Weavers Amalgamation definitely belongs, did not possess the strength they do today, nevertheless the
potential that contemporaries hoped for from the trade union movement
was far greater than today. And this is for good reason, because after all
is accounted for, the unions were the only institution in working-class
life whose ability both to survive on a permanent basis and "deliver the
goods" was well established. It is of course true that improvement through
legislation had left a long and important legacy, but legislation occurred
in spurts and clusters: For example, the working week had been shortened
by law in 1875 but not again until 1901. In addition, legislation could result in unanticipated consequences. The cloth-manufacturing unions felt
this to be the case with an act of 1891 regulating the use of steam to
raise artifically the humidity in weaving sheds, a procedure that manufacturers considered necessary to reduce yarn breakages. The unions thought
permission to use steam all but universalized what had previously been
a selective practice. Finally, even good laws required strict enforcement,
which was perhaps less than automatic when cases came before magistrates
who also had interests in mills.[3]

The performance of other working-class institutions was even more problematical than reliance upon Parliament. To be sure, both the permanence
and economic success of the cooperative movement were undoubted, but
there is reason to suppose that the inherent limitations of cooperation by

itself were becoming increasingly recognized even by cooperators themselves, as manifested by the "fusion of forces" movement.[4] The full potential of independent political action and of socialism, on the other hand,
was still far on the horizon; all authorities attest to the fact that even in
the Labour Party nobody was as yet planning for the day that Labour
would possess a working majority in Parliament.

Theory and experience, therefore, led back to the unions. Moreover,
the weavers' officials had reasons of their own for wanting the closed shop.
They appear to have felt that if collective agreements covered the entire
trade, they would be easier to enforce and service. As the secretary of the
Ashton-under-Lyne Weavers explained:

> Whenever a grievance occurs we are faced with the difficulty of
> the non-unionists. . . . When you consider that 99 percent of the
> weavers cannot calculate what they should be paid for weaving
> a piece of cloth, I think you will admit that to a very great extent
> they are at the mercy of the employer regarding their prices, and
> their remedy lies in their union. . . .
>
> The only way we have of checking the prices is through our
> members supplying me with particulars of what they are weaving.
> The employer is made to toe the line, but the non-unionist bene-
> fits at the expense of the unionists, and our members have decided
> that if the non-unionist will not pay he shall not receive. . . .
>
> Several long-standing grievances, such as bad material and low
> wages are long overdue, and if we can get a 100 percent member-
> ship it will act as a tonic to the employer whenever he is asked to
> remedy those grievances.[5]

At one level all this is merely a restatement of the appeal to a common
obligation; yet it is clear that the argument assumes that there would be
fewer attempts to "nibble" at wages in 100 percent unionized shop than
in an open shop. In addition to the closed shop having beneficial effects
within individual mills, the leaders also believed that the closed shop would
alleviate the pressures on wages and working conditions stemming from
antiunion employers: ". . . the weavers have been so often pressed and
threatened with a reduction of wages unless certain employers were compelled to pay up to the full list, and the only way to bring that about, in

the minds of our members, was the elimination of the non-member ele-ment."[6] In other words, the union had up to now *not* succeeded in making all firms in the industry pay full list wages, thereby recognizing the union, irrespective of the number of unionized workers employed by these firms. Once again the closed shop is meant to provide a remedy, presumably on the grounds that an employer confronted by a fully unionized work force would have no choice but to adhere to the common norm. In view of the weavers' uneven degree of organizing success throughout the trade—among other places, Wigan and Manchester were practically unorganized—their attempt to achieve recognition by the "shortcut" tactic of the closed shop is not surprising.

These reasons for demanding the closed shop might be regarded as gen-eral, always-in-season justifications. But there was a more specific and localized ideological problem confronting the weavers officials and mem-bers in parts of northeast Lancashire that might have also played a role in forcing the nonunionist issue. The problem took the form of a "backlash" against the Weavers Amalgamation's support of and affiliation with the Labour Party, which was taken to imply support for socialism and secular education. By 1911 a number of disquieting symptoms had appeared. In Preston the Weavers had a mini-Osborne case on their hands by virtue of an old Liberal operative weaver successfully seeking an injunction against the branch's contributing to the Labour Party.[7] In Blackburn, where a unique situation had existed since the 1880s of two branches serving the same catchment area both federated with the amalgamation, one branch, the Blackburn Weavers Protection Society, had become the trade union for Conservative weaving workers,[8] and was publicly accusing the other and larger branch, the Blackburn Power Loom Weavers Association, of having been taken over by the Socialists. In Nelson, where the Tories had unsuccessfully run an operative weaver in the January 1910 general elec-tion,[9] an organization calling itself the Nelson and District Catholic Workers Union, led by a Roman Catholic priest, Father Robert Smith,[10] had been formed. It pledged itself to the fight against socialism and secu-larism. No doubt there is a certain internal logic in these countertenden-cies surfacing in the most radical districts of the Lancashire cotton trade. The Weavers Amalgamation thus had more to tend with than just com-mon garden-variety nonunionists, acting as isolated if stubborn indi-viduals. They had to cope with organized, articulated working-class oppo-sition to the political drift of the amalgamation and the larger British

trade union movement—opposition that in the case of the Nelson organization had already crossed the line dividing mere dissent from dual unionism.[11] There is no precise way of evaluating whether the nonunionist campaign was intended to defeat this organized opposition once and for all,
and the amalgamation quite predictably maintained absolute silence on the
right-wing oppositionists within the ranks of working weavers. But however indeterminate the oppositionists' presence was as regards the causes
and origins of the nonunionist campaign, one can definitely say that the
lockout and their response to it brought them into full public view and
total opposition to the Amalgamated Weavers. As such they constituted
an important unanticipated consequence of the lockout.

There is then no doubt that the Weavers had in mind quite "functional"
goals, assuming as they did that a causal relationship existed between
complete organization on the one hand and high wages and good working
conditions on the other. Like the Cardroom Workers, the example of the
Spinners was simply too close to be ignored or overlooked, and a great
deal more was at stake than merely "keeping up with the Joneses." It was
asserted that an adult male weaver's earnings could not provide enough
to support a wife and children. Moreover, the argument was made that
low wages tended to turn the trade into a "dumping ground" for men
unable or unwilling to seek their fortunes elsewhere.[12] There are probably
several reasons why the union maintained a public silence on these points
during the closed-shop campaign, not the least of which was a reluctance
to arouse fears and a consequent resistance on the part of the employers.

Did the rank and file of the operative weavers share their leaders' strong
views regarding the closed shop? The available evidence suggests that they
did. Particularly in workplaces where the overwhelming majority of weavers belonged to the union, friction expressed in personal terms between
them and the nonunionists appears to have been a long-standing phenomenon. In these circumstances intense collective pressure of a face-to-face
nature could be exerted, which is one reason why, before 1911, strikes
over nonunionists had always been averted "in the eleventh hour,"[13] the
settlement consisting of recalcitrants either joining the union or seeking
work elsewhere. In either case 100 percent mill organization would be
achieved. Whatever other qualms the leadership may have had about initiating an industry-wide drive against nonunionists, fear of rank-and-file opposition or apathy was not one of them. On this point, if on nothing else,
they were certainly correct.

CONFRONTATION AND DEFEAT

A general predisposition in favor of the closed shop is one thing; planning and orchestrating a campaign to achieve it is something else again. Specific publicity on the nonunionist question can be traced to an article in the *Factory Times* that appeared in January 1911. The article reported a movement already afoot in several districts to drum up support for the idea of taking strike action against nonunionists, "some of whom have been guilty of the basest ingratitude toward the societies [i.e., local branches of the Weavers Amalgamation], and of cheeky and insulting conduct toward trade union members."[14] It observed that the attitude of many manufacturers was anything but friendly to this project. However, the idea that industrial action against nonunionists was and must be a concurrent act of hostility against the employers "is far-fetched and cannot be allowed to weight with the trade unionists."[15] Accordingly, the fight would continue. Realistically viewed, the notion that employers would resist was anything but "far-fetched." Yet the *Factory Times* and the weavers' leadership held fast to this public stance to the bitter end. To have done otherwise would have meant raising the ideological temperature of the dispute by many degrees, since the only logical alternative was to argue that the employers must now pay, in the form of interrupted production, the historic costs of having aided and abetted the nonunionist element down through the years.

At the local level, agitation took the form of a concerted membership drive, conditions for which were propitious, owing to prosperous trading conditions. Beginning in March 1911, prospective weavers' union members were canvassed, mass rallies were held, and speakers were brought in.[16] By December 1911 the drive had reached a crescendo, The secretary of the Colne Weavers, Tom Shaw, speaking before a gathering of weavers at Glossop, declared that for him trade unionism was a religion.[17] The word "revival" was used to describe the mood in Heywood.[18] In Great Harwood, near Blackburn, a town of 13,814 of whom 6,132[19] were textile workers, the number of nonunionists was said to be down to 3.[20] Haslingden reported that, given a few more weeks, union membership would reach 100 percent.[21] The committee of the Ashton-under-Lyne Weavers was contemplating setting a date after which a large entrance fee would be levied, in order to bring in the remaining laggards.[22] Statistically, the results were most impressive, as membership rose from 137, 196 in 1911 to 179,391 in 1912.

Nor could there have been many backsliders, for in the following year membership rose to 197,957.[23] The Lancashire weavers can thus be said to have been swimming vigorously in the mainstream of the British trade union upsurge of 1911-14, which in turn was part of the worldwide period of growth and combativeness in industrial societies.

Neither articles in the *Factory Times* nor mass enthusiasm and grass-roots activity constituted policy making. The task of framing strategies and tactics lay directly with the Central Committee and Executive Council of the Weavers Amalgamation, that is, with the key officers and full-time paid officials of the union. The nonunionist question was first formally discussed in April 1911 when it was decided to table a motion that the amalgamation provide financial assistance to union members who, in mills 95 percent or more organized, struck and refused to work alongside nonunionists. No records remain of the arguments for and against the motion.[24] But when the motion was reintroduced the following month, the 95 percent stipulation had been lowered to 85 percent: That is, the flashpoint had been reduced, so that now union members could walk out against as many as 15 percent of their mates and know that they would receive strike pay from the amalgamation.[25] Nothing in the evidence suggests that the decision of the weavers' officials to set the treshhold at 85 percent was either the result of "spontaneous" enthusiasm or a compromise between moderates and extremists. For the former to be true, one would have thought that the union would have steered for an immediate confrontation with the nonunionists. For the latter to be true, one would expect far more haggling over the precise figure, with it finally being set anywhere from 95 to 99 percent. In short, the leadership's mood in May 1911 was one of consensus and deliberateness.

It is not difficult to piece together the various strands of the officials' thinking. Tactically, the idea was to make haste slowly, so as to build up a full head of steam under the agitation and accordingly be able to confront the employers with the union's numerical and financial strength at its peak. Having decided in May to make the nonunionist question an issue, the amalgamation held off until November when it formally presented to the employers its demand for the closed shop.[26] This leisurely pace was quite unremarkable, since the nonunionist question did not require an immediate and a forceful response, as, for example, a sudden change in trading conditions would have. Far more problematical than the timing of a possible confrontation with the employers were the complex questions of the form which the confrontation should ideally (from the union's standpoint) take and the dovetailing of the nonunionist question with the question of a wage claim. Important as the nonunionist question was, the ongoing functions of trade unionism had also to be discharged, and of these none was more important than "cashing in" while the getting was good. This the weavers had failed to do on the last opportunity in 1907, having put in a wage claim only after signs of a recession had already appeared, and the union declared that they would not be caught out this time round.[27] It is plausible in retrospect that a 5 percent wage increase sought and gained *before* decisively confronting the employers with the demand for the closed shop would have effectively killed the chances of the latter being immediately obtained. The reason is that the Employers Federation would then be able to say, "this is all we can do for you now, gentlemen; and, furthermore, since you have gotten a five percent advance in wages so easily, why exactly are you bothering us with the demand for a closed shop anyway?"[28] Viewed from this perspective, the weavers' leaders acted shrewdly in bringing the nonunionist question to a head first, so that even if the closed-shop struggle failed, the union could have the issue of a wage increase to fall back on.

Did the weavers' officials seriously entertain the hope that a formal top-level agreement on the question of the closed shop could be reached without resorting to industrial action? The sources do not provide an answer, but what can be said is that if the officials thought so, any lingering illusions were dispelled once and for all in late November 1911. The Employers Federation, meeting with the union in Manchester, stated unequivocally that the furthest it was prepared to go was to consider each nonunionist case separately and that it would be a "mistake" for the union to pursue the issue in any other manner.[29] The *Manchester Guardian,* whose editorials in the period 1910-14 were usually neither otiose nor unsympathetic toward labor, commiserated with the employers because they were facing "an attack of a peculiar kind which even many of those who are firm believers in trade unionism must at present find great difficulty in justifying or even excusing."[30] The response is not surprising; it would be quite anachronistic to attribute to the employers and the *Guardian* a crystal ball that could inform them how the closed shop and traditional managerial prerogatives were really compatible. Once again, the analysis returns to the point that the weavers were demanding a new principle.

In one sense, the weavers "got the message" that the employers were indeed serious in their opposition to the closed-shop campaign. This is the meaning of their decision not to call an industry-wide strike, but rather to proceed according to the letter if not the spirit of the employers' position of discussing each nonunionist dispute one by one. Again the record does not reveal whether the tactic of simultaneously striking all mills with greater than 85 percent organization was seriously considered. What is clear is that the final tactical decision was a great deal more cautious. It consisted of forcing the issue concurrently at several mills, in the hope that the nonunionists would be eliminated on the spot. The weavers evidently felt that if all went well, they could then turn to the employers and argue that as the closed shop was coming into existence spontaneously, why not make it official?

In this case caution did not pay off. Proceeding one mill at a time carried with it the possibility that just one incorrigible nonunionist would bring on a lockout, a contingency quite beyond the amalgamation leadership's ability to predict or control in any specific case. And in the event this was precisely what happened. A Mr. and Mrs. Riley simply would not join the Accrington Weavers. The employer was equally adamant in refusing to give them the sack, thus precipitating the lockout.[31] The contemporary press made much of the fact that Mr. Riley had been a member of the committee of the Accrington weavers, only to become "disgusted with the spirit shown by trade union officials and the squabbling about getting nice jobs. . . ."[32] However, in the context of our analysis the business of Riley's having been a renegade union man is totally besides the point. Any reasons one might have put forward for not joining the union must have had the same consequences as long as the person stood his ground and the boss refused to fire him.

Thus the leadership's policy was reduced to shambles almost as soon as it had been set in motion, by virtue of the threatened lockout actually being imposed; all the evasive action of the previous months had been in vain. Playing their final card, the weavers requested that the employers immediately consider granting a 5 percent wage increase, the lockout notwithstanding.[33] The motivation was clearly that the officials could then present the membership a solid case for disengaging from the confrontation. The wage claim was intended to conciliate the employers, though the *Factory Times* adopted the casuistic line that the two issues were unrelated. Too late. The employers archly pointed out that it was impossible to deal with something as important as a wage increase in such a disturbed context,[34] which can be interpreted as a polite way of telling the union that nothing less than unconditional capitulation would be entertained. Historians who seek evidence from the early twentieth century for the complete integration of union bureaucrats and management will find no support for their hypothesis in the behavior of the Lancashire cotton cloth manufacturers.

By the first week of January 1912 there is no question but that the weavers' officials were fully prepared to liquidate the closed-shop campaign. The *Factory Times* argued that "in light of developments it may just be open to question whether it is worth while to resort to a strike to bring non-unionists to a sense of their duties and obligations. Other means to that end readily suggest themselves, maybe less Homeric, but sufficiently effective. . . ."[35] This should not be interpreted as mere cowardice or opportunism, because by this time the Weavers were under extreme pressure from many sides to capitulate. Not only were press and pulpit denouncing the weavers in full chorus,[36] but even Philip Snowden, Labour M.P. for Blackburn and a national spokesman for the ILP, explicitly abandoned the struggle, by refusing to endorse the demand for the closed shop in his weekly column and counterposing instead the diversionary notion of a thirty-shilling minimum wage.[37] Though its influence on the weavers' leaders was probably minimal, the northeast Lancashire branches of the British Socialist Party also opposed the strategy and tactics that led to the lockout.[38] Writing in *Justice,* Dan Irving, the BSP's Burnley organizer, saw the motives of the amalgamation leaders as "somewhat of a puzzle. . . . The operatives seem to me to have been lured into the worst possible position for a successful fight."[39] He went on to make the defensible case that "the cotton workers were already sufficiently well organized to obtain such advantages as it may be possible to obtain by combined Trade Union action," and should therefore be demanding the eight-hour day and a 10-20 percent rise in wages.[40] From yet another angle, the Cardroom Workers Amalgamation complained that some of their members working in vertically integrated mills were victims of a series of decisions to which they were not but should have been a party.[41]

However, the Weavers' officials could not immediately back down. In the first place, the employers would not allow them the luxury of saving face gracefully. In the second place, the struggle was unquestionably popular and enthusiastically supported by large numbers of rank-and-file

weavers and other workers as well. Brass bands were reported in Burnley;
weavers out on the streets in Nelson exuded a "holiday atmosphere."[42]
The Blackburn Trades and Labour Council, whose direct interest in the
dispute was that the Weavers were a constituent member, requested an
emergency session of the Trades Union Congress, something that the
amalgamation itself never thought of doing.[43] A deputation from the
General Federation of Trade Unions (GFTU) evidently took the initiative
in meeting with the Weavers central committee early in January, and indicated its support and sympathy for the weavers' cause (which if un-
solicited must have been welcomed by the leaders, as no end to the lockout was yet in sight).[44] A fortnight later, the council of the GFTU voted
unanimously to double the levy from affiliated unions not affected by
the lockout[45]—a gesture of solidarity that as things turned out had no
immediate consequences. The result was that despite the pressures (and
almost surely the desire of the leaders) to get out by the quickest route
—that is, unconditional capitulation—the lockout went on. The paralysis
can be seen most clearly in the amalgamation's decision made at the end
of the first week of January 1912 to turn over the task of subsequent
negotiations to the Northern Counties Textile Trades Federation.[46] This
was a body made up of all the cloth-manufacturing unions including the
Weavers, whose job in "normal" times was to bargain collectively on
matters of common concern to all sections—for instance, short-time work
and general pay claims. On strict constitutional grounds the amalgamation
officials had no right to do this, as was angrily pointed out afterward;
psychologically, the decision to pass the buck speaks volumes as to their
despair and desire to disengage from the struggle.

Given the probability of a protracted deadlock and the possibility of
escalation in the form of financial support from the larger trade union
movement, it is not surprising that Askwith intervened—not, it should
be noted, at the request of one side or the other but rather at his own
request to the employers.[47] Askwith's task was straightforward: how to
persuade the employers into sweetening the pill of defeat they were prof-
fering to the union, though in Askwith's own retrospective account this
point is obscured by a considerable overgrowth of verbiage.[48] A week of
negotiations produced a draft settlement that provided for a six-month
"cooling-off period," which meant that a minimum of one full year must
elapse before the Weavers could again take "constitutional" action on the
nonunionist question. In addition, since "each side claims a principle,"[49]

Askwith promised to bring in an opinion evaluating the respective cases for and against the closed shop.

However thin and tasteless one might think the coating on the pill, the representatives of the Northern Counties Textile Trade Federation (NCTTF) were quite prepared to accept it. No record has come down of their discussion and vote that took place in Salford on January 19, 1912,[50] but there is reason to suppose that a deeply felt consensus crystallized around the proposition that the leadership had no choice but to accept the terms as hammered out by Askwith. That conclusion was reasonable enough in view of the leadership's failure to cope realistically with the contingency of an industry-wide lockout and which was repeated over and over again as officials attempted to mollify rank-and-file union members who wanted to continue the struggle.[51] In the narrow, statistical terms by which strikes and lockouts are usually measured, it is correct to say that the lockout ended on the following Monday, January 22, 1912, when the employers reopened their mills on the explicit understanding that the Weavers Amalgamation would countenance no more stoppages against nonunionists. However, on mill floors and in union halls the nonunionist question was still very much alive.

THE CONSEQUENCES OF DEFEAT

The operatives of this district once more have been greatly disappointed that the prospect of peace in the cotton trade has been deferred, and everybody seems sick and tired of the whole thing.[52]

After a long and acrimonious meeting a resolution was unanimously adopted protesting against the settlement and condemning the Textile Federation for accepting such terms.[53]

That F. Constantine and T. Ratcliffe be instructed to get off work for the remainder of this week, and use their influence to create peace in the town.[54]

Branch reaction to the Textile Trade Federation's decision to abandon the nonunionist campaign can be listed in ascending order of opposition. Drawing an east-west line across Lancashire that passes just above Bolton, Bury, and Rochdale, one finds that in none of the branches of the Weav-

ers Amalgamation in towns located below (south of) the line was any
dissatisfaction expressed with the terms of the settlement. To the north,
no protesting voices were heard in the Preston district.[55] The reasons are
not altogether clear, but it is worth noting that these towns shared certain
common features. First, they were all "pioneer" cotton towns in which
the factory system dated back to the earliest years of the nineteenth century. Perhaps workers and union officials alike could no longer muster
enthusiasm over anything as mundane as a few nonunionist holdouts.
Second, spinning, not weaving, was dominant in these towns, with the
result that weaving workers and officials might have become accustomed
over time to proceeding cautiously and, whenever possible, in harness
with the spinning unions. Third, either despite or because of the relative
political conservatism of these towns, *organized* anti-Socialist groupings
among or close to the cotton workers did not exist. In Preston, though
apparently not in the south Lancashire towns, a de facto arrangement
had been worked out whereby Catholics were allotted a certain number
of committee members,[56] a method similar to the ethnic balancing of
the ticket in American politics.

A second variety of response was that of articulated opposition to the
settlement and the manner in which it was reached. Though it is difficult
to enumerate precisely, this might well have constituted the majority
viewpoint among operative weavers. In Blackburn, a mass meeting of
weavers held during the first week of January passed with only two dissenting votes a resolution "that this meeting of locked out operative
weavers emphatically rejects the proposed terms of settlement. We are
of opinion that our members should be at liberty to cease work rather
than work alongside non-unionists."[57] The mood of the weavers as expressed in the resolution is not easily reconciled with the statement of
a Blackburn official that "if the operatives today would be content to
live on necessities, as they were in 1878, they could carry on the present
fight for two or three months without any difficulty. 'But times have
changed,' he added, 'and now they must have their Saturday football
and their theatres, and picture shows every week. This is not the way
to fight a lockout.' "[58] This perhaps tells one more about the mood of
the leadership than the rank and file. As late as January 17, Blackburn
was still in a "no surrender" mood; one reads in the minute books "that
our delegates to the Northern Counties Textile Trades Federation meeting vote against any extension of the six-month truce."[59] However, once

the NCTTF had agreed to a one-year truce, a membership meeting in the town hall called at the request of fifty weavers passed with only 1 dissenter a vote of confidence in the committee.[60] The Church and Oswaldtwistle weavers passed a similar resolution—deploring the outcome but exonerating the officials.[61] In Rishton, the Weavers' secretary took the lead in denouncing the outcome.[62] Membership meetings in Padiham and Colne were less friendly affairs: In these branches members appear not to have upheld formally the officials in their handling of the lockout but instead moved directly to denunciations.[63] Unfortunately, documentation of what passed at postsettlement membership meetings is lacking for many branches—and in some cases meetings were apparently not called. However this may be, the important point is that the dissatisfaction led nowhere: Weavers registered their disapproval, but no further actions were planned and no personnel changes were made.

At the same time when many weavers tried to get in a "last word" at union meetings, there were several postsettlement (and therefore completely unauthorized) spontaneous attempts to fire a final shot at remaining nonunionists on the mill floor. Threats of strike action and actual short wildcats occurred in Accrington (where Mrs. Riley finally joined and Mr. Riley apparently left the trade), Ashton, Bamber Bridge, Blackburn, Glossop, Great Harwood, Helmshore, Oswaldtwistle, Ramsbottom, and Todmorden. In Todmorden one employer reacted by posting a notice threatening immediate dismissal of any worker who "leaves his or her machinery (except for a proper purpose), or neglects his or her work, or interferes with or acts in an objectionable manner toward other workpeople in any way so as to prevent peaceable working. . . ."[64] In general, however, employers appeared to treat these rumblings for what they in fact were—the final shorts in a battle recognized by the participants to have run its course.

But the short-term aftereffects were not all that nugatory everywhere. One exception was Burnley, the largest single branch of the Weavers Amalgamation, with almost 18,000 members in 1910.[65] Fred Thomas, the secretary of the Burnley weavers, was an old-style Lib-Lab alongside of whom David Shackleton looked like a positive social revolutionary. He was among the first officials to suggest that the tactics used in the nonunionist campaign had been a mistake and that the employers' terms should therefore be accepted.[66] Perhaps because of his own militant antisocialism—the Burnley Weavers had taken the trouble to withdraw from the Socialist-infested Burnley Trades Council[67]—there was no organized right-wing opposition among cotton workers in the town. Also, despite the enormous size of the Burnley branch, there was still a large minority of unorganized weavers in the branch's catchment area. Indeed, during the prelockout membership drive, more than 5,000 new members had been enrolled.[68] Whatever his exact motives, Thomas was quoted by the *Manchester Guardian* as saying that if a poll of the rank and file was taken, the results would show a five-to-one majority in favor of going back to work and abandoning the closed-shop demand.[69] As soon as the terms of the one-year truce were made public, he abruptly resigned as secretary, pleading ill health.[70]

It is impossible to verify Thomas's claim that the lockout played no part in his decision to retire. What is clear is that he had lost the ability to control the outcome of votes taken at membership meetings. Initially, the majority of the committee of the Burnley weavers, whose politics appear to have coincided with Thomas's, had not intended to call a membership meeting in order to vote upon the lockout settlement terms. This decision was strenuously challenged by enough weavers to call a special meeting of members that, on January 28, 1912, passed a resolution "that a vote of censure be passed on the Committee for not obtaining the opinion of members on the terms of settlement prior to their acceptance."[71] The leader behind this was himself a dissenting committeeman, John R. Strutt, whose fellow committeemen reacted to his flagrant breach of solidarity by suspending him from his elected position and moving "that the Committee bring before the quarterly membership meeting a recommendation that he be expelled from the society"[72]—a measure not without precedent under Thomas's regime as secretary.[73] However, the plan backfired. The quarterly membership meeting ended in an uproar over the motion to expel Strutt, but not before it passed a vote of confidence in him 111 to 0.[74] The meeting was resumed on the following night, and once again members defeated an expulsion motion "by a large majority,"[75] and Strutt was reinstated as a committeeman. Shortly thereafter, the Burnley weavers appointed a new secretary who appears to have been considerably more militant than Thomas.[76] Maybe this sharp realignment in Burnley would have taken place lockout or no lockout, but it was in fact the settlement that precipitated and determined the timing of events. One might say that the effect was one of clearing the air, of bringing the Burnley weavers abruptly into the twentieth century.

If the effects of the lockout in Burnley were a kind of settling of accounts within the union, the weavers in the neighboring borough of Nelson directed their activities toward opponents outside the union. Two crowded mass meetings denounced the settlement terms in addition to booing and hissing their own elected officials, who patiently attempted to explain the larger "realities."[77] But in the minds of the rank and file the overriding local reality was the need to continue the struggle—not so much against nonunionism in general as against the Nelson and District Catholic Workers Union. When the mills were reopened, strikes commenced immediately in several sheds aimed at smashing the Catholic organization. Angry confrontations took place in the streets, as bands of weavers—in one incident 1,000 persons were reported—harassed individual members of the Catholic Union and the police, whose numbers were hastily augmented by reinforcements.[78] Though it was denied by union spokesmen, the image of guerrilla warfare is not altogether out of place.[79]

As has already been noted, the Catholic Workers had been organized in 1906 as a reaction to the alleged Socialist turn of the weavers. As regards Nelson, their perception cannot be dismissed as runaway paranoia. The Catholics *were* outnumbered overwhelmingly—not only were there in 1910 just 184 members of the Catholic Workers as against 11,906 members of the Nelson Weavers Association,[80] but there were also 800 members of the local ILP branch[81] and several hundred more members of the British Socialist Party in the town. The ILP in turn might have commanded a majority on the Weavers' committee.[82] Given the relative strengths, it is little wonder that the Catholics felt beleaguered and that the rank-and-file militants of the union felt sure that if they took forceful measures, the opposition organization could be driven out of existence.

The leader of the Catholics, Father Robert Smith, appears to have been well aware of just how weak his side was. A Roman Catholic "labor priest," his public utterances indicate that he was a bona fide trade unionist who, unlike more frequently encountered "yellow union" operators, was as sincere in his desire for workers to enjoy the benefits of genuine trade unionism as he was no doubt sincere in his anti-Socialism.[83] To this end he proposed an offer that the Catholic Workers would make regular cash payments to the Nelson Weavers and cooperate fully on economic matters but at the same time retain organizational autonomy.[84] The Nelson Weavers summarily rejected the offer[85] on the grounds that it violated established trade unionism's cardinal tenet of one and only union per geographical district per occupation. Furthermore, the Catholic Workers were so weak numerically that there was no "pragmatic" reason to make any concession to principles. But unanimity on principles notwithstanding, the Weavers were divided over what action should be taken against the Catholic organization. A meeting of rank-and-file weavers was held in the ILP rooms in early February to make plans to continue to support the wildcat movement that was still boiling.[86] The committee and officials, however, felt that the time had come to restore some semblance of industrial peace. Their exact fears and speculations, though unpublicized, may well have turned on the likelihood that a renewed outbreak of strike action might result in another general lockout, the imposition of martial law in the town, or both. The ease with which the leadership persuaded the rank-and-file militants to call off their strikes[87] is best explained by the fact that the ILP committeemen continued to command the respect of the ranks.[88] Settling accounts with the Catholics would have to wait for another day or, more precisely, until the one-year truce had expired —a thought that though unexpressed must have been in the back of almost everyone's mind.

In one sense, then, the decision of the Nelson militants to return to work marks the end of the nonunionist campaign and of rank-and-file reaction to the settlement. In an equally real sense, it can also be judged as a temporary disengagement, preparatory to another round of conflict. For the Catholic Workers, the breathing spell gave them time to seek whatever allies they could, an obscure business[89] that in organizational terms resulted in the formal dissolution of the Nelson and District Catholic Workers and its immediate reappearance as the Nelson and District Protection Society, affiliated with the Northeast Lancashire Federation of Protection Societies.[90] In the shuffle Father Smith disappeared from public view, which can be interpreted as a shift in emphasis away from trade unionism as such and toward a more unalloyed kind of grass-roots anti-Socialist, antisecularist politics.[91]

It might appear that except for Burnley and Nelson the consequences of the amalgamation's defeat in the lockout were minimal; and, indeed, just as in the case of the Cardroom lockout of 1910, memories faded rapidly. This in itself is not surprising. Trade union members and officials are very Whiggish when it comes to their own history: clear-cut victories tend to be remembered, whereas defeats are usually forgotten or obscured.

In the short run the consequences certainly were small. First, the status of the closed-shop principle remained unchanged for both union and management. Askwith's final report, in which he concluded that "it is not possible at the present period of industrial development to appraise the value of the contending opinions of each party"[92] was, for all its essential evasiveness, an accurate enough descriptive statement. A second nonconsequence was the total absence of any measures taken toward greater centralization of the amalgamation's structure, even though a few officials made suggestions in this direction.[93] Third—and most significant—was the minimal extent to which rank-and-file morale and adherence to the leadership were impaired, considering how soundly the union had been beaten. In the wake of such a sharp defeat, one might have expected an upsurge of apathy, disillusionment, and confusion, expressed in slumping membership figures and breakaways both to the right and left. But in fact, as has been shown in Chapter 6, the weavers' unrest continued unabated throughout the rest of 1912 and 1913, almost as though the lockout and defeat had never occurred. Furthermore, amalgamation membership continued to rise, despite the decision of the Blackburn oppositionists to withdraw from the amalgamation and set up their own rival federation with branches in Preston, Clitheroe, and, as has been seen, in Nelson.[94] The amalgamation leadership's response might have been one of "good riddance" even if it meant having to put up with openly declared dual unionism. Here again one sees the effect that the lockout had in clearing the air by sorting out and readjusting the relative strengths of ideological currents within the weavers' union.

If the short-term consequences of defeat did nothing to inhibit the fighting spirit of the rank-and-file weavers, the long-range effect might well have been a failure of nerve on the leadership's part. The union had been thoroughly defeated and humiliated, having steered its way into direct confrontation only to back down when the crunch came. Although the defeat directly affected only a section of the working class, nevertheless the weavers lockout bears more than a passing resemblance to the Chartist Convention of 1839, Kennington Common, Black Friday, and the General Strike of 1926, when on each occasion labor backed down before, as it were, having climbed all the way up. Henry Pelling has commented on the extreme conservatism of the cotton unions in the interwar period and in part attributed it to a top-heavy costs-to-membership ratio.[95] His explanation is not wholly satisfactory. A high costs-to-members ratio was more the result of the industry's decline and the reluctance of small branches to merge into more efficient, larger units than a penchant for officaldom and spending money per se.[96] It is at least as plausible to suggest that the Weavers' officials, having had their fingers burnt so badly in 1912—the same year, one should note, that the Miners Federation of Great Britain succeeded by strike action in winning "half a loaf" in the shape of a district minimum wage[97]—came out of the lockout with the attitude "never again." With the exception of a strike in 1919[98] to catch up with inflation, 1911-12 saw the last industry-wide offensive strike the Weavers Amalgamation has engaged in to this day.

This raises a final question. In view of the nonunionist campaign's disastrous outcome, were not the northeast Lancashire followers of H. M. Hyndman correct in their denunciations of the entire effort and in their prescription that the amalgamation officials be removed "by order of the boot"?[99] The Hyndmanites have been severely criticized by labor historians for their rigid and unimaginative insistence that only so much good could come out of trade union organization and militancy even under optimal conditions.[100] In the case of the weavers lockout there is at least a half-measure of validity in their attack. The officials did not appear to realize that their tactics must have resulted in an industry-wide lockout. The base of public support was extremely narrow. When they finally realized the mess they had created, they indeed had no plan save that of complete surrender. But there is another side as well. Despite the half-baked strategy and the way it was implemented, one cannot accuse the amalgamation officials of willful opportunism, or of embarking upon the nonunionist campaign as a cynical diversion from more important and more difficult tasks. Nor, incidentally, can the historian assert with certainty that defeat was inevitable from the outset. Officials and members alike genuinely believed that the closed shop would be a meaningful step forward, that it would enhance the union's bargaining power, and thus constitute not so much an end in itself as a means toward larger ends. And, as the weavers of Nelson were to prove in 1913, there were ways to bring the nonunionist element to heel. For the officials, however, the loss of aggressiveness, coupled with the failure to develop new and more successful strategies, was to impede them in the struggles that lay ahead in the years following 1914.

Politics and the Labor Unrest ⏌9

So far we have examined those areas of the labor unrest in which workers and their unions fought against the employers. The industrial struggles that workers engage in do not always have direct political overtones. But in Lancashire between 1910 and 1914 political and ideological movements within the ranks of the cotton workers and the union officials and attempts by small groups of activists to influence and direct events was, upon close inspection, an integral part of the labor unrest itself. These movements are the subject of this chapter.

We must, however, begin with a warning. Despite the claims and pretensions of political scientists and sociologists, conceptual frameworks and methodologies for analyzing popular political movements cannot be said to be worked out fully and satisfactorily. To cite one very well known example in comparative labor history, answers given to the question of why a labor party emerged in Britain in the early twentieth century but failed to take root in the United States are at present little more than intelligent guesses after the fact.[1] Indeed, one can go so far as to say that no scholarly consensus exists as to what constitutes the basic components and "events" of popular political history. To make the point clear, a contrast with popular economics may be offered. In this essay we have treated strikes by the cotton workers as a basic component of popular economics. Precisely because strikes are concrete, specific, and recurring phenomena, we have been able to classify and subclassify them and offer plausible explanations of the participants' motivations and behavior. For popular politics, by contrast, the "events" that historians look at are of a quite different order, consisting usually of vote casting, party joining, the process of institution building, and the formation of leadership elites. It is little wonder that so much of the political history of popular parties has been made up of narratives that trace the activities of small (and often self-selected) leadership groups, punctuated occasionally by an analysis of election results.

In this chapter an attempt is made to break away from the practice of writing workers' political history "from the top down," which has been so trenchantly criticized by E. P. Thompson in his essay "Homage of Tom McGuire."[2] However, the politics and ideologies of official leaders will not be totally ignored. In fact, our guiding hypothesis is precisely that the cotton union leaders' conversion to the idea of a labor party was a most important "event" in the political history of the cotton workers in the early twentieth century. Accordingly, our starting point is an examination of the leaders' transition from what we call "Industrial Laborism" to that of "Political Laborism" as represented by the Labour Party and its attempt to carry the rank and file along with it. But precisely because the new Political Laborism of the leadership was not universally accepted by the workers—and this is where politics from below enters the picture—we proceed to examine instances of workers engaging in politics of their own making. These movements owed nothing to leads given by the union officials and were often in direct political and ideological opposition to them. The result was that the prewar cotton workers were engaged in not one but several political movements concurrently.

LABORISM: INDUSTRIAL AND POLITICAL

At the 1903 annual conference of the Labour Representation Committee, Thomas Ashton of the Spinners proclaimed that

> He had been connected with the Labour movement for 40 years and as an official for over 35 years; and for the first time in his life he was standing on a platform advocating the representation of Labour in Parliament. If the Trade Unionists and workers generally would only ally themselves to the movement and go upon Trade Unionist lines and keep clear of all "isms" except Labourism and Trade Unionism, he believed there was a great prospect of getting Labour members into Parliament.[3]

Ashton's remarks were aimed at the Socialists; he was telling them bluntly not to make the unwarranted assumption that cotton was "permeable," and there is little question but that the majority of the cotton trade union leaders agreed with him. Since Ashton criticized socialism in the name and cause of Laborism, it is important to grasp the positive content he assigned to the idea—that is, the practical and symbolic meanings that Laborism as an ideology held for its spokesmen.

In order to understand the Laborism of the cotton unions in the early twentieth century, it is essential to stress that, despite the profoundly conservative streak that the leadership might display on any given issue, they were solidly committed to the goals of strengthening the unions' power and independence in industrial matters. We have already observed this spirit of independence. First and foremost was the unions' liberal use of the strike weapon; and it is no exaggeration to say that upholding the right to strike and belief in the efficacy of strikes constitute the cornerstone of Industrial Laborism. From this belief flowed a unanimous opposition by the cotton unions to compulsory arbitration that was voiced almost annually in resolutions at conferences of the United Textile Factory Workers Association[4] and on the floor of TUC annual conferences.[5] For what was (and is) compulsory arbitration if not a device for waging industrial conflict without recourse to strikes and lockouts? By the same token, it is significant that the Weavers sought to obtain the closed shop not by legislation but, once again, by going on strike.

The limits of the unions' independence and noncollaboration can be measured with almost clinical precision. One measurement has already been taken: the decision of the spinning unions in 1910 to freeze the wage rates of their members rather than compromise the right to strike for higher wages or against threatened cuts in the future.[6] Another example is that of the unions' relations with the British Cotton Growing Association (BCGA), which had been founded in 1902 for the purpose of increasing raw-cotton supplies in general and developing cotton farming within the British Empire in particular.[7] In 1910 the association approached the unions, asking them to urge their members to contribute threepence per worker so that a pilot project to grow cotton in Africa could be started. The leaders happily agreed, and throughout 1910 the *Factory Times* exhorted readers to kick in their thruppences.[8] Only in radical Nelson does one find the choleric entries in the Weavers Committee Minute Books "that we advise our officials not to collect for the Cotton Growing Association,"[9] and later "that a letter from the Cotton Growing Association asking the Committee to arrange a meeting with our members not be entertained."[10] That the top union officials should have agreed to the BCGA's request, in addition to being represented among the association's numerous vice presidents, is quite understandable in terms of Industrial Laborism, since it in no way compromised the unions' freedom of action in implementing trade union tasks.

Beyond this exceedingly cautious and narrowly bounded "collaboration" the unions refused to go. A dramatic—and at the time underreported —case of a top cotton official overstepping the line occurred in 1912. William Mullin, the general secretary of the Cardroom Workers Association, whom we have already met on the Oldham bench and elsewhere, had in October 1911 acceded to Askwith's request to serve on the Industrial Council.[11] This body was a hastily conceived scheme to do something about the industrial unrest.[12] The circumstances surrounding Mullin's acceptance were not reported or commented on, either in the *Factory Times* or in the CWA's official reports, though one cannot help speculating that his decision might have in part been an act of retribution for his militant role in the lockout of 1910. But however that may be, in June 1912 the Executive Council of the CWA resolved:

1. We demand the immediate resignation of the Secretary from the Industrial Council.

2. We condemn the action of the Secretary in absenting himself from a meeting of the Executive Council . . . which he felt to be so necessary as to require the summoning of the Executive Council by telegram, and for not informing his colleagues on the Ring List Committee that he would be absent.

3. That a special Executive Council meeting be held June 27th to look into the business.[13]

A week later it was resolved "that after hearing the Secretary's explanation . . . and his future intentions in regard to the Industrial Council, he be requested to bear the charges of the abortive meeting of June 17th, 1912."[14] These powerful pressures had the intended effect, and Mullin duly resigned as demanded. Finally, as if to pound in one final nail the CWA Executive Council resolved "that we decline to give evidence before the Industrial Council."[15] Mullin's flirtation with the politics of collaboration had been decisively checked, and in doing so the union stubbornly upheld the forms and substance of Industrial Laborism.

At one level, then, Industrial Laborism implied the primacy of economic as opposed to political tactics. But at the same time its internal logic demanded that the labor movement function as an ongoing interest group and relate to the political process, which for cotton workers and their leaders had by 1910-14 a century-long history. However, interest group

politics did not necessarily imply permanent attachment to organized
Liberalism; and in any event a labor movement that pursues interest group
politics must have a perspective for relating to the government of the day
whatever its political coloration might be. This is not to suggest that the
overwhelming majority of cotton officials were at the turn of the century
anything but solidly Lib-Lab in their private political convictions. The
striking fact about the pragmatic Toryism of James Mawdesley is that
he seems to have been the only Tory spinners' union official. Rather, the
cotton men's discreetly kept distance from the Liberal Party grew out of
deeply divided electoral loyalties of the rank-and-file workers.[16] Precisely because the cotton unions, particularly in southeast Lancashire, could
not not deliver massive blocs of Liberal votes on election day (as, for example, mining constituencies were able to do), ties between the cotton
unions and the Liberal Party seem to have remained tenuous. The Liberals
thus had even less pressure on them to select union officials to stand for
Parliament than they did in other heavily urban, industrial constituencies.
And in fact no cotton union official ever stood as a Lib-Lab candidate,
despite an attempt in 1895 to put up David Holmes of the Burnley Weavers.[17]

The shallowness of Lib-Labism in most of the cotton towns is important in the context of the unions' decision to join the Labour Representation Committee (LRC). The received interpretation of labor historians has
been to stress their opposition to independent working-class politics and
to socialism throughout the 1890s, and to attribute their conversion to
fears over the implications of the Taff Vale decision.[18] One would have
thought, however, that this argument applied equally well to the Miners
Federation of Great Britain, which did not join the Labour Party until
1908. But the miners were the one section of organized labor for whom
Lib-Labism came closest to working in electoral terms. For the cotton unions, on the other hand, the decision to join the LRC, once it had been
successfully launched and once it became apparent that the Socialists
would not dominate the new body, was made with a minimum of ideological soul searching. Their decision was amply rewarded. Running under
the LRC banner, cotton union officials finally succeeded in getting themselves elected—beginning with David Shackleton in the 1903 Clitheroe by-
election and followed by A. H. Gill, secretary of the Bolton Spinners, in
1906.[19] Even in defeat the cotton candidates acquitted themselved favorably. W. H. Carr of the Cardroom Workers, standing in Preston in Decem-

ber 1910, cut the Tory percentage to 53.1 as against 56.9 percent in January in an election that showed other cotton constituencies drifting back toward the Tories.[20] In the following year, W. C. Robinson of the Beamers, Twisters, and Drawers Union contested a by-election in Oldham, and even though he polled at the bottom in a three-cornered race, the Tory candidate's 40.4 percent of the total vote, while enough to win, was lower than their 1906 showing of 40.75 percent.[21]

It might appear that the step from Industrial Laborism to Political Laborism was so small that the notion of a transition from one to the other does not apply: after all, for there to be a transition there must be a meaningful distance to be traversed. However, even if the ideological rethinking involved was minimal, one can suggest that the cotton union officials had to learn the art of working through and taking responsibility for the new Labour Party, which, unlike the great Liberal Party, was the direct creation of the labor movement itself. The evidence suggests that the older political habits died hard. The cotton unions were somewhat testily criticized by Labour M.P.'s continuing the old tradition of lobbying M.P.'s of all parties and of attempting to seek prior agreement with the employers over new legislation.[22] Also, the Oldham by-election of 1911 was marked by a singular absence of solidarity on the part of the Oldham Spinners and Cardroom unions, which did nothing on Robinson's behalf and would not even sign his nomination papers.[23] During an angry debate at the 1912 Labour Party conference, Mullin of the CWA defended the attempt to sabotage Robinson's campaign on the grounds that "the employers were doing all they possibly could to kill the insurance bill and get the Conservative candidate in. That is why he wanted the Liberal candidate to get elected."[24] No disciplinary action was taken by the conference.

At first sight this looks like backsliding with a vengeance, and it is unlikely that Robinson's membership in the ILP raised his stock in the eyes of the Oldham officials. But if Mullin was genuinely concerned about the fate of the insurance bill and with keeping the Tory out, he was equally concerned with finding an attainable parliamentary seat for his union in order achieve parity with the Spinners and Weavers, each of whom already had an M.P. of their own. Accordingly, the choice of Robinson for Oldham was unappealing to the CWA, insurance act or no. The extreme sensitivity of the CWA on the subject of parliamentary representation was made clear in 1913 when the UFTWA drew up a list of prospective parliamentary candidates, not one of whom was a Cardroom Workers official. This the CWA considered to be a palpable insult and in reaction walked out of the UTFWA annual conference.[25] Tripartite negotiations between the CWA, the UTFWA, and Arthur Henderson representing the Labour Party failed to reach agreement,[26] and the CWA rejoined the UTFWA only in 1916. Throughout this fractiousness, the important point is that the conflict turned upon mechanisms, procedures, and sensibilities and not the question of labor representation in Parliament through the Labour Party. Difficulties notwithstanding, the cotton men had cast in their lot with the Labour Party.

To what extent did the rank-and-file cotton workers make the same transition as their leaders had? Ordinarily, the only data available are election returns, and the operation of relating voting patterns to occupation is necessarily impressionistic. Sometimes even impressionistic evidence can be quite persuasive: It is, for example, inconceivable that Philip Snowden could have run up his majorities in 1906 and 1910 without considerable support from weavers in Blackburn.[27] In southeast Lancashire it seems equally clear that cotton workers' support for Labour candidates was less substantial than that of the engineers in the textile machinery trade, who in the interwar years were forced to work compulsory overtime on election day in an obvious attempt to limit the Labour vote.[28] Fortunately, we have for the cotton workers a class of evidence that allows one to probe far more accurately than is possible with election returns the degree of rank-and-file support for the Labour Party. In 1913, following the passage of a Trade Union Act, which allowed union members to contract out of paying a political levy, the three largest cotton unions polled their members on whether they approved of union funds being used for political purposes. The results are given in Table 30.

The question arises: Does an affirmative vote really mean a commitment to vote Labour? The answer is almost certainly yes. It is far more plausible to assume a penumbra of union members who abstained or even voted against their dues being used but who on election day might vote Labour after all, than it is to assume that committed Liberals or Tories should vote yes in the poll. Accordingly, the workers who voted yes must be considered hard-core Labourites.

Once more, strong sectional and geographic differences stand out. In the case of the spinners, it is interesting that solid majorities for a political levy were reported in every area except Oldham—thus substantiating the

Table 30

Vote on Use of Trade Union Funds for Political Purposes

				Spinners	
Branch	For	Against	Rejected Ballots	Total	For (%)
Accrington	61	50	0	111	54.9
Ashton Spinners	192	101	6	299	65.5
Ashton Twiners	24	17	0	41	58.5
Bamber Bridge	26	29	1	56	47.3
Bollington	21	7	0	28	75.0
Bury	62	35	0	97	63.3
Darwen	80	73	5	158	52.2
Droylsden	70	67	5	142	51.1
Haslingden	36	11	2	49	76.6
Huddersfield	50	14	1	65	78.1
Hyde	241	113	4	358	68.2
Lancaster	28	14	4	46	66.7
Macclesfield	31	8	1	40	79.5
Mossley	100	111	0	211	47.4
Rawtenstall	38	47	3	88	44.7
Rochdale	135	62	2	229	58.0
Stalybridge	44	61	2	107	41.8
Stockport	91	96	1	188	48.7
Warrington	10	0	0	10	100.0
Wigan	46	2	0	48	95.9

	Weavers			
	For	Against	For (%)	Total Membership Voting (%)
	98,158	75,893	56.3	89

Cardroom Workers		
For (%)	Against (%)	Spoiled or Rejected (%)
60.60	37.99	1.41

Table 30 continued

	For	Against	Rejected Ballots	Total	For (%)
Blackburn Province					
Blackburn	102	87	0	189	54.0
Burnley	65	14	0	79	82.3
Padiham	20	4	0	24	83.3
Church	32	33	1	66	49.7
Preston Province					
Preston	174	50	0	224	77.7
Gregson Lane	27	8	0	35	77.1
Kirkham	23	8	0	31	74.3
Bolton Province					
Bolton	1,002	649	14	1,665	60.5
Manchester	127	101	1	229	55.7
Leigh	120	112	0	232	51.3
Farnworth	156	147	2	305	51.4
Chorley	98	118	6	222	45.3
Tyldesley	55	34	0	89	61.8
Atherton	94	125	1	220	43.8
Pendlebury	47	38	0	85	55.3
Reddish	151	66	0	217	69.6
Hindley	37	2	0	39	95.0
Oldham Province					
Oldham No. 1	28	50	0	78	35.9
Chadderton	70	79	0	149	46.9
Hollinwood	52	94	0	146	35.6
Shaw	48	116	0	164	29.2
Oldham No. 2	62	79	0	141	43.9
Lees	78	83	0	161	48.4
Royton	50	22	0	72	69.5
Waterhead	50	25	0	75	66.7
Middleton	64	16	1	81	80.0
Coldhurst	51	68	0	119	42.8
Middleton Jcn.	41	22	0	63	65.1
Higginshaw	6	43	0	49	12.2
Oldham Twiners	22	14	0	36	61.2
Heywood	69	14	1	84	83.1
Failsworth	55	43	0	98	56.2
Yorkshire Province					
Ripponden	105	16	4	125	86.8

Table 30 continued

	For	Against	Rejected Ballots	Total	For (%)
Brighouse	50	12	3	65	80.7
Sowerby Bridge	62	8	0	70	88.5
Halifax	40	12	0	52	76.9
Stainland	33	4	0	37	89.3
Elland	22	4	0	26	84.7
Bradford	9	4	0	13	69.1
Dewsbury	19	1	0	20	95.0
Skipton	24	1	0	25	96.0
Totals	4,826	3,374	71	8,271	58.85

Sources: CFT, December 5, 1913, January 9, 1914. Percentages computed to slide rule accuracy.

view that large pockets of Spinner Toryism existed there. One would like to have the equivalent raw figures for the Cardroom Workers, but these data were suppressed by the union, evidently because the turnout was embarrassingly low. But it is unlikely to be mere coincidence that the percentage of cardroom workers in favor, 60.6, was almost identical to the spinners' 58.8 percent. But if apathy caused many cardroom workers to abstain, the Weavers' turnout was very high indeed, and revealed an absolute majority of union members—including even those who did not take the trouble to vote—in favor of using union funds for labor representation, again confirming the relative leftism of the weavers vis-à-vis the other cotton unions. Moreover, a majority of the Weavers' membership were women, though of course votes were not tallied along male-female lines. Yet despite the unevenness in the results, one can conclude that among cotton workers the idea of Labour representation had by 1913 reached the "tip point" necessary to ensure the continued viability of independent labor politics in the cotton towns. As in industrial matters, many cotton workers showed their willingness to follow the leadership on political questions as well.

Although a majority of cotton workers appear to have positively supported or, more passively, deferred to the leadership's conversion to the Labour Party, there was also a minority of workers who did not. There were powerful reasons for this. Leaving aside the truism that political allegiances formed and reinforced over several generations do not disap-

pear overnight, one must remember that for the cotton union officials—
whose salaries, working conditions, social security, and status were far
higher than the workers whom they represented—Political Laborism provided specific guidelines for maintaining and enhancing the power of the
unions and the Labour Party *as institutions.* For the vast majority of the
workers, however, Political Laborism did not directly address itself to
the day-to-day problems associated with being workers in a class-divided
society. Of course this did not mean that the Labour Party promised the
workers nothing. *All* political parties in advanced industrial society have
something to offer working people, however modest, demogogic, or in-
sincere these promises might be. And in fact the Labour Party promised
workers far more than the other three parties in Parliament. Rather, the
point is that the Labour Party and the cotton union officials identified
their own long-term interests as being inextricably linked to Parliament
and to parliamentary methods of advancing the workers' movement. The
workers, on the other hand, were not similarly committed.[29] It is therefore not surprising that a minority of rank-and-file workers participated
in political activities that either supplemented or, on occasion, opposed
the Laborism of the officials.

Theoretically, there is no reason why rank-and-file movements that run
counter to a dominant Laborist ideology should be all of one piece. What
stands out in the cotton workers' response to Laborism is its heterogeneity.
In the remainder of this chapter they are examined. The first response,
that of the Social Democratic Federation-led Burnley Textile Operatives,
represents the politics of a sharply defined left-wing opposition. The
second was an equally sharp right-wing opposition, again among weaving
workers, in the nearby town of Blackburn. The third involves the clash
of indigenous right-wing sentiments with the militant ILP weavers of Nelson. The final case deals with the attempts of the Middleton (between
Oldham and Manchester) branch of the spinners to win over the Spinners
Amalgamation to the ideas of militant industrial unionism. Although far
removed from the usual subject matter of labor politics as developed by
academic historians, with the emphasis upon selection and activities of
candidates, platforms, and analyses of polls, it is suggested that these
movements were all clearly political in the broad but accurate sense that
politics is about power. They also are forceful reminders that for the cotton workers "pure politics" and industrial concerns were tightly bound
together.

THE BURNLEY TEXTILE OPERATIVES: A PIONEER DUAL UNION

The cloth-weaving town of Burnley has acquired a permanent niche in British labor history because of H. M. Hyndman's four parliamentary campaigns and especially because of the 1906 results when, although he came in last in a three-way race, he polled just 350 votes fewer than the winner.[30] Although it is likely that his most consistent support came from the miners in the constituency,[31] Hyndman's good showings must have depended upon votes from other sections of the working people as well. Hopwood's history of the Weavers Amalgamation notes that the Burnley Weavers Rule Book contained a section in the 1892 edition declaring the union's goal to be the "socialization of the means of production, distribution and exchange, to be controlled by a democratic State in the interests of the entire community and the political and financial support of the Society [i.e., union] shall be used toward the creation of an Independent Socialist Party."[32] Yet when one examines the progress of socialism among the weaving workers more closely, what stands out is the fierce opposition put up by the Lib-Lab officials of the Burnley Weavers. The following terse, angry entries appeared in the minutes for January 1896.

> That J. H. Stott, L. Rippon and Thomas Southworth be summoned to appear before this committee to-morrow night.

> That the case of L. Rippon be not further entertained.

> That 3 committeemen wait upon J. H. Stott at once with regard to printed matter issued for election purposes.

> That J. H. Stott be summoned to appear before the committee to answer the charges made against him.

> That the secretary write to Stott stating he owes 15/0 minus 4/6 which we shall retain.[33]

The minutes do not indicate whether any formal explusions actually took place. What is clear is that Lawrence Rippon and an unascertainable number of other weavers left and in December 1896 formed the Burnley and District Textile Operatives, whose stated goals were:

1. To provide money for breakdowns, strikes, lockouts, & c.

2. To provide money for educational purposes, and political action on Socialist lines.

3. To awaken the workers to the importance of combining to fight the capitalist class in a scientific way, by the use of the ballot box at election times, and supporting Socialist Trade Union Candidates.[34]

In addition, Rippon ran for town council in 1906, 1908, 1909, and 1910 in the interest of the Social Democratic Federation (SDF), losing in 1910 because of the returning officer's tie-breaking vote.[35] Without doubt, then, the Textile Operatives were an ongoing, left-wing dual union and, as far as is known, the first of its kind of Britain.

The only hard data available on the union's structure and functioning are membership figures. Beginning with 60 men and 20 women, membership grew gradually to 503 in 1907, fell back somewhat during the depressed years of 1908 and 1909, and reached a peak of 515 in 1910.[36] But however gratifying the growth of the union was, it was no match for the Burnley Weavers Association, as Table 31 shows:

From this enormous differential in size between the two rival organizations it is clear that the Textile Operatives' policies and relations with the Burnley Weavers must have raised difficult problems. Since any hopes of supplanting the orthodox union as the number one weavers' society was out of the question, the Textile Operatives appear to have adopted a policy of coexistence, an interpretation strengthened by the cautious language of their advertising, which went out of the way to avoid the appearance of

Table 31

Membership of the Burnley Weavers

Year	Males	Females	Total
1896	4,726	6,414	10,690
1900	3,814	7,403	11,217
1907	7,585	10,915	18,500
1910	7,148	10,286	17,431

Sources: For 1896, BPP, 1900, Board of Trade (Labour Department) *Report on Trade Unions* (Cd. 422), p. 50; for 1900, BPP, 1906, *Report on Trade Unions* (Cd. 2836), p. 43; for 1907 and 1910, BPP, 1912, *Report on Trade Unions* (Cd. 6109), p. 31.

poaching.[37] The Burnley Weavers for their part reciprocated by extending a greater or lesser degree of toleration to its rival—possibly because they found it convenient to have left-wing "troublemakers" safely isolated in the Textile Operatives. It cannot be determined whether the Textile Operatives called strikes of their own, but it is likely that they cooperated fully in strikes and other workplace actions that the Burnley Weavers initiated. Oddly, the Textile Operatives do not appear to have been affiliated with the Burnley Trades and Labour Council, even though the "orthodox" Burnley Weavers had quit the council, and rejoined only in 1913.[38]

In short, the Textile Operatives' long-term perspective might well have been one of genuine Fabianism. Having left the Burnley Weavers under difficult circumstances, they patiently waited for the opportune time to get back in. One can even speculate that as passions aroused by the original split cooled, a policy of outright permeation was followed in order to rebuild the Left within the Weavers.. But whether or not the Textile Operatives played an active role, the fact is that by 1910 an ongoing militant left-wing presence within the Weavers had definitely been reestablished, as has already been observed in the outburst of opposition following the lockout of 1911-12.[39] Other examples are sprinkled liberally throughout the minutes:

That Ruskin College scholarships be transferred to the Central Labour College and the Burnley delegates to the Northern County Amalgamation be instructed to do the same. (Notice of motion to be presented at membership meeting.)

That we apply for 25 £1-shares in the "Daily Citizen."

Lancashire children are to-day probably as old as any children in the world; certainly they are older than they ought to be, and we shall at every opportunity endeavor to overthrow a system that adds to their care and years. (From the Secretary's Quarterly Report for the period ending 29 October 1913.)[40]

Evidently sensing the political tone, the Textile Operatives formally applied to rejoin the Weavers in 1913,[41] and after negotiations over the transfer of funds and benefits, the members of the Textile Operatives were duly admitted in full standing. A dual union had come to a successful (from its standpoint) end.

What implications does the story of the Burnley Textile Operatives have for our understanding of the politics of the cotton workers and of trends in the larger labor movement? First, the episode serves as a reminder of just how tenaciously anti-Socialist the old Lib-Lab tradition represented by union leaders such as David Holmes and Fred Thomas could be. The crackdown against the Socialists within the Weavers appears to have had no parallel in southeast Lancashire, though to be sure there were fewer Socialist cotton workers in southeast Lancashire to begin with and accordingly they might not have been perceived by the leadership as all that threatening. Nor is there any parallel in the neighboring northeast Lancashire towns of Nelson and Blackburn, where the ILP was strong but major confrontations with the cotton union leadership did not occur. It thus strongly appears that the ILP provided a sounder bridge between the old Lib-Labism and the new politics of the Labour Party than did the Social Democratic Federation. But this possibility does not automatically confirm the received interpretation of SDF sectarianism and a propensity to irritate everyone but win over nobody. It is just as plausible to argue that the antisocialism of the Burnley officials was unusually strong and that they would have also resisted the ILP had it and not the SDF been the dominant Socialist group in town, in much the same way that the Sheffield Trades Council, where Lib-Labism was also unusually powerful, did not affiliate with the Labour Party until 1920, and where the SDF was not a powerful force.[42]

Second, one's suspicions that the SDF was not totally rigid and doctrinaire are borne out by the episode of the Textile Operatives. If one supposes that the party's and Hyndman's pronouncements were Holy Writ,[43] then one should not expect to find members engaged in union building at all. Yet the SDF'ers of Burnley clearly displayed flexibility and resourcefulness in responding to a unique and difficult set of circumstances. As the membership figures show, the Textile Operatives did not degenerate into a mere rump. Rather, they maintained a viable, if obviously modest, existence. And when circumstances changed within the Burnley Weavers, following the retirement of Fred Thomas,[44] the Textile Operatives evidently had no regrets in seeing that their union had outlived its usefulness, which is not always the case with left-wing organizations caught in similar circumstances.

Third, charting the course of the Textile Operatives allows one to take the measure of the diffusion and acceptance of Socialists and Socialist ideas within the labor movement with quite as much precision as can be achieved by analyzing election returns. It seems clear that for Burnley at least a Lib-Lab counteroffensive was mounted in order to erase gains achieved by the Socialists in the early 1890s. In this sense the decision to form the Textile Operatives was an indication of Socialist weakness among the weavers of Burnley, rather than one of strength. Indeed, Hyndman never did carry the town. But the years 1910-14, when the Burnley Weavers were contributing their share to the labor unrest, marked the eclipse of Lib-Labism. It is not surprising that in December 1918 Hyndman's old colleague Dan Irving, running not as a BSP'er but as the official Labour Party candidate, should have been elected the first Social Democratic M. P. for Burnley.[45]

COTTON TORYISM: THE CASE OF THE WEAVERS PROTECTION SOCIETY

The existence of numerous Conservative cotton workers—"Tories in clogs"[46] as a contemporary source called them—is well known to labor historians. If one uses electoral data, cotton Toryism's greatest strength appears to have been Ashton, Stalybridge, Hyde, and the area between Oldham and Rochdale in southeast Lancashire; and Chorley, Bamber Bridge, and Preston in the northwest corner of the cotton region.[47] These were predominantly spinning districts. Two broad explanations have been advanced. The first, argued by E. J. Hobsbawm and more recently by P. F. Clarke, is that workers were reacting against the crude laissez-faire liberalism on nineteenth-century mill owners.[48] A second explanation, put forward by Henry Pelling, stresses more purely social factors such as the strength of the Church of England, the widespread presence of voluntary schools, and large numbers of English Roman Catholics.[49]

The two interpretations are not perhaps diametrically opposed. However, when matters are examined more closely, one finds that in the immediate prewar years the best-organized and most vocal outbursts of Toryism and antisocialism were found not in southeast Lancashire but among weavers in Blackburn, Preston, Clitheroe, and Nelson in northeast Lancashire. These were districts where the ILP was strong, and if before 1906 the Conservative vote was high in Blackburn and Preston, it certainly was not in the constituency of Clitheroe, which included the boroughs of Clitheroe, Nelson, and Colne.[50] The received interpretations, therefore, do not appear to be particularly helpful in explaining either the timing or the regional location of cotton worker Toryism. In their stead we tentatively advance the hypothesis that northeast Lancashire Toryism was essentially a backlash against the progressivism and socialism ascribed by the Tories to the cotton union officials of the Weavers Amalgamation. To be sure, a backlash hypothesis cannot satisfactorily explain either southeast Lancashire Toryism or the historical roots of working-class Toryism. But, to repeat, it has the real if limited usefulness of explaining both the timing and the regional distribution of Tory militancy.

The organizational vehicle of the prewar Toryism was the Blackburn-based Weavers Protection Society. Little is known about its origins. J. R. Clynes stated on the floor of the House of Commons that

> The right honorable Gentleman referred to the Weavers Protection Society of Blackburn, thinking that he had found a union that was representative and that was really opposed to the Labour Party. He showed that 2,000 members of that body voted against political action, while 466 persons voted for political action. He did not tell the House, probably he did not know, that this is really a Tory organization established some twenty years ago for absolutely partisan reasons. It is not representative of the textile workers or the weavers' organization, that class of work being represented by the very much larger body, the Weavers Amalgamation. . . .[51]

Clynes was in a position to know the cotton scene, what with his involvement around 1890 in trying to build a piecers' union in Oldham.[52] Moreover, it was reported in the *Factory Times* that the vice president of the Protection Society was in 1910 a delegate of the Blackburn Conservative Labour Party.[53] On the other hand, Clynes had a definite axe to grind: The context of his speech was a rebuttal of F. E. Smith's assertion that trade union members really did not want to see their funds used to support the Labour Party. In fact, despite the already noticeable Tory leanings of the Protection Society before 1910, one should not overemphasize its differences from other branches of the Weavers Amalgamation. Some time in the first decade of the twentieth century the Protection Society had reaffiliated with the amalgamation. The *Factory Times* gave the society full and "straight" coverage; no references, hostile or otherwise, were made about it in the ILP's Blackburn *Labour Journal*;

and, most surprisingly, it sent two delegates to the 1907 Labour Party annual conference.[54] For what it is worth, the original cause for the split referred to by Clynes was claimed to have been the questionable practices of the Blackburn Weavers Association, including admission to meetings by ticket only, rather than hostility to any real or imagined leftism.[55]

But institutions can change their functions and raison d'être over time, and there is no doubt whatever that by 1910 the society had become a reservoir for anti-Labour Party and anti-Socialist weaving operatives in the Blackburn district, beginning with its poll of members in 1910 whose results Clynes referred to.[56] We have already observed the circumstances of the Protection Society's withdrawal from the Weavers Amalgamation in early 1912 and its policy of active recruitment and growth in superseding the Catholic Workers in Nelson and in establishing branches in Preston and Clitheroe.[57] In the process the society also transformed itself from being strictly local in its personnel and outlook in two ways. First, out of ninety-four applicants for organizer, the winner was one J. F. Foster of Brixton, a section of south London not noted for its concentration of cotton mills, Foster was said to be a member of the Shop Assistants Union, but surely more important in the eyes of the Protection Society was his "experience of organizing as a lecturer for the Anti-Socialist Union."[58] Second, in the only internal document that has apparently survived, a circular letter from the general secretary, one learns that:

> We claim to be the first, at any rate in the cotton trade, to wage this battle inside the Trade Union ranks. We are engaged in a stupendous task. We shall feel obliged for all the influential support inside and outside Parliament that may be afforded us to continue the work and spread the movement throughout the whole cotton area.
>
> We have accomplished much and have the brightest prospect of accomplishing very much more. We have invited the influential assistance in this matter of several other M.P.'s and influential gentlemen, and if we can obtain it, will undoubtedly give a great impetus to our work.
>
> Amongst others we have asked for the support of A. Bonar Law, M.P., Steel-Mailtland, M.P., Col. George Wyndham, M.P., Harold Smith, M.P., Sir Max Aitken, M.P., Boyd Carpenter, A. Nuttal, J.P. John Whittaker, J.P., Sir Henry Hibbert, J.P., Ralph Assheton,

J.P., T. W. A. Bayley, E. A. Bayle, Sir John Randles, M.P., John
Borastan, Esq., Lord Balcarres, M.P., and Major Stanley, M.P.
Should we secure the influential support and assistance of
these gentlemen, we shall be able to do much to check and arrest
the decided Socialistic tendencies of Trade Unionism and your
valuable assistance will be much esteemed and appreciated.[59]

This bombastic rhetoric must be taken with a grain of salt (the repeated
use of the word "influence" smacks as much of cap-doffing deference as
of reporting that these worthies were actively supporting the cause).
Nevertheless, it is also clear that the Protection Society was attempting
to do its best to round up nationwide support. The society had, as it
were, come of age and had graduated into a full-blown political organization with the goal of "checking and arresting" prevailing trends in the
labor movement.

Just what was the programmatic and ideological content of the Protection Society's propaganda? The questions must be answered largely
in negatives. From the Osborne Judgment onward the group hammered
away at the use of trade union funds for political purposes, particularly
funds provided to support politicians sympathetic toward nondenomina-
tional education, socialism, or both. On occasion the ILP was singled out
as a primary target: The vice president of the Blackburn Protection Society promised to oppose "with the last breath in my body union funds to
support ILP candidates, which to me is a prostitution of trade union
principles."[60] The absence of a positive program over and above that of
calling for a restoration of the older nonpolitical stance of mid- and late
Victorian trade unionism is not surprising, since a major problem in Conservative thought has always been how to convince subordinate classes
that the maintenance of a class-divided society is really in everybody's
best interest. This is not to suggest that the Protection Society's local
spokesmen and rank and file were "dupes." Although the documentary
materials are not available to reconstruct all of the precise organizational
links between the Protection Society and non-working-class anti-Socialist
groups, it simply will not do to posit a conspiracy aimed at subverting the
cotton workers, since what must be explained is the thoroughly unforced
receptivity of Protection Society members to an anti-Socialist ideology.

How can this upsurge of working-class antisocialism be reconciled with
P. F. Clarke's thesis that by 1910 the "mainspring of Tory democracy

was running down?"[61] No doubt the simplest way is to say that Clarke
has got his timing wrong. If, on the other hand, we see the Protection
Society as a "new radical right," that is, a reaction against both socialism
and progressivism, then some of his thesis is salvageable, though it is
very difficult not to conclude that the older working-class Toryism provided a most fertile hothouse for the new growth. In any case, working-
class Toryism, although it might have been down, was not out.

Indeed, the membership figures indicate that the Protection Society
had established a solid base—far larger, one should note, than the Burnley
Textile Operatives. Blackburn had about 2,600 members in 1912 when
it withdrew from the Weavers Amalgamation, and a year later 12,000 members were claimed for all four branches, although one has no other evidence
for membership figures than the society's own assertions made to the
press.[62] In fact it is safe to say that Protection Society members outnumbered cotton workers belonging to all Socialist parties and sects in Blackburn and Preston. The same might also have been true for Clitheroe, and
the only place where Socialists definitely outnumbered them was in Nelson. Moreover, the Protection Society even in Nelson was not exclusively
Roman Catholic in either its rhetoric or its membership, although no data
are available for religious affiliation. And, religion aside, the Protection
Society's members appear to have shared all the other socioeconomic characteristics of their fellow mill workers in northeast Lancashire.

In view of the cotton workers' division along religious lines, is there
really any need for our hypothesis of a backlash against progressivism and
ILP socialism, which obviously remains to be proved? Cannot one simply
argue that where Anglican and Catholic passions ran strongly, opposition
to secularism and socialism were bound to emerge, and let it go at that?
This explanation runs up against one major difficulty. The Protection Society movement flourished in precisely those constituencies where the new
Political Laborism and a strong ILP had also emerged. Blackburn was represented in Parliament from 1906 onward by Philip Snowden; and his chief
henchman in the town, a tailor and draper named Charles Higham, appears
to have built up a local machine of considerable efficacy before surprising
all political observers by defecting to the Tories in 1913.[63] The parliamentary constituency of Clitheroe was a pioneer in Labour representation.
Preston also had a large ILP branch, and Keir Hardie ran for Parliament
there in 1900. By contrast, in southeast Lancashire, advanced progressivism and the ILP were not at all strongly represented (as an example, Old-

ham did not have a single Labour representative on the town council between 1900 and 1914), and there the Protection Society was not to be found. Returning to northeast Lancashire, it is perhaps significant that the Protection Society did not turn up in the sizable (1911 population, 106,000) town of Burnley, where the ILP was nonexistent and the socialism of the SDF stripe made the running.[64] In short, the empirical connection between the presence of the Protection Society and the presence of the ILP is so constant that one cannot avoid speculating that there was something about the ILP's style that was deeply irritating to workers who remained attached to nondissenting creeds. And given the apparent harmony with which the Weavers Amalgamation officials and the ILP worked together, it is not surprising that the Protection Society should strike a responsive chord with its propaganda that the amalgamation leadership had merged with or sold out to socialism.

Nevertheless, despite the Protection Society's proven ability to survive, and even grow, its prospects were not bright. First, the ideological leanings of Protection Society members do not appear to have been reinforced by any clearly discernible economic factors operating in northeast Lancashire. Unlike, for example, the mule spinners, whose status as contrived aristocrats might well have contributed to their Toryism, Protection Society members appear to have been occupationally identical to their fellow weavers who stayed with the official amalgamation branches. Second, since mill owners in the years before the war were clearly not in a union-busting mood, there was no practicable way for the Protection Society even to attempt ousting the Weavers Amalgamation, which therefore remained the real collective-bargaining agent for weaving workers in the industry, including those who belonged to the Protection Society. The amalgamation's charge that the Protection Society did nothing to service its membership need not be taken on its face; but surely the most powerful counterevidence would be strikes called by the society, and there is no record that any ever were called. Third, it strongly appears that for the majority of Lancashire weavers the bogy of socialism just was not all that terrifying; and since antisocialism, which electorally meant support for the Tories, was the Protection Society's self-defined claim to distinctiveness (as opposed, say, to the claim that they could provide more effective trade union services than the amalgamation), its appeal was necessarily limited. Accordingly, its ability to survive depended on the sufferance of the amalgamation, and it remained very vulnerable to a frontal attack, which, as will be examined in the next section, took place in Nelson in 1913 and wiped out the Protection Society's Nelson branch. As for the remaining branches, Preston and Clitheroe were phased out in the 1920s with help or prodding from the TUC, and the original Blackburn branch lingered on until 1949 when the amalgamation unilaterally forced it to remerge with the Blackburn Weavers Association.[65] The Protection Society's roots may have been deep enough, but in the end its appeal proved to be fatally narrow.

MILITANT LABORISM: THE NELSON WEAVERS AND THE NONUNIONIST WILDCAT STRIKES OF 1913

Viewed from afar, prewar Burnley and Nelson look essentially similar in terms of socioeconomic statistics and, indeed, in physical and visual terms as well. Both towns were newer weaving centers marked by high (for weavers) wages and a high percentage of male operatives. In both towns the anti-Tory vote in parliamentary elections was consistently high.[66] Nevertheless, the forms of political struggles engaged in by cotton workers diverged markedly. If Socialist weavers in Burnley had to work vigorously for more than a decade just to keep intact their autonomy and freedom and action, in Nelson, ILP members had successfully managed to work inside the Nelson Weavers Association with no apparent ideological friction, with the result that when the occasion presented itself, workers were able to strike powerful blows against external targets.

One such opportunity was the first anniversary of the defeat over the closed shop. On February 8, 1913, five young weavers—ranging in age from eighteen to twenty—were hauled into court and fined forty shillings and costs for badgering one William Sykes. The defendants followed him about the town, threw clinkers, lumps of clay and slush, snowballs, water and stones. Sykes's crime was that he was a member of the Nelson Weavers Protection Society.[67] When he refused either to quit the Protection Society or his job, his fellow workers at the Clover Mill came out on strike,[68] thus beginning a new round of unrest in the town that lasted until September. They key events and details can be grouped under the following headings:

Scope and Duration. Unlike the lockout of the previous year, which covered the whole industry, the nonunionist campaign of 1913 was rigorously selective and confined to mills in the borough of Nelson. From February 5 until April 14 only workers at Messrs. Pembertons' Clover Mill stayed out.[69] Following a settlement negotiated by the union officials, a somewhat confused period ensued in which workers from about six other mills staged brief wildcats over having to work with nonunionists and Protection Society members;[70] they were attempting to "get into the act," as it were. However, only two groups of weavers at the Brook Street Mill and the Albert Mills continued the struggle, which was finally settled in early September.[71] Despite threats in late March that "unless the weavers on strike at Messrs. Pembertons' return to work by next Monday, the employers will take such action as will bring the strike to a conclusion,"[72] which was interpreted as meaning either a town-wide or general lockout, no lockout took place, because of the unprecedented good trade.[73] In all, no more than 300 workers actually struck in the three sustained wildcats.[74]

Leaders, Rankers, and Supporters. The fact that the Nelson ILP meeting rooms were used throughout as headquarters for the ad hoc strike committee[75] suggests ILP dominance in the leadership, and this circumstantial evidence is further supported by the memories of Nelson residents interviewed in 1968.[76] How many of the strikers were members or sympathizers of the town's 800-strong ILP branch (making it the second largest in Britain) cannot be determined, though it is highly probable that ILP'ers and sympathizers were unevenly distributed throughout the town's weaving sheds and that the firms that were struck had a disproportionately high number of ILP'ers. Any role that the Hyndmanites (by 1913 the British Socialist Party) played is unclear, though active opposition would be unlikely to expect, and in 1913 a dissident grouping within the ILP was calling for more fraternal cooperation with the BSP.[77] Support for the strikes came from a wide range of sources including miners, foundry workers, operative plumbers, and workers in the Nelson Health Department and Corporation Yard. Workers from Nelson, Colne, Padiham, Burnley, Rishton, Great Harwood, Blackburn, Accrington, and Todmorden were among the contributors.[78] The strike committee proudly boasted that these contributions made possible strike pay averaging 7s. 3d. per worker per loom,[79] which was far higher than the union's strike pay scale with its maximum of 16s. per week.[80] In addition the strike committee in one of its weekly leaflets to the community observed that "a remarkable feature during the fight has been the determination of the women strikers. These women have not been content with merely coming out on strike, but have taken their place at the mill gates with the men, although this is a kind of work detestable to most women. . . ."[81] It appears that support for the unofficial action of 1913 was more broadly based in the working-class community than the official strike and lockout of the previous year.

The Union and the Strike Committee. Throughout the struggle the president, secretary, and committee of the Weavers continually reiterated that the strikes were totally unofficial, that not a penny of union funds was being used to support the strikers.[82] Formally this was true. However, it is equally true that the union had means of urging the wildcatters back to work that were never implemented—ranging from a promise to hold negotiations pending a return to outright explusions. That these inherent union powers were never used suggests that the officials and committee fully intended to give the strikers wide latitute to "do their own thing."

But the wildcatters did not have total freedom. Perhaps so as not to set embarrassing precedents, the Employers Association conducted its negotiations not with the strike committee but in the usual manner with the officials.[83] Similarly, the procedure followed in ratifying the settlements was impeccably orthodox—the secretary and committee put the proposed terms to the strikers, which they in turn voted upon.[84] Even more to the point, the union moved swiftly in April to keep the number of "authorized wildcats" down to a minimum following the end of the first strike by urging weavers to return to work.[85] Accordingly, the notion of a tacit conspiracy between the strikers and the officials is wide of the mark; a more appropriate formulation is that although the union fully shared the strikers' goals (which of course is not always the case in wildcats), nonetheless they did their best to limit the scope of open conflict as much as possible. Just how delicate an operation this was can be seen by examining a proposal that the union put to the Protection Society during the second round of wildcats. At the urging of the mayor of Nelson, a ballot was drawn up asking the Protection Society members whether one representative on the Nelson Weavers Committee, one representative on the Rules Revision Committee, and three dues collectors would be acceptable conditions for their disbanding.[86] Had the Protection Society members approved these terms, there is no question but that the officials would have been vehemently accused of a sellout by the wildcatters, and the results of such a ballot would have had to be accepted as final and binding. As it happened, however, the actual result was a resounding defeat for the resolution—only 60 voted for it whereas 341 rejected it—which took the

secretary of the weavers off the hook and, indeed, provided him with
ammunition against the leaders of the Protection Society for not "giving
a lead" and urging their members to vote yes.[87] In the end, however, it
is the absence of overt friction between the strike committee and the
union that should be stressed.

The Protection Society. As has been shown, the organization underwent
a transformation in 1912, and to judge from the numbers voting on the ballot registered a considerable upward jump in membership from earlier days.
At the same time, they were clearly unprepared for the direct threat the
wildcats posed to their existence, especially as there is no evidence that the
employers were in any way connected with the Protection Society movement. One must discount the strike committee's repeated propaganda that
the employers' refusal to fire Protection Society members was evidence of
collusion.[88]

Initially, the Protection Society seems to have said and done little following the first strike. Their line was well enough known, and in any event
only one of their number, Sykes, was feeling the direct effects of the strike
committee's campaign. Perhaps they felt that with the first outburst, opposition to the Protection Society had shot its bolt. However this may be,
the strike was brought to an end by Sykes's leaving town for Manchester—
pleading a bad case of nerves brought on by the harassment he had received[89]
—only to be followed by the second and equally militant round of wildcats.
The Protection Society responded with a somewhat perfunctory reitera-
tion of their offer to contribute to the Nelson Weavers for industrial purposes only, and the offer was once again rejected, on the new grounds
that the Trade Union Act of 1913, drafted to clear up the effects of the
Osborne Judgment, allowed "conscientious objectors" to contract out of
a political levy,[90] so that from the Nelson Weavers' standpoint the case
for a separate organization was weaker than ever. But most of the Protection Society's propaganda was confined to anti-Socialist attacks and an increasingly shrill assertion that they were a real trade union. The general
secretary of the Protection Society publicly threatened to sue the *Factory
Times* if the paper did not stop its suggestions that the conflict in Nelson
was over unorganized nonunionists rather than a rival and equally "legitimate" union.[91]

Indeed there was good cause for alarm. In September the second round
was settled with a promise to rehire the strikers after they had paid a fine
for breach of contract; and although no official mention was made in the

terms of settlement about the Protection Society, neither were any of its members to be found in the reopened mills.[92] Far more disturbing to the Protection Society's prospects, its president, John Stinchon, resigned, along with other members of his family who were cotton workers, and together with another committeeman went over to the Nelson Weavers, citing irregular but unspecified procedures and darkly hinting at the "hole-and-corner" methods of a "certain clique" that had gained control of the society.[93] He further asserted that the society was in fact incapable of discharging standard trade union functions and predicted that as a result of widespread rank-and-file apathy the organization would soon collapse.[94] With his defection the Protection Society was no longer heard from in Nelson, nor apparently did it raise any more hackles among the ILP'ers and other members of the Weavers. The wildcatters had done their work well.

Dr. Fred Reid has made the important point that labor historians have not put to the test Lenin's assertion that the ILP was

> really a petty bourgeois clique with a following among elements of the labour aristocracy. Did it, as a result of its social composition, pursue a wholly opportunist role in politics, that is, inhibit the development of working-class consciousness by the articulation of a policy which looked forward to a peaceful evolution of capitalism into socialism by the reconciliation of the opposing classes?[95]

Examination of the role played by the ILP weavers suggests the provisional judgment that in Nelson at least, ILP rank-and-filers acted as a vanguard in the sense that Marxists employ the terms. To begin with, they were not labor aristocrats save in the restricted sense that many strata of the British working class were aristocrats vis-à-vis the worldwide proletariat. Rather, the weavers were semiskilled operatives, and as such were perhaps analogous to the crucial position assigned to middle peasants in third world contexts. In terms of their activity the weavers demonstrated what autonomous rank-and-file militancy could achieve. This militancy was based neither on waiting for the official union leadership to take charge or on the fatalistic hope that by some spontaneous alchemy workers would, without formal leadership, rise up to the challenge of taking on the Protection Society element. The Nelson ILP'ers were saying to all who cared to take the lesson, "if you want to get rid of these troublemakers, here's how we are going about it." As a contemporary wrote:

> Here the weavers, knowing full well that the association could not support them from the funds, took action themselves, and appealed to their fellow workers to support them. This has been done admirably, clearly proving that what the strikers are out for is the desire or wish of every worker. . . . The events at Nelson are being watched by the workers of other towns, and whatever is the final issue of the present struggle, this non-unionist question has now got such a hold in all trade unions that it is bound to be kept to the front, and it is hoped that in the textile trades, in common with many other trades, the union card will eventually become a condition of employment.[96]

And if success is counted, there is no doubt but that the vanguard tactics worked more effectively than the amalgamation-led struggle of 1911-12.

But just because the Nelson ILP'ers fulfilled the vanguard criteria does not mean that they were imbued with revolutionary consciousness; and still less does it mean that any conceivable sort of revolutionary situation existed. The fact that the enemy of the hour was judged to be elements within the working class itself shows how far removed this vanguard was from mounting an assault of equal persistence upon capitalists or the capitalist state. Not that the choice of the Protection Society was a "petty bourgeois deviation." On the contrary, it really was a stumbling block whose removal was an important precondition for future advances.

As to the question of whether an active revolutionary consciousness existed, it must be noted that from there being an immediate crisis of British capitalism, either local or general, the successful militant wildcats were fought precisely because 1913 was a year of unusal prosperity during which it was possible to charge the employers all the traffic would bear, not only on economic demands but also on "intangibles" like the nonunionist question. And this brings the analysis back to Laborism, since Laborism's applicability as an ideology depends upon the stability and "healthy" working of capitalism. Now although the Nelson ILP'ers did not subordinate their efforts to the Laborist leadership of the union, neither was it ever their intention to challenge and supplant directly the leadership and its ideological foundations. Rather, their actions served to supplement and strengthen—by means of the tonic of independently led wildcats—the prevailing Laborism. Accordingly, the Nelson weavers are best seen as a Left Laborist vanguard, whose presence and successes did more to strengthen Laborist tendencies than to redirect them, by providing an important link between the rather narrowly based Laborism of the officials and the energies and aspirations of the rank and file. Whether the Nelson ILP'ers would have chosen to adopt a vanguard role in opposition to the leadership is much more doubtful.

THE MIDDLETON SPINNERS AND INDUSTRIAL UNIONISM

The first favorable mention of industrial unionism for cotton workers in the *Factory Times* came in 1913 from a staff writer for the paper, Alice Smith, who had previously in her career worked in a spinning mill outside Oldham.[97] According to her, one big union for all cotton workers was necessary because

> the great fight now lies between two classes—the working class and
> the capitalist class. Every worker who receives a wage is a wage
> slave, and his interests are diametrically opposed to the interest of
> the employer who exploits his labor. No similarity, either of poli-
> tics or religion, will bridge this chasm between the two classes.
> They are distinct bodies between which there can be no hope of
> conciliation, owing to the fact that one exists only at the expense
> of the other. The end of wage-slavery means the end of capitalism.[98]

A few favorable responses were scattered throughout the correspondence columns, including a letter from A. Heys. "Let the demand from your branch meeting be one industry, one union, one card."[99] Heys was not a mere rank-and-filer; he was president of the Middleton branch of the spinners, and in that capacity he led the only revolt against the industrial policies of the incumbent leadership fought within any of the cotton unions during the years 1910-14.

The immediate issue was again bad spinning. As has already been shown, the bad-spinning strikes of 1913 were settled with an agreement to a mor-atorium on further strikes for three months. The Middleton Spinners pro-tested by calling a special meeting of all members of the Oldham Province (i.e., of all spinners working in the area around Oldham rather than only members of the Middleton branch) at which "a resolution was unanimously passed that no agreement on the bad-spinning question should be made with the employers, and 'that we have satisfactory spinning or we close your mills .' "[100] Heys, who chaired the meeting, did not cite the number of spinners who had attended but claimed that the response was "quite beyond our expectation." He continued,

> If some of the people sitting in high places had attended that meeting instead of taking on themselves the role of absent critics, they would have received a much required education. The . . . resolution was adopted . . . with a recommendation to send a copy of same to all districts in the province that similar meetings be held. We await developments.[101]

"Developments" followed rapidly. The Executive Council of the Oldham Province voted to suspend Heys and the elected committee of the Middletown branch on the grounds of unconstitutional behavior and general rebelliousness. As the general secretary of the spinners stated in his quarterly report:

> We have . . . a class of members amongst us who are a danger to the organization, and are prone to create dissension and strife amongst the members and the officials. They seem to lose sight of the fact that no organization can be carried on without laws, regulations, system and method. . . . We find them preaching revolt in our ranks. . . .[102]

Heys was called before the Executive Council and given the choice of either submitting a full written apology or resigning with the penalty of never again being allowed to hold union office. He refused to resign.[103] As correspondents to the *Factory Times* and the *Oldham Chronicle* pointed out, it was Birchenough the general secretary who was acting unconstitutionally in suspending the Middleton men.[104] Furthermore,

> For two years bad spinning has been the biggest grievance of the operative spinner, the one most pressing of settlement, and what has been done towards its elimination? Nothing! The agitation for a breakage test . . . was dropped at the beginning of last year, at a time when trade was booming and circumstances favorable for pressing a demand on the part of the operatives. Since then

there has been nothing done except on the part of those members who, at individual mills, have struck work in desperation . . .[105]
Suspensions having failed to break the rebels, the Provincial Executive
Council tried stronger tactics. They called a meeting at the Middleton
Co-op Hall attended by 450 persons, which appears to have exceeded
100 percent of the branch's membership.[106] Before any business could
be transacted the police were called in to eject a member who demanded
that Birchenough retract statements he had made about Heys; but he
was rescued by fellow spinners. Thereupon the provincial officials walked
out of their own meeting. Once they had left, "the deposed chairman
and committee then held a meeting, at which a vote of censure was passed . . ., and the suspended officials were re-elected. A resolution was
passed requesting that the money and books seized by the Oldham officials be at once restored. . . ."[107]

At this point the provincial executive was reduced to the drastic expedient of "direct rule." Officials were sent up from Oldham every week
to collect dues only to be met by branch members picketing the Middleton Spinners clubhouse. According to Heys, only eleven members capitu-
lated to the executive's demands, a good indication of the extent of rank-
and-file support for their local officers.[108] And this support was decisive
in the end, for it was Birchenough and the provincial executive and not
Heys and the Middletonians who backed down following three months
of stalemate. As the *Factory Times* tersely reported:

> On Monday evening a special meeting of the Executive Council
> of the Oldham Operative Spinners Association was held at the
> offices of the association in Rock-street, at which the suspended
> officials of the Middleton branch attended by invitation.
>
> At the close Mr. F. W. Birchenough . . . stated that "a joint
> conference has been held to discuss the situation in regard to the
> Middleton dispute, and as a result an amicable settlement has
> been arrived at whereby the Oldham Provincial Council agrees
> to withdraw the suspension of the district officials, and the dis-
> trict officials have complied with the alternative requirements of
> the Council."[109]

A number of key questions cannot be answered by the available evidence.
First, why Middleton? What traditions of local militancy influenced the
conversion of practically an entire spinners branch to industrial union-

ism? Or was there widespread discontent against the amalgamation's policy on bad spinning in many other branches, with the result that by taking
the lead Middleton became a lightning rod attracting attention to itself
and diverting attention from elsewhere? Although the Shaw Spinners
were reported to have discussed the situation in Middleton at their monthly meeting,[110] there is no evidence of other branches' coming to Middleton's defense. In view of the fury with which the executive moved against
the rebels, this is understandable.

At the same time, positive conclusions may be drawn. First, just as in
Burnley almost twenty years earlier, one is struck by the anger exhibited
by cotton officials under pressure and criticism by their members. One
begins to wonder exactly who were the true conservatives: the workers
or their union officials? Probably the best answer is that the officials knew
that they could count on large numbers of more quiescent members to
isolate the militants and critics.

Second, the actions of the Middleton Spinners were part of the revolt
against Laborism, couched in industrial rather than political terms. Indeed,
the evil of bad spinning was itself a consequence of the spinners' traditional policy of trading off working conditions—in the form of control over
mule speeds and the quality of rovings—for wage increases. And it is important to recall that in 1910 the amalgamation had turned off that traditional safety valve. Middleton's revolt was the result, though it is interesting that the Middletonians did not include the amalgamation's wage policy
among their grievances.

Third, the Middleton Spinners' industrial unionist sentiment provides
the strongest evidence that cotton workers were indeed a constituent section of the new militancy of 1910-14 and that it simply will not suffice to
say that the strikes of 1910-14 were just like those of former years, only
there were more of them. The Middleton Spinners were insisting that the
bad-spinning strikes of former years—stately minuets of industrial conflict that they were—had failed, that the failure ought to be recognized,
and that new kinds of industrial action should be implemented at once.

But to say this raises a final point. The Middleton Spinners won an impressive victory over an entrenched and embittered incumbent bureaucracy. However, time was not on the insurgents' side. Before they could
restart their agitation over bad spinning, the war came; and with its coming, the question was no longer good versus bad spinning, but whether
there would be any spinning at all. And, *mutatis mutandis,* the same held
true for all other cotton workers.

CONCLUSIONS

Our first conclusion must be that the winds of political change were indeed blowing among the cotton workers in the years just before the war. According to P. F. Clarke, the most significant development in Lancashire popular politics was the emergence of progressivism. However, we have argued that the depth and breadth of support that the cotton workers showed for the Labour Party were equally impressive, especially when one considers that many cotton workers had been deeply committed to one or the other of the older parties before the advent of the Labour Party. The decision to "convert" to Labour must often have required a conscious and deliberate choice.

Secondly, the centripetal effects of the new Political Laborism were powerful. In Burnley militant Lib-Labism in the 1890s had created an open split within the ranks of the weavers. The demise of Lib-Labism after 1910 paved the way for reconciliation. For unlike Lib-Labism, which manifestly sought to destroy politically left-wing socialism, the fact was that the new Political Laborism tolerated Socialists. Thus in Nelson, where the combined forces of the ILP and the BSP were at least as strong as in Burnley, confrontation between the leftists and the cotton union officials—none of whom appears to have been an active Socialist—never occurred. The absence of political confrontation was not due to moderation on the part of the Socialists, since the ILP did in fact lead and independently organize industrial struggles that the leadership could not and did not wish to undertake by itself. The evidence suggests that a real, if temporary, accommodation between active Socialists and official leaders had been achieved in the years before 1914. This meant that for the Socialists the question of how and whether to function as a left *opposition* to the Laborist leadership did not arise and never had to be thought through systematically.

Thirdly, while Political Laborism smoothed and cemented relations between the union leadership and those workers to their left, the very same process produced considerable friction between the leadership and right-wing-leaning workers, culminating in the Protection Society movement. Among the cotton workers at least, it was clear from the outset that a significant minority of them simply would not support the Labour Party, just as the great Liberal Party had never succeeded in enrolling the entire working class under its banner in the late nineteenth century. (For that matter, a sizable minority of the entire British working class has continued right up to the present to support the Tories.) At the same time, though, the stridency of the Protection Society must be taken as a sign of weakness rather than of strength, heralding its inability to defeat the Political Laborism of the established union leadership.

Fourthly, just as it is somewhat surprising that northeast Lancashire was the stronghold of militant antisocialism, it comes as a surprise to note that the only case in the period 1910-14 of a left opposition to established union leaders occurred in the Middleton branch of the spinners' union over industrial policies to be followed. Although articulated hostility by local branches toward the top leadership was common enough in the weavers' union (compare the angry reactions of members following the lockout settlement in 1912), the depths of the Middleton men's anger and the repressive measures taken by the top amalgamation officials were unique. Although the available sources do not begin to provide the answers to all questions, they do shed enough light to justify the conclusion that one of the most successful and conservative trade unions of the period was not immune from the labor unrest.

Finally, one must emphasize a negative factor that underlay the activities of the left oppositionists: the apparently total absence of any interdistrict and intersectional linking up of local left-wingers. In a real sense, the unevenness of the political unrest paralleled the unevenness of the industrial unrest. In this respect one should note that the right-wing oppositionists were better organized. The strategy at Burnley, Nelson, and Middleton was evidently to throw all resources into gaining control of, or at least gaining freedom of action within, local union branches. To an extent the strategy worked. But the failure to join with oppositionists elsewhere and create a cotton trade analogue to either the railwaymen's all-grades movement or the South Wales miners' call for a radical new departure in union policies meant that at the top level of the cotton unions the Laborist leadership remained effectively unchallenged and in full command. The fact that this was so raises in the most acute form the question of just how significant the cotton workers' unrest really was. Because the question is so important, it is reserved for the next and final chapter.

Conclusion _____ 10

The main conclusion of this essay has already been stated directly and indirectly many times: The Lancashire cotton workers displayed far more restiveness during the unrest of 1910-14 than has previously been attributed to them. On the basis of our findings, they must be included in Phelps Brown's list of transport workers, unskilled workers and miners as being among the most strike-prone groups of workers in the years before World War I.[1] Moreover, unlike groups of workers like the dockers whose defeat in the summer of 1912 appears to have settled into sullen apathy, the militancy of the cotton workers continued right up to August 1914, though here one notes that the middle years of the unrest, 1911-13, witnessed the lion's share of the strike action.

How does our analysis of the cotton workers' strikes add to our theoretical understanding of strikes and protests by working people in advanced industrial society? Labor and economic historians agree that the British working class as a whole suffered an absolute decline in real wages during the first decade and a half of the twentieth century, and go on to make this downward trend a cornerstone of their analyses of the prewar unrest. As Sidney Pollard writes: ". . . basically . . . there can be little doubt that the series of extensive and often violent industrial disputes that occurred in Britain between 1908 and 1914 was called forth by the failure of real wages to rise and by the actual decline of some of them, at a time when the wealthy classes were evidently becoming richer.[2] Peter Stearns has suggested that the same was true for French workers between 1900 and 1910.[3] To an extent, cotton workers also felt the pressures of falling real wages, particularly during the 1908-09 recession when, as has been shown, average money earnings slumped so badly as to fall below the figures for 1891-93. Late in 1910, however, earnings began an upward movement, which continued to a record (for the time) peak in 1913.[4] The evidence suggests that the usual definition of offensive and defensive strikes is inadequate, and that the idea of *counteroffensive* strikes in order to make up lost ground and gain new ground is called for. This conclusion certainly fits the cotton workers' experience, and examples can also be found elsewhere, as in the American workers' upsurge of the 1930s when, having been battered by years of unprecedented depression, they found their collective second wind and built the industrial unions of the CIO.

However, our analysis has also shown that the single variable of wages is inadequate to explain the cotton workers' strikes. Instead the political economy of work was clearly decisive. Because *several* factors operated concurrently—(1) brisk trade and high employment, (2) wage levels well above subsistence for most workers, (3) inroads into working conditions, (4) a trade union officialdom at the very least either unwilling or unable to crush rank-and-file initiatives, and (5) the will and ability of the workers themselves to articulate grievances and set objectives—the result was trade union militancy and the sense of collective self-assertiveness that goes along with it. This conclusion is quite compatible with Tilly's and Shorter's argument that organization is somehow the key factor in workers' propensity to strike. In both style and substance, the strikes of the cotton workers would have been inconceivable without generations of union organization and experience. It strongly appears that the best training school for unofficial strikes is official ones.

But we have also insisted that the cotton workers' trade union militancy had its limits. As has been shown, every one of the nearly 250 strikes shared certain characteristics. First, they were directed solely against the bosses and not the state. Second, they all made concrete demands that in theory could have been granted at a moment's notice. Third, if granted, the socioeconomic identity of both labor and management would not have been altered. Trade union tactics and trade union consciousness on the part of the strikers were wholly sufficient to carry on the struggles, and indeed trade union tactics and consciousness could wage only these kinds of struggles. In short, the strikes were quintessentially economist in the sense that Lenin developed and used the concept.[5] His main point was that trade union consciousness, however militant in waging industrial conflict, could never spontaneously develop into revolutionary consciousness, a line of argument that both the Webbs before him and labor theoreticians like Selig Perlman after him fully endorsed.

However, it will not do to say that the cotton workers were engaging in mere economism and leave matters at that. In the first place they simply were not unique in this respect. In January 1912 the cotton and woolen workers of Lawrence, Massachusetts, turned out in a massive strike whose leadership was quickly and brilliantly taken over by the Industrial Workers of the World (IWW). It is accurate to say that the Lawrence strike is better known to both laymen and experts than all of the 1910-14 Lancashire unrest put together. The Lawrence strikers achieved a momentous victory in the face of tremendous odds, first because of the revolutionary élan and commitment of the IWW, but, as importantly, because the demands and tactics used in Lawrence ran diametrically counter to syndicalist orthodoxy. The strike lasted for two full months. It was largely nonviolent, except for violence initiated by agents of the state. The demands centered directly on wages, hours, and working conditions.[6] In other words, revolutionary leadership notwithstanding, Lancashire and Lawrence workers were waging industrial struggles over essentially the same grievances and making the same kinds of demands. Of course there were enormous differences in style between the American and Lancashire workers, since in Britain the employers had come to accept ongoing trade unionism and collective bargaining as a fact of industrial life, whereas the Lawrence employers had not. The point is that in both countries the impregnable strength of industrial capitalism doomed any tactics other than those of militant trade unionism to failure.

In the second place, there is reason to suppose that the potential for a transition from sectional strikes to industry-wide movement indeed existed in Lancashire. The five-year freeze was scheduled to end in September 1915 and in all likelihood a new round of fierce struggle would have followed. In addition, as Hinton has shown for the Glasgow engineers, their last prewar agitation was for a closed shop,[7] just as the weavers were demanding in 1911-12. If in Glasgow the demand for the closed shop turned out to be the herald of the shop stewards' movement, so might it also have been for the cotton workers, whose need for workshop organization independent of the union bureaucracy was every bit as great. The prewar unrest of the cotton workers did not reach the threshhold of a shop stewards' movement, but if the impact of war upon the industry had been anything like that in engineering, the results might have been very similar.

For many sections of British working people, their history in the early twentieth century is periodized from 1906 to 1926—the General Strike marking the "end of an era." Two decades that saw the emergence of the Labour Party from a pressure group in Parliament to the government of the day, a massive growth of trade unionism, and at times, particularly

in 1919 and 1926, open, unmediated class conflict, gave way to the sober
realities of mass unemployment and Britain's decline as a world economic
power, and the recognition by labor statesmen of the urgent need to cooperate with government and industry in the "national interest." But for
the cotton workers August 1914 is not a wholly artificial watershed.
Before the war the *Factory Times* devoted very little attention to foreign
affairs and the Empire. Indeed, one of its rare comments was to run down
the Imperial Vision: "We should remember first our responsibilities—the
little children in the street, the unemployed, the hovels, and the slums—
and afterwards talk about the greatness and glory of the Empire."[8] As
late as August 7, 1914, after war had already been declared, the main
issue was:

> Depending as we do for the whole of our raw material upon other
> countries, and upon our export trade for the disposal of 80 per-
> cent of our production any interference with seagoing traffic is
> at once translated into stoppages of spindles and looms in propor-
> tion to the extent of that interference.[9]

Other labor spokesmen took a less parochial view. The Church and
Oswaldtwistle weavers passed a resolution protesting "against the Government not maintaining strict neutrality in the present warfare of the
European powers." The secretary of the Todmorden weavers announced
a meeting to urge British neutrality. The Oldham Labour Party and the
Ashton Trades Council also passed resolutions.[10] But these voices were
quickly drowned out:

> Sit tight, old boy! Buck up and try
> With all your heart and soul;
> What, though you've cause to mourn and sigh
> You're not yet up the pole!
> Your sons are fighting for your case,
> They'll beat this monster vile,
> They've fixed their bayonets and their jaws,
> So set your teeth and smile. . . . .[11]

The impact of World War I on the industry was disastrous, as the export figures in Table 32 show. They reveal in the most glaring terms that
the rest of the world could in a pinch readily make its own yarn and cloth

Table 32

Raw-Cotton Consumption and Exports, 1913-19

	Piece Goods (Million Yards)	Twist and Yarn (Million Pounds)	Cotton Consumption (Million Pounds)
1913	7,075	210	2,178
1914	5,736	178	2,077
1915	4,748	188	1,931
1916	5,254	172	1,972
1917	4,978	133	1,800
1918	3,699	102	1,499
1919	3,524	163	1,526

Source: B. R. Mitchell, *Abstract of British Historical Statistics*, pp. 179, 183.

and that in the conditions of total war, fuel, transport, agriculture, heavy machinery, and, eclipsing all else, the instruments of war were the new key sectors of the economy. Had it not been for the mushrooming growth of munitions factories in the region and the war's insatiable demand for fighting men, Lancashire might have become a depressed area as early as the autumn of 1914.[12] This is not to say that the cotton workers disappeared overnight. As late as 1924 the industry still had 528,000 workpeople. But the aggressiveness of the prewar years now had to be rechanneled into fighting round after round of wage cuts and speedups as the bottom fell out of the coarse- and medium-goods market in 1920, followed by a partial and fitful recovery in the mid-1920s, only to suffer a general relapse in 1930. By 1941 only 220,000 looms were licensed by the government to run—down from the 1914 total of 808,000.[13] In the precipitous decline of the industry and afterward, the days of 1910-14 and their militancy were all but forgotten. And yet in their waging of explosive, unofficial, and, above all, unpredictable strikes along sectional lines, which more often than not achieved part or all of their aims, like the strikes of British workers in the 1960s and 1970s,[14] the Lancashire cotton workers were clearly part of our time. They deserve to be remembered.

METHODOLOGICAL NOTE ON COMPILING STRIKE DATA

The data in Appendixes 1-5 have been drawn from two sources. Those without an asterisk are from the *Cotton Factory Times*, January 1910-August

1914. A single asterisk indicates the source as the BPP, Board of Trade (Labour Department), *Report on Strikes and Lockouts*, 1911, Cd. 5850, pp. 90-91; 1912, Cd. 6472, pp. 106-7; 1913, Cd. 7089, pp. 96-97; 1914, Cd. 7658, pp. 128-131. Two asterisks indicate that the strike listed can be found in both sources.

It should be noted that the *Factory Times* listed far more strikes than did the *Reports on Strikes and Lockouts*. This cannot be explained fully simply by pointing to different criteria. Although it is true that the Labour Department's standard for inclusion was that of 300 or more working days lost and that the *Factory Times* appears to have used no fixed criteria at all, there were at least 14 strikes listed in the *Reports* that did not turn up in the pages of the *Factory Times,* and at least 36 strikes falling within the Labour Department's criteria that the *Factory Times* noted but did not turn up in the *Reports.* No doubt these lapses in data gathering can be attributed to haphazardness on the part of reporters to both sources, but the question then becomes why such sloppiness should occur in the first place. It has been suggested in Chapter 1 that in industrial society strikes constitute a departure from the norms laid down by the dominant value system and are accordingly—to one degree or another—a source of embarrassment for the concerned parties. It appears at least arguable that in order to ensure full and complete recording of such goings on, society must have administrative machinery backed by the force of law to collect and record data. But in fact prewar Britain was content to leave the reporting of strikes to the Labour Department largely up to the volition of the involved parties. As for the coverage in the *Factory Times,* it is permissible to assume that some of the union officials upon whom the paper relied for news from the individual districts had their own ideological reasons for sending in news of strikes. But here too cooperation was entirely voluntary. The obvious conclusion follows that the figures presented in Appendixes 1-5 are almost surely incomplete.

If sole reliance on the Labour Department's printed statistics must result in undercounting the true number of strikes in the cotton industry, there is every reason to suppose that this is equally true for other industries. For this reason the present writer has not attempted to compare the strike data generated in this essay with strike data for other industries as recorded in the *Reports.* Until assiduous research into strike statistics for other industries has been undertaken, it would appear that comparative analysis must result in incomplete or misleading conclusions.

APPENDIX 1
Disputes Involving
Workers in Weaving Processes

PLACE	STRIKERS	DURATION	STATUS
1910			
1. Preston	180	4 months	official
2. Preston	92	2 months	official
3. Nelson*	300	1 day	n.a.
4. Stockport	n.a.	n.a.	official
5. Stockport**	233	1 month	official
6. Padiham**	520	2 months	official
7. Oldham**	60	5 months	official
8. Haslingden**	310	4 days	n.a.
1911			
9. Accrington	n.a.	1 day	unofficial
10. Nelson	n.a.	1 day	unofficial
11. Bolton**	460	16 days	official
12. Padiham	4,500	1 week	unofficial/lockout
13. Accrington**	460	2 days	unofficial
14. Littleborough	n.a.	n.a.	n.a.
15. Manchester**	318	n.a.	official
16. Hebden Bridge	n.a.	3 months	official
17. Northeast Lancashire	n.a.	1 day	unofficial
18. Oldham	650	1 day	unofficial

ISSUE	RESULT
Underpayment of union piecework list.	Three out of five firms agreed to recognize list.
Ten percent reduction sought; "local disadvantages."	"Satisfactory" terms conceded.
Imposition of fines for alleged bad work.	Work resumed unconditionally.
Bad material	"Amicable" settlement.
Works reorganization, 30 percent cut in piece rates to "compete with Northrop looms."	Unspecified but "amicable" settlement. Union noted "danger" of ceding principle of rate reduction on "competitive" grounds.
Bad material, resulting in loss of earning.	Compensation of two shillings per loom to those workers who struck.
Bad material.	Compensation offer refused: "too small"; strikers prosecuted for intimidation. Work resumed on boss' terms.
Alleged bad materials.	Firm promised to improve material.
Weavers were not provided full complement of warps.	Negotiated settlement.
Overly exact clothlooking.	Boss promised to attend to grievance.
Bad material, underpayment.	Compensation offered; standard rate to be paid.
Strike at one mill over firing of a worker without a reason being given. Town-wide lockout in retaliation.	Worker promised a job at first vacancy.
"Driving" of workers.	"Firm promised to endeavor to remedy grievance."
Demand that extra tasks be performed.	N.a.
Bad material.	Work resumed pending inquiry by two persons appointed from each side.
Piece rates; union recognition.	Production continued by scabs and boss' kinfolk. Recognition denied.
Turnout when manager speeded up the mill engine.	Joint conference and return to work the following day.
Summary dismissal of a weaver; backlog of other grievances.	Worker to seek job in another mill.

PLACE	STRIKERS	DURATION	STATUS
19. Burnley	n.a.	n.a.	official
20. Burnley	150	6 weeks	official
21. Nelson	150	1 day	unofficial
22. Bamber Bridge, near Preston	200	1 day	unofficial
23. Bury	300	1 day	unofficial
24. Shaw, near Oldham	n.a.	1 day	unofficial
25. Nelson	n.a.	1 day	unofficial
26. Blackburn	n.a.	1 day	unofficial
27. Burnley	n.a.	1 day	unofficial
28. Burnley	150	3 days	unofficial
29. Burnley	93	1½ months?	official
30. Skipton**	1,500	1½ months	official
31. Haslingden	n.a.	3 days	unofficial
32. Bury	n.a.	1 day	unofficial
33. Northeast Lancashire	3,000?	1-5 days	unofficial
34. Preston	200	1 day	unofficial
35. Northeast Lancashire	n.a.	1-5 days	unofficial/lockout
36. Haslingden**	310	2 days	n.a.
37. Westhoughton	50	1 day	unofficial
38. Wigan	69	4 months	official
39. Padiham	n.a.	2 days	unofficial

ISSUE	RESULT
Bad material.	Agreement to 7½ percent compensation pay for four weeks.
Dismissal of a loom tackler.	Production resumed with scab labor.
Working conditions.	Union official persuaded workers to return; complaints to be investigated.
Working conditions.	Boss subsequently brought court action against two workers for refusing to obey orders.
Various grievances.	Union secretary persuaded workers to return; agreement reached on grievances.
Overnight change in machinery.	Interview by union officials restored status quo ante.
Sacking of workmate; working conditions.	Weaver reinstated.
Claim that boss had pulled down Coronation decorations in shed and refused to make proper reparation.	N.a.
Working conditions.	N.a.
Working conditions.	N.a. Weavers "returned to work."
Bad material.	Boss agreed to pay compensation of 1s. 9d. per loom.
Recognition of union piece rate list.	Agreement reached with assistance of Board of Trade mediators.
Unsatisfactory conditions.	Negotiations with head manager produced a settlement.
Certain grievances.	Union secretary "arranged terms."
Heat wave; temperature of 102° reported.	At some mills operatives ceased work; at others, joint agreement to stop.
"Strong language" by overlooker.	Return to work.
Another heat wave.	Two lockouts in reaction to turnout; elsewhere joint agreements, at some mills lemonade and warm tea.
Alleged bad materials.	Compensation was granted.
Dispute over piece rates on a new sort.	Work resumed on old terms.
Union recognition.	Small pay rise induced most workers to return. Summonses for riotous conduct against strikers and supporting miners.
N.a.	Agreement reached between weavers and firm.

PLACE	STRIKERS	DURATION	STATUS
40. Oswaldtwistle	n.a.	1 day	unofficial
41. Rawtenstall	273	4 months	official
42. Weaving industry**	200,000	4 weeks	official/lockout

1912

42a. Various towns**	n.a.	1-6 days	unofficial
42b. Leyland, near Preston	250	1 day	unofficial
43. Bacup	35	1 month	official
43a. Bacup	35	n.a.	n.a.
44. Accrington**	n.a.	1 day	unofficial
45. Todmorden	n.a.	1 day	unofficial
46. Radcliffe, near Bury	n.a.	n.a.	unofficial
47. Burnley	n.a.	3 days	unofficial
48. Padiham	n.a.	1 day	unofficial
49. Blackburn	n.a.	2 days	unofficial
50. Edgeworth	80	8 weeks	official?
51. Ashton**	385	1 day	unofficial?
52. Blackburn	n.a.	1 day?	unofficial
53. Patricroft, near Eccles	n.a.	1 day?	unofficial

ISSUE	RESULT
Complaints against new clothlooker.	Threat to fine each weaver onepence per loom per hour; union secretary effected settlement.
Compensation claim for bad material.	At first boss refused to negotiate until work was resumed. Agreement to pay 5 percent extra for four weeks and 2½ percent extra for another eight weeks.
Closed shop.	Demand was refused; return to work negotiated by G. Askwith.
Refusal to work with nonunionists.	In most cases, holdouts either joined or sought work in other mills.
Refusal to work with nonunionists.	All but two joined; firm had never recognized union.
Recognition of union piece rate list.	A list was negotiated, possibly for just the one firm.
Feeling that firm had reneged on a promise to rehire all hands.	N.a.
Working conditions.	Union secretary arranged a meeting, and work was resumed.
Refusal to work with nonunionists.	The nonunionists were successfully persuaded to join the union.
Bad work.	The union secretary advised returning.
Alleged nepotism in promotion of tenters to power loom weaving.	The status quo ante was restored.
Alleged unfair treatment of a worker.	A settlement was arrived at.
Alleged "driving" of workers by management.	Union secretary visited the mill and negotiated.
Irregularity of employment.	Several joint meetings were held, and an agreement was reached.
Proposed change in "making-up day" because of Insurance Act.	Status quo ante was restored.
Complaints over temperature in the mill.	Joint meeting was held; boss said it was impossible for him to comply with new temperature regulations.
Higher wages.	"[D]isaffected ones were paid up and discharged."

PLACE	STRIKERS	DURATION	STATUS
54. Accrington	n.a.	1/2 day	unofficial
55. Nelson	n.a.	1/2 day	unofficial
56. Darwen	n.a.	1 day	unofficial
57. Nelson	n.a.	1 day	unofficial
58. Burnley	n.a.	n.a.	unofficial
59. Haslingden	n.a.	2 days	unofficial
60. Nelson	n.a.	1 day	unofficial
60a. Nelson	n.a.	1 day	unofficial
61. Accrington	n.a.	1 day	unofficial
62. Church, near Accrington	n.a.	1 day	unofficial
63. Blackburn	n.a.	n.a.	unofficial
64. Ramsbottom	n.a.	2 weeks	official
65. Kearsley, near Bolton	80	4 months	official
66. Blackburn	n.a.	2 days	unofficial
67. Preston	n.a.	1/2 day	unofficial
68. Church	n.a.	3 days	unofficial
69. Burnley	n.a.	1 day	unofficial
70. Foulridge, near Colne	200	6 weeks	official

ISSUE	RESULT
A weaver who had lost a half-day's work through illness was told she must pay the employer's insurance contribution.	After union negotiations, work was resumed.
Unspecified grievances.	Union officials advised strikers to send a deputation to the manager.
Unspecified grievance.	Union secretary urged a return to work, which was done following a meeting outside mill gates the next morning.
Time off before breakfast to fetch hot water for tea.	Workers granted the right to stop at 7:50 A.M.—ten minutes before "official" break.
Working conditions.	On returning to work weavers were mulcted threepence per loom for room and power charges. Suit was filed against firm for this; information about outcome n.a.
Bad material.	Firm made a compensation offer, which was accepted.
Unspecified grievances.	Firm gave assurance that complaints would be looked into.
One weaver was sacked at a neighboring mill.	A "satisfactory arrangement" was made.
Working conditions.	A settlement was arranged after a "long interview."
Unspecified grievances.	Union secretary arranged an interview following return to work.
Unspecified grievances.	n.a.
Unspecified grievances.	A settlement was negotiated.
Union recognition?	Information about outcome n.a. Mill continued to operate; schoolmaster and vicar offered to help arbitrate.
Unspecified grievance.	Resumption of work after union secretary negotiated.
Bad material?	Union officials held an investigation, pending a return to work.
Working conditions.	Work resumed after union secretary reported his findings.
Bad material.	Work resumed pending further inquiries.
Compensation for extra and/or unusually difficult work.	Principle of compensated was conceded: Weavers to receive 5% extra for work still in looms. Firm had not been a member of the Employers Federation.

PLACE		STRIKERS	DURATION	STATUS
71.	Burnley**	200	2½ months	official
72.	Padiham	n.a.	2 days	unofficial
73.	Blackburn	n.a.	1 day	unofficial
74.	Padiham	n.a.	2 days	unofficial
75.	Ashton	n.a.	1 day	unofficial
76.	Haslingden	n.a.	1 day?	unofficial

1913

77.	Burnley	n.a.	6 weeks	official
78.	Barnoldswick, near Colne	n.a.	1 day?	unofficial
79.	Accrington	n.a.	1 day?	unofficial
79a.	Accrington	n.a.	3 days?	unofficial/lockout
80.	Macclesfied**	605	1 day	unofficial?
81.	Blackburn*	635	1 day	unofficial?
82.	Rochdale*	530	2 days	unofficial?
83.	Brierfield, near Nelson	n.a.	1½ weeks	unofficial
83a.	Brierfield	n.a.	1 week	unofficial
84.	Nelson**	90	2 months	unofficial
84a.	Nelson	90	2 months	unofficial
84b.	Nelson**	175	4½ months	unofficial
85.	Eccleston, near Leyland	n.a.	6 weeks	official
86.	Great Harwood, near Blackburn	n.a.	10 days	unofficial

ISSUE	RESULT
Working conditions.	A negotiated settlement was arrived at.
Working conditions.	Work was resumed.
"Continued complaints."	A joint inspection was held following resumption of work.
"Unsatisfactory conditions."	An interview was held between the boss and a deputation of workpeople.
Equal payment for the same sort of cloth.	A negotiated settlement was effected.
Turnout after a worker with forty years' service was sacked.	Head manager promised to investigate; the worker decided to leave anyway.
Working conditions.	Negotiated settlement. See also no. 71.
Summary dismissal of a woman weaver.	N.a.
Bad material, resulting in lower earnings.	Work resumed, conditional upon negotiations.
Firm locked out the workers after they had struck over bad materials.	Joint committee will investigate.
Bad material.	Improvement promised by firm.
Payment for an operative process called pick-finding.	Demand conceded, meaning an advance in wages.
Dispute over supplying weavers with warps.	"Satisfactory" agreement reached.
Compensation for bad material.	Ten percent extra for one month was agreed to.
Newly imposed working conditions.	"Reasonable terms" were granted.
Refusal to work with members of the Anti-Socialist Protection Society.	Objectionable person left the town. See Chapter 9.
Refusal to work with nonunionist.	Person joined; strike occurred immediately after settlement of no. 84, above.
Weavers from two mills refused to work alongside Protection Society members.	Strikers claimed victory, but did not say what became of the nonunionists; president of Nelson Protection Society resigned, criticizing "hole and corner" methods.
Union recognition and payment of union piece rate list.	Firm offered terms that the union accepted.
Bad material?	Negotiations and a joint inspection were held.

PLACE	STRIKERS	DURATION	STATUS
87. Glossop	391	2 days	unofficial?
88. Haslingden	n.a.	1 day	unofficial
89. Whitworth	n.a.	1/2 day	unofficial
90. Oswaldtwistle	n.a.	n.a.	unofficial
91. Burnley**	250	2 days	unofficial
92. Padiham	n.a.	1 day	unofficial
92a. Padiham**	n.a.	1 week	unofficial
93. Haslingden	n.a.	1 day	unofficial
94. Haslingden	n.a.	2 days	unofficial
95. Haslingden	n.a.	2 days	unofficial
96. Ramsbottom	n.a.	1 day?	unofficial
97. Haslingden*	300	n.a.	unofficial
98. Todmorden	n.a.	n.a.	unofficial
99. Whittle,** near Chorley	500	6 months	official/lockout
100. Todmorden	300	1/2 day	unofficial
101. Todmorden	n.a.	1 day?	unofficial
102. Accrington	n.a.	1 day	unofficial
103. Todmorden	n.a.	1 day?	unofficial

ISSUE	RESULT
Weavers' refusal to work with a nonunionist.	Man given a job in another part of the mill.
Reduced earnings for winders, blamed on working conditions.	The union secretary interviewed the manager, who promised compensation and correction of the difficulty.
Dispute between weaver and loom tackler.	The union secretary intervened and effected a settlement.
A weaver, returning to work after illness, was provided with a less remunerative class of work.	Status quo ante restored?
"Differences arose between the operatives and management."	Work was resumed, "pending a settlement of the differences."
Similar complaints about working conditions at both mills.	An investigation was promised in both cases.
Similar complaints about working conditions at both mills.	An investigation was promised in both cases.
Working conditions.	Firm promised to remedy grievances; some workers opposed striking without notice.
Unequal distribution (regarding wages) of sorts given workers to weave.	Some operatives contended that the distribution was fair. "Satisfactory arrangement" arrived at.
Working conditions.	"Some arrangement was made."
Alleged favoritism shown toward one worker.	N.a.
Production interrupted because of fighting among weavers.	Six workers from two feuding families sacked. Firm had the reputation of being a model employer.
Payment of a particular sort.	Agreement was reached to pay one shilling more per cut.
Five percent compensation claim.	Boss refused on principle to entertain the claim. Union claimed that a "settlement" was reached.
Ten percent compensation demanded.	Five percent was offered and accepted.
Recognition of union piece rate list.	Firm agreed to enter into negotiations; Thirty-four weavers joined the union on the spot.
Working conditions.	Negotiations after work resumed led to a settlement.
Dismissal of a worker.	He was reinstated.

PLACE		STRIKERS	DURATION	STATUS
104.	Preston	n.a.	1 day	unofficial
105.	Wigan*	450	2 months	official/lockout
106.	Horwich, near Leigh	n.a.	1 day	unofficial
107.	Blackburn	250	n.a.	official
108.	Ramsbottom	n.a.	1½ days	unofficial
109.	Todmorden	n.a.	1 week?	unofficial
110.	Golborne,** near Leigh	n.a.	6 months	official
111.	Earby, near Colne	200	3 days	unofficial
112.	Earby, near Colne	n.a.	9 weeks	official
113.	Littleborough	100	6 weeks	official
114.	Brierfield	n.a.	1 day?	unofficial
115.	Bollington, near Macclesfield	n.a.	n.a.	official

1914

116.	Turton, near Bolton	n.a.	1 month	official
117.	Nelson	200	n.a.	n.a.
118.	Haslingden	n.a.	1 day	unofficial
119.	Haslingden	n.a.	3 days	unofficial
120.	Bury	300	1 day	unofficial
121.	Padiham	n.a.	3 days	unofficial
122.	Darwen	200	3 days?	unofficial

ISSUE	RESULT
Bad material.	Firm agreed to pay 5 percent compensation for two weeks and improve material.
Reduction in wages, amounting to nonrecognition of union.	Union was defeated.
Girl winders, aged fourteen to sixteen, struck over depressed earnings, were supported by older workers.	Wage rise granted.
Bad material?	N.a.
Unfair treatment of a worker.	Union officials negotiated a settlement.
A weaver was sacked for leaving his looms too frequently.	Worker was reinstated.
Recognition of union piece rate list.	Final offer of firm accepted.
Highhanded methods of overlooker.	Complaints to be looked into.
Union recognition?	Firm was sold; new owners expected to resume production.
Working conditions.	Arrangements made.
Dissatisfaction over reduced earnings.	N.a.; workers at this mill had struck before.
Winders and reelers demanded higher wages.	Increase of two shillings was granted.
A new firm insisted on paying less than list wages because of "local disadvantages."	A 2 percent advance on old wages was granted.
Weavers claimed that firm was not paying union list.	N.a.
Broken warp threads reduced weavers' earnings; compensation demanded.	Ten-pound compensation was "equitably distributed" among the workers.
Compensation payment for bad material: 5 percent demanded, 2½ percent offered.	Five percent conceded.
Walkout occurred when manager told workers to quit if they did not like the conditions.	Union secretary effected a settlement.
Weaver sacked for producing oil-stained cloth.	The worker was reinstated.
Alleged favoritism toward a weaver and his kinfolk.	Management promised to equalize conditions.

PLACE	STRIKERS	DURATION	STATUS
123. Hadfield	100	7 weeks	official
124. Saddleworth, near Oldham	n.a.	n.a.	official
125. Haslingden	n.a.	n.a.	unofficial?
126. Ramsbottom	n.a.	n.a.	unofficial
127. Church	n.a.	n.a.	unofficial
128. Bolton	n.a.	2 weeks	unofficial?
129. Heywood	n.a.	1 day?	unofficial
130. Glossop	n.a.	2 weeks	n.a.

ISSUE	RESULT
An elderly weaver had her complement of looms reduced from four to two.	Status quo ante restored.
Wages and working conditions.	N.a.
Winders dissatisfied with working conditions.	N.a.
Winders turned out over working conditions.	Work was resumed on unstated terms.
Weavers who assisted tackler in lifting full warps into the looms of women weavers demanded more money for this task, and refused to do the work. work.	N.a.
Loom cleaners demanded a two-shilling pay raise.	Satisfactorily settled; workers to receive twenty-three shillings per week.
Teenage girls, working as winding frame doffers, objected to a newly hired girl being given a job out of turn.	Work was resumed; the girls decided to join the union, which for them was a new experience.
Piece rates for new winding machinery.	Union officials negotiated a settlement.

APPENDIX 2
Disputes Initiated by Piecers

PLACE	DURATION
1911	
1. Glossop	n.a.
2. Bolton	1 day
2a. Bolton	1 day
3. Hyde	1 day
4. Oldham	4 days
5. Bollington	2 weeks?
6. Mossley	5 days
7. Bolton**	n.a.
8. Bolton	n.a.
9. Oldham	1 day
10. Bolton	n.a.
11. Turton, near Bolton	3 weeks
11a. Ashton	2 days
1912	
12. Dukinfield	3 days?
13. Ashton	1 day

ISSUE	RESULT
Manager ordered a piecer to be shifted to a lower-paying pair of mules.	N.a.
Alleged favoritism in promotion from little piecer to big piecer.	N.a.; union secretary persuaded them to return.
Alleged favoritism in promotion from little piecer to big piecer.	N.a.; union secretary persuaded them to return.
Bringing in of an outsider to mind a pair of mules.	New man stayed; promise that all future vacancies would be filled by piecers.
Wage reduction of sixpence to one shilling sought.	The proposal was withdrawn.
Wage rise of 12½ percent demanded.	Demand was conceded, to come wholly out of minders' pocket.
Unspecified grievances; boss refused a request to intervene on grounds that piecers were employees of minders.	Union secretary effected an unspecified settlement.
Dispute over promotion.	Union secretary arranged settlement.
Little piecers struck when an outsider was brought in to fill a vacancy for big piecer.	Union secretary arranged settlement.
Piecer was given the sack; twenty mates struck in consequence.	Replacements found at Labor Exchange; minders successfully sued piecers for lost wages.
Out-of-turn promotion to big piecer; see also no. 2.	N.a.
Nepotism in promotion from piecer to minder.	Outsider to stay. Arrangement worked out for future promotions.
Demand that spinners pay piecers for cleaning mules during meal hour.	Work resumed unconditionally.
Working conditions.	Joint meeting with firm resulted in an agreement.
Outsider brought in as big piecer.	Union secretary intervened: Outsider was stopped and "proper promotion was arranged for."

PLACE	DURATION
14. Ashton	n.a.
15. Oldham	n.a.
16. Manchester	2 days
17. Blackburn	1 day
18. Heywood	2 days?
19. Bolton**	1½ days
20. Bolton	1½ days
21. Higginshaw, near Oldham	n.a.

1913

22. Oldham	4 days
23. Manchester	3-4 days
24. Bolton	1/2 day
25. Middleton	1 day
26. Bolton	1 day?
27. Hadfield**	6 weeks
28. Oldham	n.a.
29. Middleton	1 day
30. Oldham	1 week?
31. Hyde**	n.a.
32. Ashton	1 week?
33. Ashton	n.a.

ISSUE	RESULT
Scavengers, i.e., little piecers, demanded a shot at big piecing. See no. 13.	Outcome n.a. Lads chastised by *Factory Times* to learn the trade first.
Dispute over promotion.	Striking piecers were sacked.
Working conditions.	Union secretary persuaded them to return.
Dispute over bringing in an outsider.	"Satisfactory" arrangements were made.
Working conditions.	N.a.
An outsider was brought in to substitute for a sick minder.	He was sent back to his own mill.
An ex-minder wanted his job back.	Status quo ante restored; minder found work at another mill.
Dispute over big piecers' claim that a vacancy for minder existed and promotion should therefore be made.	N.a.
Out-of-town promotion.	Status quo ante restored; piecers fined five shillings each for walking out.
Wage rise of one shilling demanded.	Work resumed on old terms except for three or four who were given the sack.
Outsider brought in as minder.	"Amicable arrangement."
Out-of-turn promotion.	Unspecified settlement.
Alleged unfairness in promotion at several mills.	N.a.
Nepotism in promotion; undermanager's relative given a pair of mules.	Piecers' action strongly supported by other workers and community; firm agreed to comply.
Outsider was brought in.	Settlement whereby he took his proper place in the queue.
Spinner was brought in to fill a vacancy.	Promotion by seniority was the custom at this mill; "satisfactory settlement" arrived at.
Unfair promotion and compensation to be paid to piecers in bad-spinning cases.	Firm agreed to establish rules for promotion.
Working conditions.	N.a.
N.a.	Forty piecers brought to court and fined 7s 6d. each and costs for breach of contract. Firm promised to rehire them.
Bringing in an outsider to fill a minding vacancy.	N.a.

PLACE	DURATION
34. Oldham**	1 week?
35. Oldham	1 week?

1914

36. Hyde	1 week?
37. Bolton	n.a.
38. Bolton	1 day
39. Rochdale	n.a.
40. Bolton	1 day
41. Manchester	n.a.
42. Manchester	n.a.
43. Burnley	n.a.
44. Glossop	1 day?
44a. Glossop	n.a.

ISSUE	RESULT
Outsider brought in to fill a minding vacancy.	N.a.
Leveling up of wages.	Strike collapsed, as the firm filled the vacancies created by the strikers.
Unspecified complaints.	Firm promised to deal with grievances; piecers promised not to strike without notice.
Disputes over promotion at four mills.	N.a.
Unfair promotion from big piecer to minder.	Union secretary negotiated a settlement.
Outsiders brought in to fill minding vacancies.	Negotiated settlement.
Unspecified grievances.	N.a. Lads brought to court and made to pay costs.
Dispute over promotion to big piecer.	N.a. Minders and boss could not agree who should initiate legal action; none was taken.
Unspecified grievances and claims, referred to as an "epidemic."	N.a. Most piecers in Manchester were women.
Unfair promotion.	Union officials said they had worked out a settlement, but the piecers did not return.
Piecers claimed that the firm was not implementing an agreed-upon system of promotion.	Firm agreed that the piecers had a good case.
Same business of piecers' complaining that guidelines were ignored.	Arrangement made "for the time being."

APPENDIX 3
Disputes Initiated
by Mule Spinners

PLACE	STRIKERS	DURATION	STATUS
1910			
1. Glossop**	150	1 day	official
1911			
2. Hyde	50	n.a.	unofficial
3. Accrington	n.a.	n.a.	n.a.
4. Sowerby Bridge*	30	11 months	official
1912			
5. Hyde	n.a.	3 weeks	unofficial
6. Oldham**	177	5 months	official
7. Hyde	n.a.	less than one month?	official
8. Hadfield	n.a.	1 day	unofficial
9. Haslingden	8	1 week?	unofficial
10. Padiham	n.a.	n.a.	official?
11. Padiham	n.a.	n.a.	official?
12. Heywood	223	2½ months	official
13. Manchester**	244	6 months	official
14. Oldham	200	2½ months	official
1913			
15. Oldham** and district	1,500	6 months	official
15a. Mossley**	560	7 months	official
16. Padiham	n.a.	"several weeks"	official?
17. Colne	n.a.	1 day	unofficial
18. Preston	89-90	2 days	unofficial?

ISSUE	RESULT
Dismissal of workmen.	Reinstatement.
Working conditions.	N.a.; spinners were not union members.
Wage dispute.	N.a.
Number of spindles to be tended by each worker.	New hands replaced the original workers.
Working conditions.	Work was resumed on old terms; spinners were not union members (see no. 2).
Dismissal of a spinner.	Worker not reinstated, but employers agreed not to blacklist him.
Reduced earnings.	Firm promised to make full compensation.
Bad spinning?	Union secretary arranged for a joint inspection.
Working conditions.	A settlement was reached.
Working conditions?	N.a.
N.a.	N.a.
Bad spinning.	Joint committee to investigate.
Bad spinning.	Joint committee to investigate.
Bad spinning.	Joint committee to investigate.
Bad spinning at ten firms operating sixteen mills.	Spinners Amalgamation had withdrawn from Brooklands Agreement. New procedure agreed upon for handling bad-spinning claims.
Bad spinning.	Minimum wages guaranteed.
Working conditions.	A settlement was reached.
Firm refused to talk with workers about working conditions.	Spinners agreed to leave negotiations to their officials.
Dismissal of a spinner without traditional fourteen days notice.	Firm promised to reconsider if men returned.

PLACE	STRIKERS	DURATION	STATUS
19. Skipton**	100	5 months	official
20. Bolton**	168	2 months	official
21. Bolton	n.a.	more than 2 weeks	official?
22. Padiham	n.a.	3 months	official
23. Heywood	150	30 weeks	official
24. Droylsden	41	2 months	official

1914

25. Mossley	n.a.	1 week	n.a.
26. Oldham	n.a.	n.a.	official?
27. Hyde	n.a.	15 weeks	official
28. Bamber Bridge	n.a.	1 day	unofficial
29. Cicely Bridge, Yorkshire	n.a.	1 day	unofficial
30. Stockport	68	2 weeks	unofficial
31. Oldham	n.a.	n.a.	official
32. Ashton	n.a.	9 weeks	official
33. Stalybridge	n.a.	more than 19 weeks	official?
34. Hyde	60	2 days	unofficial?

ISSUE	RESULT
Ten percent wage increase demanded.	Firm agreed to pay Yorkshire List.
Tyrannical conduct of overlookers.	Employers Federation agreed that the men had a case; amalgamation threatened to cut off strike pay if men did not return.
N.a.	N.a.
Working conditions.	An unspecified settlement was reached.
Compensation for making up reduced earnings.	Improvements in machinery were made; strike prolonged when firm insisted on pocketing part of piecer's wages when spinner worked without one.
Compensation for bad spinning.	A satisfactory settlement was reached.
Sacking of two spinners who were members of the Woollen Workers Union; payment of union scale.	The two dismissed men were not reinstated; wage increase was granted.
Bad spinning.	N.a.
Bad spinning at two mills.	Firm granted compensation after six weeks; spinners stayed out when coppackers struck over a wage claim.
Reduced earnings, caused by a change in the type of yarn being spun.	Union official explained that reduction was justified; the men apparently quit.
Men walked out, thinking a mate had been sacked.	Firm decided to close the mill "for several weeks."
Compensation for bad spinning.	Union officials advised men to give official notice.
Working conditions.	N.a.
Bad spinning.	A satisfactory agreement was reached.
Working conditions?	N.a.
Reduced earnings, related somehow to a new batch of Egyptian cotton.	Union officials negotiated a satisfactory settlement.

APPENDIX 4
Strikes Initiated by Cardroom Workers

PLACE	STRIKERS	DURATION	STATUS
1910			
1. Oldham**	200	3½ months	official
1a. Lancashire and Cheshire**	102,000	1 week	lockout
1911			
2. Bury**	300	1 month?	official
3. Manchester**	300	3 months	official
4. Rawtenstall	n.a.	3 months?	official
5. Stockport	n.a.	1 day	unofficial
6. Bollington	n.a.	1 week	official
1912			
7. Wigan	n.a.	n.a.	n.a.
8. Bury	40	1/2 day	unofficial
9. Oldham*	223	4 months	official
10. Makerfield*	330	1 month	official
1913			
11. Bolton	n.a.	1 day	unofficial
12. Littleborough*	80	4 days	n.a.
13. Wigan	120	4 days	n.a.
14. Rochdale	n.a.	n.a.	unofficial
15. Bury*	70-80	1 day	unofficial

ISSUE	RESULT
Demand that a cardroom operative perform extra tasks; worker sacked when he and union refused to comply.	Job found for worker at a neighboring mill; otherwise, status quo ante restored. See Chapter 7.
Wage claim for ring spinners.	An increase was granted.
Wage rise of 12 percent demanded for ring spinners.	An advance of 9 percent was granted.
Wage rise demanded for ring spinners.	An unspecified increase was made.
Dissatisfaction over working conditions.	Union officials promised to negotiate with management.
Lower earnings caused by rearrangement of machinery.	A "considerable advance" was granted.
Ring spinners' working conditions.	N.a.
Back tenters' protest over one of the lads not being promoted to piecer.	Spinners' secretary promised to look into the matter.
Refusal of firm to negotiate an accident compensation claim under the terms of the grievance machinery.	Agreement that such cases should be heard in the courts.
Wage increase demanded by ring spinners.	One shilling per week advance was conceded.
Wage increase demanded by tenters.	A partial advance was promised if the workers went back.
Advance in wages.	Wages to remain as before, but bonus system rearranged.
Cardroom hands demanded reinstatement of a dismissed overlooker.	Firm refused to reinstate the overlooker.
Wage increase demanded by doffers.	N.a.
Extra payment demanded by doffers.	Only one striker was a union member; cardroom officials persuaded them to return.

PLACE		STRIKERS	DURATION	STATUS
16.	Bury	n.a.	1 day	unofficial
17.	Stockport	60	1 day	unofficial
18.	Hyde	n.a.	n.a.	unofficial

1914

19.	Padiham	n.a.	n.a.	n.a.
20.	Manchester	n.a.	n.a.	official/lockout

ISSUE	RESULT
Cardroom operatives had unspecified grievances.	N.a.
Working conditions of ring spinners.	N.a.
Various grievances.	N.a.
Unspecified grievances of ring spinners.	N.a.
New strippers and grinders brought in, apparently not union members.	N.a.

APPENDIX 5
Strikes Initiated by
Miscellaneous Cotton Workers

PLACE	OCCUPATION	STRIKERS	DURATION	STATUS
1911				
1. Middleton*	cop-packers in spinning mills	n.a.	2 days	official?
1912				
2. Ashton	ring doffers	n.a.	n.a.	unofficial
1913				
3. Bury**	weaving overlookers	320	2 weeks	official
4. Oldham**	cop packers and spinning-mill warehousemen	1,300	1 month	official
5. Todmorden	doffers	30	n.a.	unofficial
6. Manchester	reelers and doublers	200	n.a.	n.a.
7. Radcliffe	warpdressers	n.a.	n.a.	official?
8. Chorley	loom over-lookers	n.a.	n.a.	official

ISSUE	RESULT
Unspecified dispute over wages.	"Acceptable settlement" was reached.
Wage advance of fourpence. Juvenile workers.	N.a.
Refusal of overlookers to deliver the weavers' wages.	Weavers to be paid directly from office.
Advance in wages and union recognition.	Union scale to take effect on August 1.
Additional pay for extra duties. Juvenile workers.	N.a.
General underpayment.	N.a.
N.a.	Negotiated settlement.
Dispute over new procedure for installing beams.	N.a.

Notes

CHAPTER 1

1. E. Halévy, *A History of the English People in the Nineteenth Century,* vol. 6, *The Rule of Democracy* (New York, 1961); George Dangerfield, *The Strange Death of Liberal England* (New York, 1961).

2. E. H. Phelps Brown, *The Growth of British Industrial Relations* (London, 1959).

3. Henry Pelling, *Popular Politics and Society in Late Victorian England* (New York, 1967).

4. S. Meacham, "The Sense of an Impending Clash: English Working Class Unrest Before the First World War," *American Historical Review,* vol. 77, no. 5 (1972), pp. 952-70.

5. P. N. Stearns, *Revolutionary Syndicalism and French Labor* (New Brunswick, 1971). See especially p. 104.

6. R. J. Holton, *British Syndicalism, 1900-1914* (London, 1975).

7. J. Hinton, *The First Shop Stewards' Movement* (London, 1973).

8. Halévy, op. cit. pp. 451, 462.

9. Dangerfield, op. cit., pp. 237-38, 288. According to him the weaving trade lockout of 1911-12 "had frightened the country almost out of its wits" (p. 288). Characteristically, no authority is cited for this conclusion.

10. Brown, op. cit., p. 334, and in general, pp. 294-343.

11. H. A. Turner, *Trade Union Growth, Structure and Policy* (London, 1962), p. 392.

12. G. D. H. Cole and R. Postgate, *The British Common People* (London and New York, 1961), p. 493.

13. K. G. J. C. Knowles, *Strikes: A Study in Industrial Conflict* (New York, 1952), pp. 167-71, 203-7, 307.

14. See Chapters 2 and 3 for a fuller discussion of the workforce and divisions within it.

15. Henry Pelling, *Social Geography of British Elections, 1885-1910* (London and New York, 1967), pp. 252-65.

16. Alvin W. Gouldner, *Wildcat Strike* (Yellow Springs, 1954), especially pp. 18-22.

17. C. Kerr and A. Siegel, "The Interindustry Propensity to Strike," in A. Kornhauser, ed., *Industrial Conflict* (New York, 1954).

18. C. Tilly and E. Shorter, *Strikes in France, 1830-1968* (London, 1971), especially pp. 66-74 and 194-235.

19. M. Perrot, *Les Ouvriers en Greve, 1871-1891* (Paris, 1971), p. 353.

CHAPTER 2

1. Frederick Merttens, "The Hours and Cost of Labour in the Cotton Industry at Home and Abroad," *Transactions of the Manchester Statistical Society*, 1893-94, pp. 178-79. Merttens was not an academician but a businessman who evidently owned the firm of Merttens and Company, general commission and shipping merchants, Manchester. See *Slater's Manchester, Salford and Suburban Directory* for 1895 (London and Manchester, 1895). Is the thrust of his argument that of the "New Liberalism" or does it echo the older ideas of, say, Lord Brassey or the young Alfred Marshall?

2. John Worral, Ltd., *Cotton Spinners' and Manufacturers' Directory* (Oldham, 1914), p. 19.

3. R. Robson, *The Cotton Industry in Britain* (London, 1957), pp. 332-33.

4. P. Deane and W. A. Cole, *British Economic Growth, 1688-1959* (Cambridge, 1962), p. 297.

5. Historical statistics for the cotton industry, although abundant, are surprisingly oblique when it comes to using them to compute total production. One major difficulty flows from the fact that annual statistics for value and output of yarn and cloth exist only for exports. There is no reason why the ratio of exports to total production should remain constant over time. Another difficulty that crops up if one relies solely upon machinery is that there is always some (incalculable) surplus capacity. At first glance one would seem to be on reliable ground in using raw-cotton consumption, since the amount wasted and lost in production processes did remain constant throughout the nineteenth and early twentieth centuries. However, a given quantity of raw cotton could be used to turn out either low-value coarse (i.e., thick) yarn or higher-value fine yarn. In the Lancashire cotton industry during our period the tendency was unquestionably toward finer yarn, and it is no surprise that the increase in the number of spindles should be greater than the increase in cotton consumption. The point is that the statistics are useful only to indicate rates and direction of change, and are not to be construed as anything other than approximations.

6. David Landes, *The Unbound Prometheus* (Cambridge, 1969), p. 211, n. 1.

7. S. Ecroyd, comp., *Cotton Year Book*, Manchester, "Textile Mercury," 1911, passim; F. Jones, "The Size and Construction of Cotton Spinning Mills, 1896-1914," Manchester University M.A. thesis, 1959, ch. 2.

8. J. Jewkes and E. Gray, *Wages and Labour in the Cotton Spinning Industry* (Manchester, 1935), pp. 82 ff.

9. BPP, "Wage Census of 1906," Cd. 4545 (1909), p. xxv; BPP, 1912-13, "Fifteenth Abstract of Labour Statistics," pp. 300-301.

10. This is true because producing fine yarns requires slower-running mules and higher-priced, long-staple cotton, which must result in a higher selling price relative to coarser counts.

11. CFT, 13 January 1911, 17 October 1913.

12. Board of Trade, Labour Department, *Labour Gazette*, July 1912; CFT, 5 July 1912.

13. See Chapter 5.

14. B. R. Mitchell and P. Deane, *Abstract of British Historical Statistics* (Cambridge, 1962), p. 344.

15. Merttens, op. cit.; G. von Schulze Gaevernitz, *The Cotton Trade in England and the Continent* (London, 1895), ch. 9 and passim; G. H. Wood, *History of Wages in the Cotton Trade During the Past Hundred Years* (London, 1910), pp. 147 ff.

16. BPP, 1911, "Board of Trade Earnings and Hours Enquiry," Cd. 5814, p. xiii.

17. Harold Catling, *The Spinning Mule* (Newton Abbot, 1970), p. 149. Catling's book is an admirable example of what historians can accomplish by working at the interface of technological and social history.

18. See note 16.

19. J. Haslam, "Life in a Lancashire Factory Home," *The Englishwoman* (May 1910): 215; S. J. Chapman and F. J. Marquis, "The Recruiting of the Employing Classes from the Ranks of the Wage Earners in the Cotton Industry," *Journal of the Royal Statistical Society*, 1912, p. 301n. Remains of pianos can easily be seen by anyone who takes the trouble to check out auction rooms and secondhand shops in the cotton towns.

20. BPP, "Pauperism, England and Wales," HC 263, 1912, p. 30.

21. Haslam, op. cit., p. 215.

22. BPP, 1909, "Board of Trade Earnings and Hours Enquiry," Cd. 4545, p. xxx.

23. BPP, 1913, "Census of England and Wales," Cd. 7019, p. 205.

24. How then is the presence of pianos in the sitting room to be explained? The answer must surely run as follows: For years you do without one; during the period of peak earnings you buy it; and because a piano is truly a consumer durable, it remains, regardless of subsequent ups and downs. For a discussion of the earnings and poverty cycle of working-class households, see B. S. Rowntree, *Poverty: A Study in Town Life* (London, 1899). Holidays at Blackpool are an example of "saving for a sunny day." See N. Dennis, F. Henriques, and C. Slaughter, *Coal Is Our Life* (New York, 1969).

25. In Wigan 8.0 percent of the town's population, 7,115 out of 89,152, was employed in cotton; in Manchester 2.4 percent, 16,824 out of 714, 333. By comparison, Bolton had 19.4 percent, Oldham, 24.2 percent, Burnley, 31.8 percent, Blackburn, 34.0 percent, and Nelson, 42.6 percent. See BPP, 1913, "Census of England and Wales," Cd. 7018.

CHAPTER 3

1. BPP, 1909, "Board of Trade Earnings and Hours Enquiry," Cd. 4545, p. xxviii; G. H. Wood, op. cit., p. 47.

2. See "Children and the Half-Time Question" in Chapter 3 and "The Piecer Problem" in Chapter 6.

3. Wood, op. cit., p. 61

4. Ibid., p. 74.

5. The total depends upon the method used. According to the 1911 census there were 39,476 women engaged in spinning processes, 48,459 women and 17,117 men engaged in "winding, warping, etc.," processes. This includes all workers aged ten and older. According to S. Ecroyd, comp. *Cotton Year Book*, 1911, an 80,000-spindle spinning mill employed 50 tenters and a 350-loom weaving mill 18 winders. Cross-multiplying by the figures of 59 million spindles and 805,000 looms in 1914 given in Worrall's *Directory*, one arrives at a total of 78,400.

6. Wood, op. cit., pp. 47, 61; BPP, 1911, "Earnings and Hours Enquiry," Cd. 5814, p. xxx.

7. CFT, 18 April 1913.

8. The 1911 census is practically useless, as one cannot tell what occupations are meant by the term "weaving processes," which the census employs, so that if one wants to estimate the number of power loom weavers, the best approach is to take the 1914 figure of 805,000 looms and assume an average work load of one weaver per four looms.

9. Taking all men and women cotton workers, the average wages for men in 1906 were 29s. 8d., 19s. 0d. for women. BPP, op. cit. (see note 6), p. xxix.

10. "In every mill we see both men and women at work, often at identical tasks. But . . . as a whole, the great majority of the women will be found engaged on the comparatively light work paid for at the lower rates . . . A majority of the men will be found practically monopolizing the heavy trade, priced at higher rates. . . ." S. and B. Webb, *Industrial Democracy* (London, 1901), p. 501. This means that in the aggregate men's wages and women's wages were not strictly comparable to begin with and cannot therefore be taken as prima facie evidence that men were more skilled and efficient. The possibility that this might have been true becomes even more remote when one notes that three-loom women weavers in Bolton and Accrington actually earned *more* than their male counterparts: 18s. 3d. and 18s. 5d. versus 16s. 10d. and 17s. 4d. BPP, op. cit. (see note 6), p. xxxiv.

11. H. Pelling, *Popular Politics and Society in Late Victorian Britain* (New York, 1968), pp. 46-52.

12. See Chapter 3. For an analysis that casts an international net, see C. Kerr and A. Siegel, "The Inter-Industry Propensity to Strike," in A. Kornhauser, ed., *Industrial Conflict* (New York, 1954).

13. Wood, op. cit., p. 149.

14. E. J. Hobsbawm, *Laboring Men* (New York, 1964), p. 273

15. Ecroyd, op. cit.

16. H. A. Turner, *Trade Union Growth, Structure and Policy* (London, 1962), p. 151.

17. Wood, op. cit., p. 74.

18. See Appendix 5.

19. Catling, op. cit., p. 150; Turner, op. cit., p. 111.

20. A. Clarke, *The Effects of the Factory System* (London, 1913), p. 63; CFT, 19 July 1912.

21. Catling, op. cit., p. 170; CFT, 25 December 1936. According to D. Hunter,

The Diseases of Occupations (Boston, 1969), p. 823, some 1,989 cases were reported by 1955.

22. In January 1912 the spinners of the Oldham Cotton Spinning Co., Ltd., sued four piecers for 3s. 9d. each, the sum representing wages lost during a wildcat strike of the piecers. The judge awarded damages on the grounds that a contractual relationship indeed existed between spinner and piecer. In addition another spinner sued his piecer for 9s. 0d., a day's lost wages, brought about when the piecer turned off the main gas valve, causing the spinner to twist his ankle in the ensuing darkness (CFT, 12 January 1912). For a formulation of the piecer-spinner relationship closer to industrial realities, see CFT, 25 October 1912.

23. Turner, op. cit., pp. 209-10; CFT, 12 January 1912, and passim.

24. See also the discussion of piecers and spinners in "Who Broke the Brooklands Agreement?" and "Honorable Compromise via Militancy" in Chapter 7.

25. Webb Trade Union Collection, Section A. Vol. 34, interview dated March 31, 1892.

26. Wood, op. cit., pp. 47, 74.

27. Hobsbawm, op. cit., p. 274; H. Pelling, *Social Geography of British Elections, 1885-1910* (New York, 1967), pp. 259, 424. Pelling also stresses the fact that the spinning towns of southeast Lancashire were strongholds of voluntary education. He makes no attempt to relate this fact to the spinners in any concrete way.

28. Our threefold division of the cotton aristocracy is liable to the objection that it is essentially a jargon-laden restatement of Hobsbawm's theory of the labor aristocracy. Subaristocrats appear very much like "ordinary skilled workers and suchlike" (*Laboring Men,* p. 275); contrived aristocrats like the spinners "defended positions of privilege in an industry in which, under normal circumstances, they would have stood much lower" (p. 287). The objection is certainly justified in the sense that the analysis presented here is not intended to be counterposed to Hobsbawm's. What is asserted is that in the concrete instance of the cotton industry the gap between "ordinary skilled workers" like the strippers and grinders and those below them was unusually wide—with the result that strippers and grinders are best treated as a separate entity. As for the spinners, the point being made is that the defense of their privileges was carried to such extreme lengths that it threatened to become downright counterproductive—a theoretical possibility quite compatible with Hobsbawm's discussion, but one that he himself does not develop.

29. Amalgamated Spinners, *Proceedings of the Executive Council* for the quarter ending April 30, 1911; ibid., for the quarter ending January 31, 1912.

30. Webb, op. cit., p. 497; Turner, op. cit., p. 143.

31. In 1910 the Cardroom Workers Amalgamation's membership was 43,351 women and 9,209 men. BPP, 1912-13, "Board of Trade Report on Trade Unions," Cd. 6109, p. 25.

32. Ecroyd, op. cit.

33. The figures for 1910 are: men, 43,370; women, 104, 742 (BPP, op. cit. [see note 31], pp. 30-33).

34. BPP, op. cit. (see note 6), p. xxx.

35. See Table 12.

36. But not always, as in the case of women mule spinners and compositors. See BPP, op. cit. (see note 23), passim.

37. The employment of women for secretarial and other nonretailing work had not gotten very far by post-World War II standards. It is quite possible that earnings and working conditions often compared favorably with work in the mills. See, for example, C. Stella Davies, *North Country Bred* (London, 1961), who greatly enjoyed her job just before the war as a telephone switchboard operator for a private firm in Manchester.

38. BPP, 1911, Board of Trade, Labour Department, "Accounts of Expenditures of Wage-Earning Women and Girls," Cd. 5963, p. 4 ff.

39. The possibility that many women might have supported themselves constitutes a fascinating challenge to the social historian in view of (1) the marriage boom of the twentieth century, which has greatly reduced the social visibility of unmarried working-class women, and (2) the absence of either a literary tradition or the nuclear family to serve as a "conveyor belt" for distinctive values. See also R. M. Titmuss, *Essays on the Welfare State,* (Boston, 1969), ch. 5.

40. "Uncertainty" may be too mild. The fact is that attempts to predict demographic trends in advanced industrial societies have not been accurate: ". . . a glance at a college faculty . . . will show . . . the associate professors already have more children than the full professors . . ." (P. A. Samuelson, *Economics,* 5th ed. [New York, 1961], p. 33). According to the U.S. Census Bureau, the net reproduction rate fell to unity around 1970 and continues to fall.

41. Webb, op. cit., p. 638.

42. For a good discussion of this point see E. H. Phelps Brown, *The Growth of Industrial Relations* (London, 1959), ch. 1, and especially p. 28.

43. See the discussion of poverty in "Wages" in Chapter 2.

44. J. Haslam, "Women and the Nation," *The Englishwoman* (February 1910): 269.

45. One does not find women articulating the demand that their husbands help out with child care in our period.

46. Haslam, op. cit., p. 269.

47. Once again the incompleteness of the analysis must be stressed. One should like to know far more about the social effects of factory work upon women regarding, among other things, religiosity, the propensity to join voluntary associations, and relations between the sexes. Another question affecting both men and women is the assertion that cotton workers were peculiarly liable to mental illness. See A. Clarke, *The Effects of the Factory System* (London, 1913), pp. 56-57. The conceptual and methodological difficulties of probing these questions are staggering.

48. Webb Trade Union Collection, sect. A, vol. 67.

49. Trades Union Congress, *Annual Report* (London, 1913), p. 330.

50. Webb, op. cit., p. 495.

51. Ibid., p. 496.

52. Ibid., pp. 495-96.

53. Ibid., p. 500n.

54. Ibid., pp. 497-98.

55. Ibid., pp. 499-500.
56. Ibid., p. 497n.
57. Ibid., p. 505.
58. Ibid., p. 506.
59. See Appendix 1.
60. Webb Trade Union Collection, op. cit. However, the weavers' union sent 8 women delegates to the TUC annual conference between 1901 and 1914, 6 of them between 1901 and 1906, and 2 (both from Oldham) in 1910 and 1912. Over the same period more than 125 male delegates attended (TUC, *Annual Reports* [London, 1900-1915]).
61. CFT, 1 May 1914.
62. See Nelson ILP Minute Books, 1913-16, passim, in the possession of Stanley Iveson of Nelson.
63. BPP, 1906, "Report on Trade Unions," 1902-14, Cd. 2836, p. 44; BPP, 1909, Cd. 4651, p. 34; BPP, 1913-14, Cd. 6109, p. 33.
64. BPP, 1912-13, Cd. 6109, p. 33.
65. CFT, 7 January 1910.
66. Ibid.
67. CFT, 27 January 1911.
68. CFT, 8 December 1911.
69. CFT, 15 December 1911.
70. CFT, 20 December 1912.
71. CFT, 2 August 1912.
72. CFT, 8 September 1911; 1 May 1914.
73. CFT, 17 January 1913, 24 January 1913, 4 April 1913.
74. Nelson Weavers Minute Books, 17 September 1913, 10 December 1913.
75. CFT, 24 October 1913.
76. Cf. M. Royko, *Boss: Richard J. Daley of Chicago* (New York, 1971), p. 214.
77. E. and R. Frow, *A Survey of the Half-Time System in Education* (Manchester, 1970), p. 57.
78. Brown, op. cit., pp. 58-59. The *Factory Times* published a different version of this incident. "Mr. Churchill also paid a compliment to Mr. D. J. Shackleton when he pointed to him as an example proving that the alleged hardships of half-time did not prevent those who went through it from making their way in after life. No doubt Mr. Shackleton would appreciate the compliment, but he would probably be the last person in the world to cite his own career as a reason why the half-time system should be continued. Whilst he was an official of the Weavers Amalgamation he was an advocate of its abolition, and there is no reason to believe that he has changed his views" (24 February 1911).
79. In 1895 there were 31,510 children under fourteen at work in cotton mills. By 1907 the number had fallen to 19,501. In 1911 in Lancashire only, 15,976 children under fourteen were employed. For 1895-1907, see BPP, "Fifteenth Abstract of Labour Statistics," p. 300; for 1911, BPP, 1913, "Census of England and Wales," Cd. 7019.
80. For example, in Great Harwood, Brierfield, and Nelson, the percentage of

the *total* populations of these towns employed in mills was 44.4, 42.4, and 42.6 respectively. By contrast, in Bolton 19.4 percent of the town's population were cotton workers, and Oldham was only a bit higher, with 24.2 percent. Percentages calculated from BPP, 1913, "Census of England and Wales," Cd. 7018.

81. BPP, 1902, Interdepartmental Committee on Employment of Children, "Minutes of Evidence," Cd. 895, Questions 156-94.

82. Ibid., Questions 9883-10,023. See especially question 9,883.

83. The Webbs, op. cit., p. 769, have only one thing to say on the half-time question. Remarking on how Britain appeared to be losing the lead in progressive factory legislation—they cite Geneva's fourteen-year entrance age for factory work—they favored the *extension* of the half-time system to age sixteen on the grounds that an educated work force is a more efficient one. The root and branch abolition of half-time in 1918 was a more radical solution.

84. TUC, *Annual Report*, 1901.

85. Quoted in Frow, op. cit., pp. 59-60.

86. United Textile Factory Workers Association, *Report of the Annual Conference*, 1909; Ibid., 1914. The only known file is located in the offices of the Oldham weavers.

87. Oldham Trades and Labour Council, *Annual Report* for 1913.

88. CFT, 3 May 1912.

89. UTFWA, *Annual Report* for 1910.

90. CFT, 6 October 1911, and passim.

91. CFT, 29 December 1911.

92. Ibid.

93. CFT, 3 October 1913; Clarke, op. cit., p. 95.

94. J. R. Whiteley, *How to Become a Successful Operative Cotton Mule Spinner*, 2nd ed., (Oldham, 1903), pp. 2, 5-6.

95. CFT, 8 July 1910, and passim.

96. *Oldham Chronicle*, 5 May 1914.

97. *Oldham Chronicle*, 20 May 1914.

98. *Oldham Chronicle*, 25 May 1914.

99. The Independent Labour Party and the Social Democratic Federation denounced the half-time system consistently and frequently. Their performance is covered well in Frow, op. cit. However, the difficult problem is not the Socialists' position, but rather why they met with so much resistance.

CHAPTER 4

1. S. and B. Webb, *Industrial Democracy* (London, 1897), passim; S. J. Chapman and F. J. Marquis, "The Recruiting of the Employing Classes from the Ranks of the Wage Earners in the Cotton Industry," *Journal of the Royal Statistical Society* 75 (1912): 305. H. A. Turner, *Trade Union Growth, Structure and Policy* (London, 1962), endorses this judgment without adducing new or different evidence.

2. Communist Party of Great Britain, Historians Group, *Our History 21*, records reminiscenses of share-buying mania in Bolton during the boom of 1919. Cf. A.

Clarke, *The Curse of the Factory System*, 3rd ed. (London, 1913): ". . . most of these new mills are joint stock affairs, and any cotton operative desirous of getting employment within them has really to buy his berth—he must take up at least one share (generally £10)" (p. 133).

3. Chapman and Marquis, op. cit., pp. 296-97.

4. Ibid.

5. Ibid.

6. Public Record Office, Government Board of Trade (BT) 31, 14475/8102, 14428/5677, 14429/5727, 14430/5751, 14439/6327, 14459/7448, 31749/8080, 14452/7161, 14463/7639, 14465/7652, 14194/80259, 14481/8190, 14480/8164, 14483/8211, 14484/8248, 14485/8293, 8274, 14486/8310, 14488/8341, 14495/ 8474, 15855/54564, 17167/79729,17204/80420, 17286/81828, 14511/9076, 14518/9155, 14520/9196, 14521/9199, 17348/82924, 17230/82404, 17363/83217, 17409/83891, 17447/84482, 17459/84639, 17555/85837, 17670/87471, 14521/ 9199, 17692/87826, 17743/88519, 17893/90540, 17959/91444, 17990/91970, 18006/92134, 18248/95338, 30737/2334c, 30851/8953.

7. Some figures are given in R. E. Dyson, "The Sun Mill Cotton Spinning Company" (unpublished University of Manchester M.A. thesis), 1961, which tend to bear out the argument advanced here and, indeed, strengthen it, since the Sun Mill was founded by working men.

8. The large number of persons defining themselves as cotton spinners reflects the tendency for private mills to be reorganized under the provisions of the new limited liability acts.

9. The attempt has not been made to match the names of the twenty-three gentlemen with persons of the same name appearing earlier, a laborious and somewhat inconclusive undertaking, as there is no method for unmasking coincidental namesakes.

10. CFT, 25 August 1911.

11. CFT, 18 July 1913.

12. CFT, 10 November 1911.

13. CFT, 24 November 1911.

14. BT 31, 15855/54564.

15. CFT, 19 September 1913.

CHAPTER 5

1. BPP, 1915, "Seventeenth Abstract of Labour Statistics," Cd. 7733, cited in H. A. Clegg, A. Fox, and A. F. Thompson, *A History of British Trade Unionism Since 1889* (London, 1964), p. 468.

2. BPP, 1912-13, "Report on Trade Unions," Cd. 6109, pp. 24-27.

3. Amalgamated Association of Operative Spinners, *Annual Report* for 1914.

4. Cardroom Workers Amalgamation, *After Fifty Years* (Ashton, 1936), p. 5, pamphlet located in the Webb Trade Union Collection.

5. BPP, op. cit. (see note 2), p. 24.

6. Cardroom Workers Amalgamation, *Quarterly Report* for the period ending September 26, 1914.

7. Amalgamated Weavers Association, *Annual Reports,* 1910-14.

8. E. Hopwood, *The Lancashire Weavers Story* (Manchester, 1969), pp. 53-55.

9. Cf. H. A. Turner, *Trade Union Growth, Structure and Policy* (London, 1962), p. 138. See also pp. 108-68 and 233-68 for a definitive treatment of the cotton unions' structure, one that renders the Webbs obsolete.

10. See Chapter 8.

11. S. and B. Webb, *Industrial Democracy* (London, 1902), p. 195.

12. Ibid., p. 203.

13. Presently it is a common practice for the union official himself to calculate the piece rate when a new sort goes into production, management being either unable to make the accurate calculations or trusting the skill and fairness of the union official, or perhaps both. Interview with Fred Hague, general secretary of the Weavers, July 1972.

14. The text of the original Brooklands Agreement can be found in BPP, "Report on Wages and Hours of Labour," Cd. 5767, p. 10.

15. Ibid.

16. Ibid. The cloth-manufacturing unions did not conclude an industry-wide agreement on the machinery for processing grievances until June 1910. Its main provisions are broadly similar to those of the Brooklands Agreement. The text can be found in the Webb Trade Union Collection, sec. C, vol. 101.

17. From a theoretical standpoint, unvarnished collective bargaining, that is, a state of affairs in which each side has the opportunity to demand all the traffic will bear, appears to have a logical coherence that surpasses any scheme to link wage levels to another factor, be it selling price, profit, productivity, or anything else. For the drawback of using selling price, cf. Webb, op. cit.: "There seems no valid reason why the wage-earner should voluntarily put himself in a position in which every improvement in productive methods . . . all of which are calculated to lower price should automatically cause a shrinking of his wages" (p. 577). The trouble with using profit is that wages and profits are two entirely different kinds of income. For production to take place, wages must be paid; profits, on the other hand, are residual income. Because profits are not a necessary consequence of production, it is not the responsibility of labor to help maintain them at a "satisfactory" level. For a fuller discussion see T. Cliff and C. Barker, *Wages, Incomes Policy and Shop Stewards* (London, 1966). Attempts to link wages to productivity likewise run into trouble over the question of whose responsibility increased productivity is, as well as the question of the instance of increased productivity and falling profits occurring at the same time. In such a case could industry "afford" pay rises?

18. See L. L. Price, "Conciliation in the Cotton Trade," *Economic Journal,* 1901.

19. *Justice,* 11 June 1910, et. seq. The negotiations and correspondence can also be followed in the *Cotton Factory Times* and the *Manchester Guardian.*

20. Calculated from figures in *Tattersall's Cotton Trade Circular,* 10 January 1910, et seq.

21. *Justice,* 11 June 1910.

22. Clegg, Fox, and Thompson, op. cit., pp. 458-60.

23. Sir Edward Clarke, Q.C., 1841-1931, Conservative M.P. for Southwark, 1880; M.P. for Plymouth, 1880-1900; solicitor general, 1886-92; M.P. for the City of London, 1906. Prior to 1908 Clarke appears to have had no firsthand experience in industrial relations or arbitration *(Dictionary of National Biography, 1931-40* Supplement, pp. 179-81).

24. Clarke to Macara, 21 October 1909. Text in *Justice,* 18 June 1910.

25. Macara to Clarke, 25 October 1909, in *Justice,* 25 June 1910.

26. Macara and Smethurst to Clarke, 12 November 1909, in *Justice,* 2 July 1910.

27. Clarke to Macara, 16 November 1909, in *Justice,* 9 July 1910.

28. Joint union letter to Clarke, in *Justice,* 16 July 1910.

29. CFT, 14 January 1910.

30. This in turn was unlikely, owing to the strength of the unions. It is perhaps significant that while the weavers' officials entertained sliding-scale proposals for the spinning mill workers whom they had organized, they appear to have displayed no interest in a sliding scale for the 200,000 power loom weavers.

31. CFT, 15 April 1910.

32. CFT, 3 June 1910. A difficulty in assessing the motives of the employers is that their records were destroyed in the Blitz.

33. The *Factory Times* leaked the offer on May 27, 1910. After the settlement the paper revealed (July 22, 1910) that Lord Brassey had agreed to mediate. Given the bad experience with Sir Edward Clarke, one can appreciate the reluctance shown toward taking up the offer.

34. *Factory Times,* 13 May 1910.

35. *Factory Times,* 22 June 1910.

36. Included with the "Report of the Executive Council for the Quarter Ending July 31st, 1910," in the offices of the Amalgamated Spinners, Manchester.

37. Amalgamated Weavers "Report of the Council" for 1910.

38. CFT, 22 July 1910.

39. *Manchester Guardian,* 25 July 1910.

40. CFT, 5 August 1910

41. CFT, 29 July 1910.

42. Ibid.

CHAPTER 6

1. CFT, 27 September 1912.

2. BPP, Board of Trade (Labour Department), "Report on Strikes and Lockouts," 1911, Cd. 5850, pp. 90-91; 1912, Cd. 6472, pp. 106-7; 1913, Cd. 7089, pp. 96-97; 1914, Cd. 7658, pp. 128-31.

3. H. A. Turner, *Trade Union Growth, Structure and Policy* (London, 1962), p. 392.

4. See Chapter 2 and especially the sections on differentials and women in Chapter 3.

5. This was the only instance of workers outside the cotton industry providing direct, physical support to a strike of cotton operatives.

6. H. Pelling, *Social Geography of British Elections, 1885-1910* (New York, 1967), pp. 255-56, 263.

7. A good introductory discussion of "wage drift" can be found in T. Cliff, *Wages, Incomes Policy and Shop Stewards* (London, 1966), pp. 59-62.

8. CFT, 10 July 1914, et seq.

9. CFT, 24 April 1914; 3 July 1914. However, the Farnworth (near Bolton) Trades Council, which included representatives from the cotton unions, passed a resolution that "the time is long overdue when all workers should receive their wages for all recognized general holidays . . ." (CFT, 31 July 1914).

10. See "Cotton Toryism" in Chapter 8 and Chapter 9.

11. CFT, 10 July 1914; 17 July 1914.

12. CFT, 8 December 1911. Piecers came in two sizes: little and big. A lad would begin as a little piecer, and his job consisted of keeping the mules and surrounding work area clean and free from loose cotton and helping to unload yarn and replenish the rovings. Upon promotion to big piecer, the spinner trained him to operate a pair of mules; and once he learned, the big piecer performed essentially the same job as the spinner. In the Bolton district little and big piecers were called creelers and side piecers, respectively.

13. S. and B. Webb, *History of Trade Unionism* (London, 1920), p. 7; Turner, op. cit., pp. 141-42.

14. CFT, 12 January 1912.

15. Occasionally, officials of the spinners' union wrote articles on the piecer question in the *Factory Times,* as in the July 17, 1914, issue.

16. CFT, 10 May 1912.

17. CFT, 20 March 1914; 10 July 1914.

18. CFT, 5 July 1912.

19. CFT, 27 December 1912.

20. J. R. Clynes, *Memoirs,* vol. 1 (London, 1937), p. 72.

21. BPP, "Report on Trade Unions," 1912, Cd. 6109, pp. 26-27.

22. CFT, 24 October 1913; 28 November 1913.

23. CFT, 27 December 1913.

24. CFT, 19 June 1914.

25. Ibid.

26. CFT, 26 June 1914.

27. See "Women" in Chapter 3.

28. CFT, 17 November 1911.

29. *United Textile Factory Workers Association, Annual Report,* 1910 and 1911.

30. CFT, 10 July 1914.

31. CFT, 5 December 1913.

32. CFT, 12 June 1914.

33. CFT, 8 January 1937.

34. Turner, op. cit., p. 255.

35. The definitive description and analysis of the spinner's working day is H. Catling, *The Spinning Mule* (Newton Abbot, 1970, ch. 9, "The Life of the Spinner."

36. CFT, 1 November 1912.

37. Amalgamated Association of Operative Spinners, *Quarterly Report of Proceedings of the Executive Council* for the period ending October 31, 1912; CFT, 3 January 1913.

38. CFT, 10 January 1913.

39. CFT, 3 January 1913, et seq.

40. The Spinners' president, Thomas Ashton, had a thorough command of the language of trade union militancy: "We have just settled seven strikes, and we have a clean sheet . . ., and here you see (picking up a list of mills) we have 20 bad spinning complaints. The employers say they won't meet us. What shall we do? Why, we shall do something. . . . The fine weather is coming on, and any future strikes will be much longer than the seven which were settled last week. You may depend upon that" (CFT, 14 February 1913).

41. CFT, 28 February 1913.

42. Amalgamated Spinners, *Minutes of Sub-Council Meeting,* April 21, 1913; *Minutes of Executive Council Meeting,* April 26, 1913.

43. Amalgamated Spinners, *Report of the Executive Council* for the period ending July 31, 1913.

44. Amalgamated Spinners, *Annual Report* for 1913.

45. Amalgamated Spinners, "Terms of Settlement," circular dated October 17, 1913.

46. Amalgamated Spinners, circular dated September 10, 1913.

47 G. H. Wood, *History of Wages in the Cotton Trade During the Past Hundred Years* (London, 1910), p. 152. The Webbs concluded that the wages of ring spinners were not large enough to reproduce their labor power (*Industrial Democracy* [London, 1901], p. 753).

48. CFT, 4 October 1912.

49. See R. Blauner, *Alienation and Freedom* (Chicago, 1961), ch. 2, for an interesting discussion of alienation and textile workers in the United States. Blauner does not investigate whether or how trade union militancy has any countereffects on alienation in work situations that are "objectively" alienating.

50. As a Weavers' official put it, "Fifties to sixties count weft yarn heaped together and soaked with paraffin would make a gigantic and magnificent bonfire to celebrate the weavers' revolt over bad material" (CFT, 6 October 1911).

51. N. J. Smelser, *Social Change in the Industrial Revolution* (Chicago, 1959); see in particular, ch. 12, pp. 313-14.

52. E. J. Hobsbawm, "Custom, Wages, and Work-load," in A. Briggs and J. Saville, eds., *Essays in Labour History,* vol. 1 (New York, 1960), pp. 113-39.

53. Ibid., p. 114.

54. Webb, *Industrial Democracy,* p. 260.

CHAPTER 7

1. G. Dangerfield, *The Strange Death of Liberal England* (New York, 1936), is a good example. E. Halévy, *A History of the English People in the Nineteenth*

Century, vol. 6, *The Rule of Democracy* (New York, 1961), regards the lockout as "important" (p. 453). Neither account adds anything new to our knowledge.

2. G. R. Askwith, *Industrial Problems and Disputes* (New York, 1921), p. 137.

3. Ibid., p. 138.

4. Ibid.

5. Ibid., p. 140.

6. Askwith (1861-1942) was a barrister and an expert on labor law. From 1911 to 1919 he was comptroller general of the Labour Department and chief industrial officer, and served as chairman of the Industrial Council. E. H. Phelps Brown, *The Growth of Industrial Relations* (London, 1959) p. 368. A famous account of his negotiating style can be found in Ben Tillett, *History of the Transport Strike* (London, 1912), p. 30.

7. For his assumptions and approaches in industrial relations, see in particular Chapters 6 and 19 of *Industrial Problems and Disputes*.

8. G. H. Wood, *History of Wages in the Cotton Trade During the Past Hundred Years* (London, 1910).

9. Comparison of the similarities between the new and growing cotton unions in the 1880s and the New Unionism should not be pushed too far. In the case of the Cardroom Workers Amalgamation, two important differences with the New Unionism should be noted. First, none of the founding leaders was a Socialist; the union itself remarked fifty years later that the founders were trade unionists of the "old-fashioned" school. Cf. *After Fifty Years: The Amalgamated Association of Card, Blowing and Ring Room Operatives Golden Jubilee Souvenir, 1886-1936*, p. 45, in the Webb Trade Union Collection. Second, although the union's policy of organizing workers who in the productive process came "before and after" the strippers and grinders can be seen as an intelligent response to the challenge of building a powerful union, there was never any doubt that the strippers and grinders came first in terms of priorities. In our period complaints are recorded that only men were allowed to run for union office. As a general union, then, the CWA was both reluctant and imperfect.

10. The wages of strippers and grinders in fact caught up with the spinners' wages in the mid-1960s, though union policy was only one of several factors. There were strong reasons for the CWA to pursue a leveling-up policy, having to do with the peculiar relation between worker and machine that characterized many jobs during the "classical" phase of the Industrial Revolution. In both preindustrial society and contemporary industry a good case can be made for the distinction between skilled and unskilled—for example, craftsman and laborer, programmer and keypunch operator. Wage differentials are accordingly easy to justify. In a cotton factory during our period, one would be hard-pressed not to conclude that the overwhelming majority of jobs were "semiskilled" and that wage differentials arose from factors other than difficulty, complexity, training, education, or native ability. It thus made good sense for unions representing lower-paid sections to set their sights on catching the leader.

11. Comparison with the situation of workers on piece rates will clarify the point. Under piece rates the question of tasks actually performed is subordinated to the

question of maximizing output, since it is output that determines wages. Thus if management insists upon new tasks and procedures, workers are likely to object only insofar as they reduce output, which in a well-managed trade is rather unlikely, since it is in everyone's interest that output be increased.

12. CFT, 23 September 1910.

13. *Quarterly Report* of the Cardroom Workers Amalgamation for the period ending December 23, 1911; *Minutes of the Executive Council*, November 9, 1911; *Minutes of the Representatives Meeting*, October 28, 1911. Unlike an end product, for instance, yarn or cloth, or raw materials, which can simply be stored when there is overproduction, carded cotton is to be regarded as a moment in a continuous-flow process. It cannot be stockpiled.

14. *Times* (London) 15 September 1910.

15. *Manchester Guardian*, September 1910. I have lost the exact date.

16. J. H. Porter has shown that wages as determined by the Brooklands Agreement failed to keep pace with the cost of living. Although it is true that the cotton unions did not drive a particularly hard bargain in this respect, it remains to be proved that the Brooklands Agreement was for its time peculiarly moderate. After all, an unlimited cost-of-living escalator clause is even today a rarity. See Porter, "Industrial Peace in the Cotton Trade, 1875-1913," *Yorkshire Bulletin of Economic and Social Research* 19, no. 1 (May 1967).

17. The text of Clauses 6 and 7 are in the Board of Trade *Labour Gazette*, October 1910, p. 331.

18. The union issued its version by releasing a series of documents in pamphlet form, which can be found found with the union's minute books. Excerpts can be found in the CFT, 30 September 1910.

19. *Manchester Guardian*, 10 September 1910.

20. *Labour Gazette*, October 1910, p. 331.

21. Askwith, op. cit., p. 140.

22. For assertions that the employers had been "taking advantage" of the Brooklands Agreement for some time, see CFT, 17 June 1910.

23. CFT, 30 September 1910.

24. CFT, 7 October 1910.

25. CFT, 16 September 1910. The president of the CWA stated: ". . . we decline arbitration because there is absolutely no necessity for it. Our position has been clear from the start. . . . We have maintained all along that the employers have broken the Brooklands Agreement.

26. Text of letter from W. Mullin (general secretary of the CWA) to J. Smethurst (secretary of the Employers Federation), 26 September 1910, in CFT, 30 September 1910.

27. CFT, 16 September 1910.

28. Smethurst to Mullin, 28 September 1910, in CFT, 30 September 1910.

29. Mullin to Smethurst, 29 September 1910, in CFT, 7 October 1910.

30. *Manchester Guardian*, 4 October 1910.

31. CFT, 23 September 1910.

32. *Times* (London) 22 September 1910.

33. CFT, 30 September 1910.

34. CFT, 7 October 1910; Askwith, op. cit., p. 131.

35. I have found only one published account, A. Rothstein, *From Chartism to Labourism* (London, 1928), which argues that the outcome was a clear victory for the workers.

CHAPTER 8

1. There are exceptions in twentieth-century British labor history. In cases where a section of the labor movement is itself an employer—e.g., a consumers' cooperative or Labour Party controlled public authorities—here "management" has on occasion given a lead. There is also the case of closed-shop privileges being granted to one union so as to avoid having to deal with another one, as appears to have been the case in 1946 when the London Passenger Transport Board recognized the Transport and General Workers Union (T&GWU) as the sole bargaining agent for all London Transport workers employed in operating and servicing vehicles. For both, see W. E. J. McCarthy, *The Closed Shop in Britain* (Berkeley, 1964), pp. 57-58. In McCarthy's account the T&GWU initiated the request, which while apparently formally true tends to obscure the community of interests at work: Both the London Passenger Transport Board and the T&GWU were equally eager to suppress the more militant National Passenger Workers Union, which had broken away from the T&GWU following the "coronation strike" of 1937.

2. The cogency of the common-obligation argument has been called into question by McCarthy. He cites as a counterexample the instance of a voluntarily financed organization whose activities might benefit the entire community. He goes on to suggest that the case for the closed shop is far stronger when it is made on "functional" grounds, that is, when the closed shop can be shown to be necessary in order for a union to operate effectively. However, the analogy does not quite fit, because the common-obligation argument rests on the assumption that non-unionists are just as able to pay dues as are workers who have joined the union. For "philanthropic" associations, on the other hand, it is precisely an inequality of means that makes differential support by the community legitimate.

3. According to the mayor of Oldham, "we have them magistrates with interests in mills imposing miserable fines of five shillings and costs in black smoke cases—such a small sum for the serious pollution of the atmosphere, which could be altogether avoided. They are too lenient in such cases. The Health Committee have frequently complained of the uselessness of sending mill cases before the magistrates" (CFT, 26 September 1913).

4. In February 1913 a joint conference of representatives from the Cooperative Union, the TUC Parliamentary Committee, and the Labour Party met in Manchester, passed a resolution calling for close mutual support and effort, and indicated the desirability of a subsequent conference, which apparently was never held. Three cotton union leaders attended (CFT, 14 February 1913). Although there does not appear to be any direct connection between this "fusion of forces" movement, as it was called, and the formation of the Cooperative Party in 1917, it does stand out as an indication of the lines along which certain sections of the labor movement were thinking.

5. CFT, 17 November 1911.

6. Amalgamated Weavers Association, *Annual Report* for 1912.

7. W. V. Osborne, who was secretary of the Walthamstow (North London) branch of the Railway Servants union and a Liberal, successfully sued to prevent the union from using its funds to help support the Labour Party. Not until 1913 was legislation enacted allowing union members to "contract out." See H. Pelling, *A History of British Trade Unionism* (Baltimore, 1963), pp. 130-32.

8. CFT, 12 August 1910; 17 February 1911; et seq.

9. P. F. Clarke, *Lancashire and the New Liberalism* (Cambridge, 1971), p. 334. It is interesting to observe that the Tories allowed a working-class Conservative to stand in Lancashire's most solidly anti-Tory constituency rather than in a marginal or safe Tory seat. In the post-World War II years the Labour Party has been accused of "generously" adopting middle-class left-wingers to run in solidly Tory constituencies.

10. BPP, Board of Trade, "Report on Trade Union," Cd. 6109, pp. 32-33.

11. H. A. Turner's discussion in *Trade Union Growth, Structure and Policy* (London, 1962), is muddled and confused. As will be shown shortly, his statement (p. 315) that they received a "relative toleration" from local established branches in false, unless the term is used so flexibly as to include long and bitter strikes waged to remove them. Although he correctly notes that the Blackburn Weavers Protection Society rejoined the Blackburn Weavers in 1949, one does not learn from his account that until May 1912 the Protection Society was affiliated with the Weavers Amalgamation. The terminology adopted here is that as long as it remained affiliated, the Protection Society is best called an oppositionist branch, but that after it left, it functioned as a dual union. Following this definition, the Catholic Workers were a dual union from the outset.

12. CFT, 18 October 1912; 19 January 1913. The important point is not whether it was "possible" to live on a weaver's wage, but rather the perception that weaving was a "dishonorable" trade.

13. CFT, 20 January 1911. See also the Amalgamated Weavers *Annual Report*, op. cit., for 1909, for an instance of weavers in five Heywood mills expressing dissatisfaction over having to work with nonunion mates.

14. CFT, 20 January 1911.

15. Ibid.

16. CFT, 24 March 1911.

17. CFT, 8 December 1911.

18. Ibid.

19. BPP, 1913, "Census of England and Wales," Cd. 7018.

20. CFT, 15 December 1911.

21. Ibid.

22. CFT, 1 December 1911.

23. AWA, *Annual Reports* for the years ending April 30, 1912, April 30, 1913, and April 30, 1914.

24. AWA, *Report of Council Meeting*, April 11, 1911.

25. AWA, *Report of Council Meeting*, May 20, 1911.

26. AWA, *Report of Council Meeting*, November 18, 1911; CFT, 24 November 1911.

27. CFT, 23 June 1911.

28. What would have prevented the employers from agreeing to the closed shop but subsequently refusing to entertain or concede a wage increase, thus leaving the union holding the bag? The answer is that the union could have responded that since the closed shop per se cost the employers nothing, the demand for an increase could be decided on its merits.

29. AWA, op. cit. (see note 26).

30. *Manchester Guardian*, 23 December 1911.

31. *Manchester Guardian*, 21 December 1911; CFT, 22 December 1911.

32. CFT, 29 December 1911.

33. CFT, 5 January 1912.

34. CFT, 12 January 1912.

35. CFT, 5 January 1912.

36. See *Burnley Express*, 10 January 1912, for the remarks of the vicar of St. Andrew's Church, comparing the union's campaign to a heresy hunt; see also the *Times* (London), 26 December 1911, et seq.

37. *Nelson Leader*, 5 January 1912. J. R. Clynes, M.P., told his Manchester constituents that the nonunionist campaign was an attack by unionized workers upon another body of workers *(Manchester Guardian, 19 January 1912)*. Clynes at least can be said to have held his tongue until the battle was almost over.

38. BSP, Padiham Branch, "A Word of Council and Remembrance to the Locked-Out Workers," printed leaflet in the Webb Trade Union Collection.

39. *Justice*, 6 January 1912.

40. Ibid.

41. CFT, 5 January 1912; Askwith, op. cit., p. 188.

42. *Burnley Express*, 13 January 1912.

43. CFT, 12 January 1912.

44. CFT, 12 January 1913.

45. CFT, 19 January 1912.

46. CFT, 12 January 1912; AWA, *Annual Report* for the year ending April 30, 1912.

47. Askwith, op. cit., p. 188.

48. Ibid., pp. 187-92.

49. Ibid., p. 190.

50. *Manchester Guardian*, 20 January 1912; CFT, 26 January 1912.

51. CFT, 26 January 1912.

52. CFT, 19 January 1912, reporting on the mood of weavers in Stalybridge.

53. CFT, 26 January 1912, reporting on the reaction of the Padiham weavers.

54. Nelson Weavers *Minute Books*, entry for February 7, 1912.

55. CFT, 26 January 1912.

56. *Manchester Guardian*, 3 February 1912.

57. CFT, 12 January 1912.

58. *Manchester Guardian*, 8 January 1912.

59. Blackburn Weavers *Minute Books*, entry for January 17, 1912.

60. Blackburn Weavers *Minute Books*, entry for January 31, 1912; CFT, February 2, 1912. According to the *Factory Times*, the vote was unanimous.

61. CFT, 2 February 1912.

62. *Manchester Guardian*, 20 January 1912.

63. See note 53; *Manchester Guardian*, 22 January 1912, et seq.; CFT, 26 January 1912, et seq.

64. CFT, 2 February 1912.

65. AWA, *Annual Report* for the year ending April 23, 1911.

66. *Manchester Guardian*, 22 January 1912.

67. "That the committee be instructed to take steps to rejoin the Trades Council," notice of motion on the agenda of the quarterly membership meeting, Burnley Weavers *Minute Books*, December 10, 1913.

68. CFT, 1 December 1911; *Nelson Leader*, 19 January 1912.

69. CFT, 19 January 1912.

70. Ibid.

71. Burnley Weavers *Minute Books*, entry for January 28, 1912.

72. Burnley Weavers *Minute Books*, entry for February 1, 1912.

73. Burnley Weavers *Minute Books*, entry for January 2, 1896, et seq.

74. Burnley Weavers *Minute Books*, entry for March 19, 1912.

75. Burnley Weavers *Minute Books*, entry for March 20, 1912; CFT, 29 March 1912.

76. See in particular Burnley Weavers *Minute Books*, quarterly report for the period ending October 29, 1913, quoted later in the chapter.

77. CFT, 26 January 1912; *Nelson Leader*, 26 January 1912.

78. *Manchester Guardian*, 3 February 1912.

79. CFT, 16 February 1912.

80. BPP, Board of Trade, Labour Department, "Report on Trade Unions, 1908-1910," Cd. 6109, pp. 30-33.

81. *Labour Leader*, 30 January 1913.

82. One cannot tell for sure. Although the names of Weavers' committeemen are available, similar data are lacking for the ILP branch.

83. CFT, 2 February 1912. He is remembered in Nelson as having been a legitimate labor spokesman and leader. Interview with Mr. Stanley Iveson and the late Euclid Voltaire Thursby, both of Nelson, August 1968.

84. *Nelson Leader*, 2 February 1912.

85. Nelson Weavers *Minute Books*, entry for January 20, 1912.

86. *Nelson Leader*, 9 February 1912.

87. CFT, 16 February 1912. The committee took firm action in the form of lunch-time meetings at the mills.

88. See note 54.

89. It was also obscure to the members of the Weavers' committee: ". . . that as much information as possible in reference to that society [i.e., the Protection Society] be got," Nelson Weavers *Minute Books*, entry for August 14, 1912.

90. CFT, 3 May 1912.

91. This topic has been neglected, but see J. Saville, "Trade Unions and Free Labour: The Background to the Taff Vale Decision," in A. Briggs and J. Saville, ed., *Essays in Labour History*, vol. 1 (London, 1960).

92. Askwith, op. cit., p. 192.

93. CFT, 26 January 1912.

94. CFT, 24 May 1912.

95. H. Pelling, *A History of British Trade Unionism* (Baltimore, 1963), p. 203.

96. Turner, op. cit., pp. 322-23.

97. Pelling, op. cit., pp. 137-38.

98. Turner, op. cit., p. 392.

99. *Nelson Leader,* 23 February 1912, quoting from an article in the *Nelson Socialist.*

100. See H. Collins, "The Marxism of the S.D.F.," in Briggs and Saville, op. cit., vol. 2 (London, 1972).

CHAPTER 9

1. The pot continues to boil vigorously over the question of whether the emergence of the Labour Party was "inevitable." For a recent contribution see P. F. Clarke, *Lancashire and the New Liberalism* (Cambridge, 1971). For a critique of Clarke's thesis see Joseph White, "A Panegyric on Edwardism Progressivism," *Journal of British Studies,* vol. 16, no. 2 (May 1977).

2. E. P. Thompson, "Homage to Tom McGuire," in A. Briggs and J. Saville, eds., *Essays in Labour History,* vol. 1 (London, 1960), pp. 276-316. Perhaps because of this essay's formidable brilliance historians have not seen fit to apply Thompson's approach to other persons and periods, despite Thompson's clear inference that there were many "Tom McGuires" and that it is utterly misleading to suppose that if you have seen one, you have seen them all.

3. Labour Representation Committee, *Report of the Annual Conference* (London, 1903), p. 19. For the scanty biographical data on Ashton that could be found, see "Women" in Chapter 3.

4. United Textile Factory Workers Association, *Report of the Annual Conference* for 1910, 1912, and 1914.

5. Trade Union Congress, *Annual Report* (London, 1911), p. 311.

6. See Chapter 5.

7. W. F. Tewson, *B.C.G.A. Golden Jubilee* (Manchester, 1954), pp. 20-21.

8. CFT, 17 June 1910; 1 July 1910; and passim.

9. Nelson Weavers *Minute Books,* entry for March 16, 1910.

10. Nelson Weavers *Minute Books,* entry for April 27, 1910.

11. G. R. Askwith, *Industrial Problems and Disputes* (New York, 1921), p. 313.

12. Ibid., p. 306; E. H. Phelps Brown, *The Growth of Industrial Relations* (London, 1959), p. 341; V. L. Allan, *Trade Union Militancy* (London, 1965), pp. 66, 97.

13. CWA, *Minutes of the Executive Council,* meeting June 19, 1912.

14. CWA, *Minutes of the Executive Council,* meeting of June 27, 1912.

15. CWA, *Minutes of the Executive Council,* meeting of June 29, 1912.

16. H. Pelling *Social Geography of British Elections, 1885-1910* (London, 1967), pp. 252-57, 260-65.

17. CFT, 19 April 1895.

18. Cf. H. Pelling, *Origins of the Labour Party* (New York, 1966), p. 302.

19. F. Bealey and H. Pelling, *Labour and Politics, 1900-1906*, (London, 1958), pp. 98-124.

20. Clarke, op. cit., p. 412.

21. Ibid., p. 386; A. Bennett, *Oldham Trades and Labour Council Centenary* (Oldham, 1967 [no pagination]).

22. CFT, 27 January 1911; 22 November 1912.

23. Labour Party, *Report of the Annual Conference* (London, 1912), pp. 70-71.

24. CFT, 26 January 1912; 17 May 1912; 28 February 1913.

25. UTFWA, *Report of the Annual Conference*, 1913; CFT, 1 August 1913 et seq.

26. CWA, quarterly report for the period ending March 28, 1914.

27. Blackburn was a two-member constituency. In all of his three victorious elections there Snowden polled second, with pluralities over the third candidate of 1,350 in 1906, 2,609 in January 1910, and 948 in December 1910. Clarke, op. cit., pp. 433-34.

28. Interview with Fred Hague, the general secretary of the Weavers Amalgamation, August 1972.

29. This analysis draws heavily on R. Miliband, *Parliamentary Socialism* (London, 1973), pp. 13-14, 152-57, 348-49, and passim. His argument that the Labour Party has tenaciously adhered to parliamentary methods and tactics over the entire twentieth century appears to be irrefutable, so that the only cogent criticism of his thesis is either the historicist argument that the Labour Party must inevitably have evolved in a parliamentary direction, or the ideological argument that the party's steadfast rejection of revolutionary politics was the only rational choice it could have made.

30. C. Tsuzuki, *H. M. Hyndman and British Socialism* (Oxford, 1961), p. 158.

31. Ibid., pp. 156-59; Pelling, op. cit., p. 262.

32. E. Hopwood, *The Lancashire Weavers Story*, (Manchester, 1969), p. 41.

33. Burnley Weavers *Minute Books*, January-February 1896.

34. *Nelson Socialist Journal*, March 1903, p. 8. The wording is identical to that on the actual membership card, one of which was shown to me by the late Roger Shackleton of Nelson.

35. *Labour Leader*, 11 November 1910; County Borough of Burnley *Year Book*, 1906-11.

36. BPP, Board of Trade, Labour Department, "Report on Trade Unions," 1901, Cd. 773, pp. 52-53; 1906, Cd. 2838, pp. 44-45; 1909, Cd. 4651, pp. 34-35; 1912, Cd. 6109, pp. 32-33.

37. This can be seen from the advertisement announcing the first meeting: ". . .persons who are engaged in the weaving industry . . . *for whom there is no present organization* . . . are requested to attend" (emphasis added) (*Burnley Express*, 1896). I owe this reference to Mavis Williams, who most generously answered my request in the *Burnley Express* for information about the Textile Operatives.

38. Burnley Weavers *Minute Books*, "Notice of Motion for Quarterly Meeting," December 10, 1913.

39. See above, pp. 140-141.

40. Burnley Weavers *Minute Books,* entries for August 14 and January 20, 1913.
41. Burnley Weavers *Minute Books,* entry for September 21, 1913; CFT, 17 October 1913.
42. S. Pollard, *History of Labour in Sheffield* (Liverpool, 1959), pp. 199-200.
43. H. Collins, "The Marxism of the Social Democratic Federation," in A. Briggs and J. Saville, eds., *Essays in Labour History,* vol. 2 (London, 1971), pp. 47-69.
44. See "Cotton Toryism" in Chapter 8.
45. Tsuzuki, op. cit., p. 220.
46. Oldham Industrial Co-operative Society *Record,* April 1913.
47. According to Pelling, op. cit., pp. 252, 260, the average Conservative percentage in the six-election period from 1886 to 1910 was: Ashton, 51.3; Stalybridge, 51.2; Hyde, 49.5; and Preston, 57.9.
48. E. J. Hobsbawm, *Labouring Men* (New York, 1964), p. 287; Clarke, op. cit., pp. 84-94.
49. Pelling, op. cit., pp. 212-27.
50. Ibid., p. 260. The Tories averaged 54.6 percent of the votes in Blackburn, but only 36.7 percent in Clitheroe, which was accordingly the most anti-Tory constituency in all Lancashire.
51. *Hansard,* 6 August 1912.
52. J. R. Clynes, *Memoirs* (London, 1937), pp. 69-70.
53. CFT, 25 November 1910.
54. Webb Trade Union Collection, sec. B, vol. 95, item 14. This document consists of four cyclostyled sheets containing J. R. Clynes's speech in Parliament, a correspondence between Clynes and W. A. Duckworth, general secretary of the Protection Society, which ran in the *Factory Times,* 30 August 1912, et seq., a circular letter of Duckworth's, and headnotes. Neither the authorship nor the political agency of the document is indicated.
55. Labour Party, *Report of the Annual Conference* (London, 1907), p. 6.
56. CFT, 16 December 1910.
57. CFT, 15 March 1912; 3 May 1912; 2 July 1912.
58. CFT, 15 August 1913.
59. Webb Trade Union Collection, sec. B, vol. 95, item 14, op. cit.
60. CFT, 2 December 1910.
61. Clarke, op. cit., p. 406.
62. CFT, 12 July 1912.
63. *Blackburn Labour Journal,* February 1898, et seq; CFT, 13 June 1913.
64. County Borough of Burnley, *Year Book,* 1906-14, passim.
65. Turner, op. cit., p. 316; interview (July 1972) with Fred Hague, who was secretary of the Blackburn Weavers Association in 1949.
66. Pelling, op. cit., p. 26
67. CFT, 14 February 1913.
68. Ibid.
69. BPP, 1914-16, "Report on Strikes and Lockouts," Cd. 7658, pp. xxxvi ff.
70. CFT, 25 April 1913; 2 May 1913.
71. BPP, op. cit. (see note 69); CFT, 2 May 1913; 9 May 1913.

72. Penciled ms. dated March 26, 1913, in the files of the Nelson Weavers.

73. *Lancashire Daily Post,* 5 April 1913.

74. BPP, "Report on Trade Unions, 1914-16," op. cit.

75. CFT, 14 February 1913; *Nelson Leader,* 14 February 1913.

76. Interview (August 1968) with the late Euclid Voltaire Thrusby and Roger Shackleton, both of Nelson.

77. *Nelson Leader,* 9 May 1913. Although a Liberal paper, the *Leader* gave full, if not always fair, coverage to the ILP and carried Philip Snowden's weekly column. The ILP branch in turn advertised its public meetings in the *Leader.*

78. Leaflets issued by the Joint Strike Committee, in the files of the Nelson Weavers Association; CFT, 9 May 1913, et seq.

79. CFT, 18 April 1913.

80. Nelson Weavers *Rule Book* (n.d.), in the files of the Nelson Weavers.

81. CFT, 18 April 1913, quoting the "Final Report" of the Pemberton Strike Committee.

82. CFT, 11 April 1913.

83. Nelson Weavers *Minute Books,* February 5, 1913; "that the matter in dispute at Pemberton's be left to the Secretary,"

84. CFT, 18 April 1913.

85. CFT, 25 April 1913; 2 May 1913.

86. CFT, 25 July 1913.

87. CFT, 1 August 1913.

88. Strike Committee leaflets, passim.

89. CFT, 18 April 1913.

90. CFT, 20 June 1913.

91. CFT, 5 September 1913. One leaflet put out by the Protection Society urged "all trade unionists who object to religious and political interference in trade union affairs not to contibute to to the collection of the Nelson strikers . . . . While these people shout so much about the idle rich they themselves do not object to live on the earnings of others." (leaflet in the files of the Nelson Weavers Association).

92. CFT, 5 September 1913.

93. CFT, 19 September 1913; 26 September 1913.

94. CFT, 3 October 1913.

95. *Bulletin* of the Society for the Study of Labour History, no. 24, p. 69.

96. CFT, 22 August 1913.

97. CFT, 14 February 1913.

98. CFT, 13 June 1913.

99. CFT, 15 November 1913.

100. CFT, 6 March 1914.

101. Ibid.

102. CFT, 13 March 1914.

103. CFT, 27 March 1914.

104. CFT, 3 April 1913, et.seq. *Oldham Chronicle,* 2 April 1914; 20 April 1914.

105. CFT, 3 April 1914, article by Alice Smith.

106. Only eighty-one Middleton spinners voted in 1913 on the question of using

trade union funds for political purposes; the percentage of all spinners who cast votes was 34.9 (CFT, 5 December 1913).

107. CFT, 24 April 1914. According to the *Oldham Chronicle*, 20 April 1914, two members of the Executive Council sent for the police, but they did not enter the hall.

108. CFT, 1 May 1914; *Oldham Chronicle*, 20 April 1914.

109. CFT, 3 July 1914; *Oldham Chronicle*, 30 June 1914.

110. *Oldham Chronicle*, 14 May, 1914.

CHAPTER 10

1. E. H. Phelps Brown, *The Growth of Industrial Relations* (London, 1959), p. 334.

2. S. Pollard, *The Development of the British Economy, 1914-1950* (London, 1960), p. 30; Brown, op. cit., pp. xxxi, 337-38.

3. P. N. Stearns, *Revolutionary Syndicalism and French Labor* (New Brunswick, 1971), pp. 111-20.

4. See "Work" and "Wages" in Chapter 2.

5. V. I. Lenin, "What Is to Be Done?" in *Collected Works*, vol. 4, bk. 2 (New York, 1929), pp. 114-15 ff.

6. For a sound recent treatment of the Lawrence strike, see M. Dubofsky, *We Shall Be All: A History of the Industrial Workers of the World* (New York, 1969), pp. 227-62.

7. J. Hinton, *The First Shop Stewards' Movement* (London, 1973), p. 104.

8. CFT, 13 January 1911.

9. CFT, 7 August 1914. An absolute majority of exports went to the Empire.

10. Ibid. See also A. Marwick, *The Deluge* (New York, 1970), pp. 31-32.

11. CFT, 14 August 1914.

12. CFT and *Manchester Guardian,* September-October 1914, passim. On the political economy of total war see Pollard, op. cit., chap. 2, and A. Marwick, *Britain in the Century of Total War* (New York, 1971).

13. E. Hopwood, *The Lancashire Weavers Story* (Manchester, 1969), pp. 191-92; R. Robson, *The Cotton Industry in Britain* (London, 1957), p. 340.

14. For an analysis of postwar strike trends see R. Hyman, "Strikes and the Political Economy," in R. Miliband and J. Saville, eds., *Socialist Register 1973* (London, 1974), pp. 101-53.

Index

Accrington, 96, 135, 140, 168
Air pollution, 242n
Albert Mill (Nelson), 168
Alienation, 109-10
Amalgamated Association of Operative Mule Spinners, 32, 36-37, 39, 59, 74, 101, 130, 156; negotiations on sliding wage scale, 80-86; rank-and-file opposition to, 173-76, 178; strikes led by, 104-08; structure and membership figures, 75-76. *See also* Cotton unions; Cotton workers; Piecers; Spinners
Amalgamated Weavers Association, 32, 34, 40, 76, 78, 86, 115, 148; alleged socialistic leanings of, 162-66; policy of collectivist laissez faire, 78; rank-and-file attitudes toward, 131, 137-43, 167; strategy and tactics in 1911-12 lockout, 136-45; strikes led by, 94-98; structure and membership figures, 77. *See also* Cotton unions; Cotton workers; Weavers; Weavers branches in individual towns
Anti-Socialist Union, 163
Arbitration and mediation, 82-87, 112-14, 117-24, 127-28, 148. *See also* Askwith, G. R.
Ashton, Thomas, 59-60, 147, 239n
Ashton-under-Lyne Trades Council, 182
Ashton-under-Lyne Weavers, 129, 132, 140, 161

Askwith, G. R., 112-13, 117, 120, 122, 124, 137-38, 143, 149; biographical note, 240n
Aughton, W. H., 98. *See also* Nelson Weavers Association

Bamber Bridge (near Preston), 161
Bardsley, S. J., 54-55. *See also* Amalgamated Weavers Association; Women
Beamers, Twisters, and Drawers Union, 151
Bell, James, 60-61
Birchenough, F. W., 174-75. *See also* Middleton spinners
Blackburn, 30, 40, 91, 130, 136-37, 139, 152, 156, 160-62, 165, 168
Blackburn *Labour Journal*, 162
Blackburn Power Loom Weavers Association, 130, 139, 162-63, 167
Blackburn Weavers Protection Society, 130, 144, 162-67, 177-78. *See also* Dual unionism; Conservatism among cotton workers
Black Friday, 144
Blackpool, 229n
Boardman, John (age 14), 62-63
Boardman, John (Senior), 62-63
Bollington (Cheshire), 91, 101
Bolton, 25, 40, 56, 58, 101, 103, 138
Bolton Spinners, 50, 150
Brass bands, 137

About the Author

Joseph L. White is Associate Professor of History at the University of Pittsburgh. His special interests include comparative labor movements, and leisure and society.

DATE DUE

30 505 JOSTEN'S			